Altl
fun
sto
nec
inv
an

Llyfrgelloedd
Libraries

el, it also
ading the
d, is not
homicide
y pursues

MASK OF BONE

Janson Mancheski

To James "Exy" Exferd, my old University of Wisconsin-Oshkosh roommate, whose motto—"If the right one don't get you, then the left one probably won't either"—has proved a valuable life lesson for me over the years. RIP, old friend.

"Trail of evil, mask of bone, drink the blood and hear the moans; When shadows rise at full moon's toll, I'll take from you your living soul."

— *Nzambi* hex of witch doctor Tazeki Mabutu

CONTENTS

PART ONE:

A CAUL BABY

PART TWO:

THE BARCELONA TWIST

PART THREE:

A LONG DAY'S JOURNEY INTO NIGHT

PART ONE:

A CAUL BABY

CHAPTER 1

Green Bay, Wisconsin

The serial kidnapper stood at the top of the concrete steps outside the Brown County courthouse. Gone were the orange jailhouse jumpsuit and lace-less canvas shoes he'd been wearing hours earlier. They'd been replaced by gray khaki slacks, a light button-down shirt, and a sports jacket. He was shaved, his hair a little longer than his arrest photos from four weeks ago, and he was leaning on what the cops were calling a "sympathy" cane.

The man was positioned, strategically, a pace behind his attorney, who was addressing the crowd. A brown-shirted county deputy stood on each side, and the eyes of the lawmen scanned the angry, restless crowd that had gathered across the concrete walkway and clipped courthouse lawns.

From this agitated group of citizens, occasional shouts rang out: "Murderer!" "Scumbag!" "You're gonna fry, Crenshaw!"

The members of the media, their recording devices and cameras and cell phones angled to capture every nuanced word, had formed a semi-circle at the bottom of the courthouse steps. This designated "safety arc" was enforced by another pair of uniformed city patrolmen, ensuring that the man speaking—an attorney with glasses and a grandfather's wreath of gray hair—was allowed his personal space near the top of the steps.

The weather report had verified the conditions: one of those hazy May days, the sky trying to decide what to do. Cement-colored clouds could be seen approaching from the west, casting traces of shadow, bringing with them the metallic hint of coming rain. So far, the drizzle had held off, but for how long was anyone's guess.

The attorney requested quiet, putting an end to the crowd's insolent jeers. When the voices abated, he proceeded to speak in a solemn tone about evidence, due process, and the importance of examining the relevant facts, so nothing could exist beyond a reasonable doubt. He sounded as if he were delivering a lecture on legal ethics.

"Screw you, Crenshaw! You murderer!" someone shouted.

"Hope you burn in hell—you bastard!"

Positioned behind the attorney, Tobias Crenshaw kept his expression blank. He'd been schooled at keeping it that way for this event, and he stood frozen, feigning disinterest, as the small crimson dot appeared just below the hairline on his forehead. His demeanor remained unfazed as the back of his head exploded. At this same instant, he dropped to the ground like a life-sized puppet whose strings had been snipped.

Those who had been listening close might have distinguished a faint coughing sound in the same millisecond the crimson dot had appeared on the target's forehead. But this mild idiosyncrasy was forgotten by most everyone who'd chanced to hear it; and it was no surprise, for an instant later, pandemonium broke loose.

——

The shooting on the courthouse steps had taken place yesterday.

After a day of techno analysts consolidating the data, putting together a timeline from a variety of digital sources, reviewing every angle and shadow and movement, the detectives were at last viewing the finished production.

Inside the Green Bay Police Department's Electronic Forensics/Tech Analysis lab, Detective James "Slink" Dooley watched the replay of the grisly event unfold. Five other tech officers inhabited the room, walking him through the various sequences. They were focused on the first monitor on the left of a bank of eight. Slink watched Tobias Crenshaw—the man charged with being the infamous serial offender dubbed "The Chemist"— take the bullet to his head and disappear from view.

It was Friday morning now, just after eight o'clock. Having joined the group of video-techs, standing behind them as they viewed the display monitors, Slink shifted his eyes away from the screen showing Crenshaw's prone body. The assassination, he knew—if one chose to call it that—had taken place yesterday, around noon.

The next monitor over was showing a different angle of the same event. It was a high-angle crowd shot from the left wing of the courthouse steps. At the precise instant Crenshaw fell, three shots rang out like tossed firecrackers. The sounds were captured by media microphones, along with multiple crowd members' mobile phones. The echo of the shots was smothered an instant later by the shouts and screams of panic-stricken citizens.

A third monitor down the row showed Detective Dooley the observers' reactions to the shooting. Those persons gathered on the south lawn were beginning to scatter. The sight of a young female shooter and the *pop-pop-pop* of gunshots caused them to flee like pond geese.

Slink watched four seconds elapse on the monitor's timer. A pair of men—one college-age in plaid cargo shorts, one older and wearing blue jeans—was grabbing the female shooter, wrestling her to the ground. The event was fast descending into chaos.

Detective Dooley's focus shifted to a fourth monitor, where now it was the media's turn to panic. Shocked into reality, they began turning and fleeing from their staked-out positions at the base of the courthouse steps. Some were bent halfway over as if ducking invisible bullets. Others scooted across the courthouse lawn, covering their heads, searching for whatever shelter they could find.

Slink returned his gaze back to the first monitor. The prone figure of Tobias Crenshaw lay in the middle of a group of people, and they appeared to be assessing his dire health status. Since the man had suffered a point-blank shot to the forehead, and dropped backward on the concrete steps, unmoving, Slink figured it would turn out less than positive.

"There! Right there!"

Sergeant Pete Rosera called out to his quartet of coworkers. Their heads turned as he pointed up at the fifth monitor, where it showed a magnified, Hi-Def image. "Watch the foam covering. Right there! On the mic attachment."

Slink focused where the sergeant was indicating. Rosera was fiddling with the joystick, clearing the picture on the flat-screen. He had zoomed in tight, magnifying the image by twelve, backing the time up to moments before the shots were fired. It was yet another camera angle, a high-angle view from behind the target, which focused on the gathered media.

The camera shot was locked on a foam-covered, solitary, extended microphone. And the mic was attached to the video camera that a BET cameraman aimed at the courthouse steps.

The sergeant magnified the image another two clicks.

"Fifteen-point-four seconds," Sergeant Rosera said, pointing at the screen. "The felt covering is intact." He eased the joystick forward a fraction. "There! Right there...fifteen-five..."

On the screen, the enlarged image showed the microphone's foam fragmenting into pieces. Over his shoulder, for Slink's benefit, the sergeant said, "I was going over the CCTV feeds, trying to freeze the instant of the weapon's discharge. Match it with the time-differential on the other digitals. I discovered this angle on the cameraman."

"I'll be damned," Slink said, impressed.

Pointing to the monitor again, Rosera added, "It gives us irrefutable visual evidence. The round was fired from his disguised firing apparatus."

The other techs *oohed* and *aahed*, praising their sergeant. A few claps sounded. They reversed it and played it again.

Slink took a sip from his coffee mug. The video room had a door cracked open at the far end, and it gave off a long slash of light. The smell of fresh coffee and day-old French crullers drifted in from the back room. Returning his eyes to the monitor, he watched the microphone foam disintegrate into frayed and ragged bits, as each fraction of a second passed in super-slow motion.

"Ballistics is confirming a frontal entry wound," Slink said solemnly. "Through-and-through shot. We're guessing a nine-mill, that close a range."

"I checked the CSU log," Rosera said, without turning. "They discovered a single nine-millimeter casing. Found on the sidewalk near the street curb."

"Not the firing point. Judging from your video here." Slink motioned at the monitor.

"Scene techs are guessing it was kicked around by fleeing shoes."

Slink was silent for a beat, thinking. "The Hulbreth girl was carrying a .38-caliber. Off in the wings, on the lawn. Impossible angle."

"From what we're seeing here."

"So, this rules her out as the shooter," Slink suggested.

The techs in the room were silent.

"Not entirely," Tiara Thorp said after a pause, turning her head toward Slink. She had dark, pulled-back hair and high cheekbones. "There's no getting around the three rounds she unloaded toward center stage, is there?"

"Three rounds that didn't hit anything." This counter came from Rosera.

"You're right," Slink said. "No reports yet on what she might've hit on the other side of the main stage. No other GSWs."

"Might've hit a tree. Even a squirrel or a car tire. CSU's still combing the area. They should have something today."

"Still—her rounds did not strike Crenshaw." Rosera spoke in a bold voice. "That's the main thing."

"I'll break down the trajectory of the shots." This was offered by an Asian-looking tech named Sudzinski. "Our angle-pattern software can pinpoint where they might've wound up. I'll feed the data over to the scene techs."

Slink gave the young man a nod.

"Might've been working together," Thorp said, arching dark eyebrows. "Assassin team. Make a name for themselves...offing a high-profile bad dude."

"Like the guy who murdered Dahmer. In prison."

"Too much *CSI*, Thorp," said Sudzinski, adding a snicker.

"Sudsy's got a point," Slink allowed, giving Thorp a smile to show he wasn't playing favorites. "No limit to dickheads scheming for a second of fame."

Sergeant Rosera sighed. "At any rate, we've got a lone frontal shooter. Time-sequentials sync with the target angle." He pointed to the monitor showing the courthouse steps, where Tobias Crenshaw remained hidden by hovering bodies.

"*Another one bites the dust...*" Sudsy sang off key.

Slink turned and departed from the video room.

6

—— ——

The evening before, Slink Dooley had forwarded the enhanced photo images of the BET cameraman to a pair of sources. The first set was sent to the Black Entertainment Television Network headquarters in Atlanta. The second copies were issued to the FBI's evidence processing lab in Quantico, Virginia.

Slink arrived at his desk in the detectives' bullpen, flicking on his computer. He discovered a pair of fresh emails in his box. The first one stated that the BET Network's Human Resources Department was denying the individual in the photo was either a current or past employee. No surprise there.

The second email proved more fruitful. The FBI's facial recognition software had provided them with a hit on their suspect. A match came back positive for a fugitive already in their database: an existing "Wanted for Questioning" warrant. It belonged to a Liberian national, who went by the solitary name of "Kinsella."

"You've got to be kidding," Slink said out loud, to no one.

At his desk across the aisle, Detective Anton Staszak was sipping from a tiny orange bottle: a reputed energy concoction. His large lumpy head was shaved (due to recent cranial trauma and consequent surgery, injuries he'd received in the Chemist case), and he swallowed the concoction, making a face like a man who'd just been tasered.

"What, Dooley? You lose the Powerball again?" Staszak asked, his eyes still watery.

"This is even crazier odds."

Slink clenched his jaw. Grabbing his desk phone, he punched in the number for Agent Eddie Redtail in Milwaukee. Redtail was head of the FBI's Wisconsin Bureau, and a friend of theirs. The agent had helped fast-track Slink's partner, Detective Cale Van Waring, on his current search-and-rescue mission to Europe. Attempting to locate a pair of trafficking victims of the Chemist—two local girls: Leslie Dowd and Mary Jane Moore. He'd assisted in green-lighting Cale's clearance through the State Department—helped expedite his passport, inoculations, credentials, travel plans—the whole nine yards. Agent Redtail was providing as much support for Cale as he could manage, within the boundaries of his authority.

The FBI man answered on the second ring. Slink said, "You're not going to believe this one."

Agent Redtail spoke in a measured voice. "I'm FBI. I'm beyond surprise."

Slink's smirk went unseen. "Our Crenshaw shooter? Guy we're attempting to ID? It turns out he's the same perp Cale Van Waring's trying to locate on his trip: the Liberian national— *Kinsella*."

Agent Redtail was silent for a beat. "You mean the suspect Crenshaw fingered? In the murder of your Vanderkellen girl?"

"Bingo!"

Agent Redtail allowed a degree of intrigue to season his otherwise stoic voice. "That would mean the tip Crenshaw gave you guys? It was on the money, right?"

"So much so, that he's now lying in the trauma unit. Brain-dead, from what I'm hearing." Slink paused. "Our boy Kinsella doesn't take too kindly, it would seem, to being narced on."

"The understatement of the year." The hint at dark humor was the closest Agent Redtail came to levity. "Does Cale know about this?"

Slink glanced at his watch. "Not yet. Just got it. His phone's been down. *Incommunicado.* I'll keep trying to reach him."

"In the meantime, I'm going to contact Homeland. Your courthouse shooting took place, what, noon yesterday?" Agent Redtail was tabulating of the fly. "It's not too late to issue an APB. But odds are your suspect's well in the wind, Detective."

"No surprise."

"I'll also notify ICE. Tell them they're dealing with a confirmed murder suspect. Along with the human trafficking angle. It should ramp their antennas up toward this Kinsella character."

"You'd think, wouldn't you?" Slink, like many local cops, had little confidence in how federal law enforcement chose to prioritize their efforts.

"Your case appears to have suddenly gone international in scope, Detective." Agent Redtail stated the obvious. "It's beyond anything we can handle at our level."

"You're right." Slink exhaled with frustration. "Don't suppose there's much chance our shooter stuck around to guzzle beers with the locals." He imagined he could picture Agent Redtail's wooden face cracking the barest of grins.

"In the wind—like I said." Redtail paused for a breath. "When you talk to your partner, Detective Dooley, better tell him to watch his ass."

"I'll do that." Slink decided the agent knew Cale well enough to add, "It's a position he's quite familiar with."

CHAPTER 2

Anzio, Italy

The steady *whup-whup-whup* of rotating chopper blades—Cale Van Waring was being jostled about like a man trapped in the trunk of a speeding getaway car. As he awoke, the dream was quick to fade, and yet the pain remained. Every muscle of his body was singing a chorus of protest.

The rotating blade sound became a rhythmic knocking on the door to his small sleeping quarters. As luck would have it, when Cale opened his eyes, he saw that Cheetah was standing in the doorway, ready to usher him back to reality. She reminded him where he was, why he was there, and how close he'd come to not waking up with a pulse at all on this day.

If she only knew the half of it, Cale reminded himself grimly.

When he moved, slow at first and continuing to groan, she said with a clap, "Let's go, Detective. Chop, chop."

Cale lifted himself to one elbow, then into a sitting position, shifting on the mattress, which sat on the small room's dingy floor. "What time is it?"

"Friday afternoon. You slept over nine hours." She gave him an impatient look. "Better get a move on, or you'll miss the bus."

After he'd showered, re-bandaged his injuries, and donned a fresh set of military camos provided by Jacek—boots included— Cale limped his way down the hallway like a geriatric war veteran. He felt ninety years old as he entered the wide central area of the warehouse.

The inner area was a huge and shadowy expanse of open space, complete with support beams and upper rafters. The ceiling was thirty feet high. The walls were undecorated concrete. A good distance away from where Cale emerged, in a central zone, a trio of computer monitors had been set up on a pair of long tables. Jacek Tumaj, the Czech mercenary functioning as Cale's European contact-*slash*-guide-*slash*-bodyguard, was sitting at one station, logging in data. Next to him sat his partners: to one side Cheetah, and Pharaoh on the other side. They were Jacek's more-than-capable assistants, meaning they could each shoot the heart out of a hummingbird at fifty meters, as well as break whichever limb of yours they chose in hand-to-hand combat.

Turning at the sound of his limping approach, Jacek shouted, "Ah! If it isn't Detective Lazarus, back from the grave to join us."

With a shake of his head, Cale said, "If you're calling me a vampire, Jacek, trust me. I've been called worse."

"Not my intention, but I'm a Czech, am I not? We believe in the lore of the *vampyr*." He pronounced these last words like Bella Lugosi.

Cale's thigh and ribs were bandaged. His forehead and jaw showed superficial lacerations, and his eyes were still puffy from sleep, so Jacek wasn't far off the mark: he *did* appear to be a member of the walking dead. Still, Cale could only roll his eyes at the man who'd saved his life less than twenty-four hours earlier. More than once, as a matter-of-fact.

"Whatever," Cale conceded with a grimace. "At any rate, you look better than I feel."

"*Pshee*." Jacek waved away the compliment. "Haven't we all seen better days, eh?"

"Two legs and upright—my motto till the end."

"Speaking of which," Jacek said after a pause. He spun in his chair to make a full appraisal of Cale. "After everything we were put through the past few days, well, don't think less of me if I thought you might pack it in. Maybe catch a comfy flight back to the States today, eh?"

Cale touched his bandaged ribs carefully with his fingertips. He wondered if Jacek might be testing him, seeing if he still had the mettle to continue his mission.

"After our encounter with Colonel Mabutu, I decided I'd better stay." Cale confessed this in the even tone of a man resigned to performing his duty, however unsavory it might be. "We stared him right in his evil eye and didn't blink." He exhaled, his face bearing a sober expression.

"That we did, my friend. That we did."

"In my book," Cale added, "you run from a fight with the devil, you end up his little bitch for the rest of your days."

Pharaoh, the large mesomorph with olive-toned skin, half-smiled while continuing to plug data into his computer. Cheetah shot him a sidelong glance, snickering in silence. Cale noted them both. He wondered if they were bestowing upon him a silent blessing for not bailing out on his mission. If so, he'd consider it a feather in his cap. Winning the simplest praise was a positive when it came from people who faced down serious bad guys for a living.

"There's the spirit," Jacek said, grinning. He turned back to his computer, thick fingers tapping at the keyboard.

"By the way," Cale said. "Can I borrow one of your mobile phones? Mine fried yesterday, you might recall." He took a moment to study Jacek and his partners: Cheetah, the petite, cocoa-skinned African with the weapons-grade fingernails; and Pharaoh, the oversized Turk or Samoan tree trunk—or whatever-the-hell ethnic mix he might be.

It was Jacek who responded with a head jerk. "On the table over there. Near what's left of our lunch buffet."

Cale limped away from the computer station. He walked the thirty feet to the side of the warehouse, following his nose as it led him toward the lingering smell of food. His mouth salivated as he spotted a solitary cold meatball sub on a sandwich tray. It was sitting there taunting him, daring him like a drunk at a party.

One of Jacek's mobile phones sat near the tray. Cale glanced at his watch. Six hours ahead here in Italy. Back in the Midwest, his partner would be at the station by this time.

He powered the phone on and punched in the familiar number. Detective Slink Dooley answered on the second ring with his customary: "Dooley."

Cale recalled Maggie's information, which she'd passed along very late last night. It all came rushing back to him now in a flash of disjointed memory:

The Chemist—a.k.a. Tobias Crenshaw—had been shot in the head. The shooting had taken place on the steps of the Brown County Courthouse, in Green Bay, Wisconsin. This news had been relayed to Cale very late last night—like four a.m. late—while he was still groggy and barely coherent, just returning from the all-night flight back from Africa.

Maggie Jeffers, Cale's fiancée, had been the bearer of the grim revelation. Since it was Maggie, Cale decided there was little doubt the event had occurred. His trust in her was implicit. But there remained an outside chance he might've dreamed the entire scenario. Maybe even hallucinated it. He had been sparring with delirium, like a rubber-legged boxer in the late rounds, by the time their airplane had touched down in Naples.

Therefore, what Cale needed was confirmation—confirmation from Slink Dooley that the shooting had, indeed, taken place.

His partner didn't waste any time. Slink dove right in with the information about Crenshaw's assassination: shot point-blank in the forehead; and at this moment, was lying in ICU on life-support. In all probability the Chemist would be a vegetable, even if his body did manage to survive the internal trauma.

"Pity I'm not there to yank the plug, myself," Cale said, his demeanor morbid.

"No need to worry, *muchacho*. There'd be fifty people in line ahead of you." Slink's remark lacked humor. "Another fifty behind—including his fentanyl suppliers. But who's counting?"

"Including yourself, I take it?"

"Damn straight. My hands, his neck," Slink said determinedly. "I'd choke the last living breath out of the bastard."

Cale pondered his partner's dark sentiment. "A very personal way to end someone's life—choking."

"It'd be personal, all right. Very, very personal."

Slink went on to report that with the FBI's assistance, they had employed facial-recognition software to ID the primary shooter of Tobias Crenshaw. "Our man Kinsella—the one and only," Slink said, his tone flat. "Believe it or not."

He allowed Cale a moment to process this fact over the many miles between them, before adding, "So wouldn't you know it? Looks like we're both working the same case, after all."

Kinsella? Cale was dumbfounded by the news. He almost failed to recognize his own voice: "You're yankin' my chain, right?"

"I'm not yankin' anything. We ID'd him via CCTV cameras, on the lawn outside the courthouse. Quantico verified the ID via facial rec."

Cale frowned. The news Maggie had provided him about Tobias Crenshaw being shot had been surprising enough. But how, he wondered, could Kinsella—the man he was pursuing five-thousand miles away in Italy—show up in Green Bay, Wisconsin, the day before? Pulling off a public assassination?

"He's been a step ahead of us. No doubt." Slink's tone didn't disguise his frustration. "Maybe two or three steps."

"Son of a bitch."

"That'd be a right-on summation."

Cale felt a sense of unease wrap around him. Kinsella had played them for fools. While he, Cale, was chasing halfway around the world trying to find the guy, the conniving killer had doubled back to the Midwest and—what—done a hit on Tobias Crenshaw? Shot him in the head?

It appeared to be the case.

Maggie's words arose in his mind now, a version of the old I-Told-You-So. Earlier in the week, as Cale had been contemplating his trip to Europe in search of their suspect—as well as the two missing victims in the case—she had warned him pointedly: "You can't go off trying to save the world, Cale. Besides, it's not a very healthy job description."

He was glad she wasn't on the line right now to rub it in.

And yet, he couldn't escape the gnashing pain in his gut. In light of the grim news, there still seemed to be something he was missing.

After considering the puzzle for a few moments, Cale felt a premonition rising. He had the feeling, dark and intense, that Colonel Tazeki Mabutu—the evil Liberian head of national security, and the man who had attempted to end his life three times already on this trip—had likely known the whereabouts of his henchman, Kinsella, all along. Even *before* the colonel had sprung the trapdoor, which had sent Cale dropping forty feet down into a pool of hungry moray eels.

He had been fortunate to survive.

If it hadn't been for Jacek, they never would have made it out of Africa in one piece. Looking back just days ago, considering Slink Dooley's information, it was apparent Mabutu had known far more than he'd revealed during their interview with him.

In fact, Cale was getting the sickening realization that the shooting in Green Bay, as well as the attempts on his life in Liberia, had been orchestrated by one master conductor: the crazy colonel.

Forty minutes ago, when he had woken up sore and confused on his lumpy mattress, Cale imagined that his mood would rally with a newfound sense of optimism. Like a ballplayer who couldn't wait to get to the stadium on game day. Now, however, reality was slapping him in the face. They were back to square one; back to chasing invisible ghosts.

And ghosts, in Cale's experience—even if you did manage to corner one—seldom, if ever, came quietly.

CHAPTER 3

Positioned at the bank of computers, Jacek Tumaj was logging in the data they were receiving from their American ICE contact, SAC (Special Agent in Charge) Amy Fronteer. The agent had promised to send over anything relevant to the human trafficking case they were working on, the case Detective Cale Van Waring was spearheading. Thus far, to Jacek's surprise, Agent Fronteer had been generous in sharing her information with them.

"She's not getting in hot water by sending this, is she?" Cheetah asked. She was at her monitor, next to Jacek, and noted how her screen showed the identical data display. "We don't have US security clearance."

Jacek said, "You don't. But I do. She's feeding it to my encrypted IP address. Your systems happen to be interfaced with mine." He smiled, and the lines creasing his forehead and crinkling the corners of his eyes made his retreating hairline appear more evident. "Besides, she trusts me."

"Silly girl," Cheetah mumbled, not bothering to shade her grin.

"No doubt she's doing this off grid." On the other side of Jacek, Pharaoh's voice conveyed his seriousness.

"Of course, she is. But our friend Cale here is running out of time. Maybe four days tops, before he has to return to the States." Jacek paused. "If Agent Fronteer follows strict protocol, the steam runs out of this investigation, and we all go home."

They were silent for a minute, watching as more data rolled in.

"Look at those…images. Is that—"

"Prince Mir Al-Sadar," Jacek said, agreeing. He was staring at the identical photo on his screen. The prince was standing on a walking path on his magnificent estate, locked in conversation with a large, dark-skinned man in a too-tight sports jacket. The man's sleeves were rolled up to his elbows—a man they had previously ID'd as Kinsella.

"This is a separate time-stamp from the previous photos of them together."

Jacek was quiet for a moment. "It might be the game-changer we're looking for here, my friends." He glanced over his shoulder toward the back of the warehouse. He shouted in a loud voice for Cale's benefit: "Has our detective friend fallen asleep back there?"

"On the phone, still." Cheetah reported, matter-of-fact in her clipped British tone. "Might be having girlfriend problems. You know? Back home?"

They could hear Cale's low voice echoing off the crates and inner concrete walls.

Jacek narrowed his eyes at her. "Girlfriend?" He snorted. "He was close to having his bollocks eaten off by eels yesterday. Then shot at; then almost decapitated... And he picks *now* to worry about his love life?"

"Fiancée. I should've been more specific."

"I don't care if he's dating Kate Middleton! He better get his arse over here. We're running short on time."

"You're the boss," Cheetah said.

Jacek spun in his chair and shouted for real this time, "Hey! Detective. You'll have plenty of time to play with your dingy on your plane flight home. Get over here. *Pospes si*!"

Cale's voice echoed off the high ceiling of the warehouse. "Finishing up. Be there in a minute."

After five minutes had passed, sensing Jacek's growing impatience, Pharaoh pushed his chair back and rose to his full height. His shadow was the size of a Kodiak bear, and it covered them like a shroud. From the pocket of his camo pants he produced a hefty, black-handled knife. And when he pressed a small dark button on the handle, six inches of deadly blade *snicked* free.

Peering across the warehouse at where Cale was standing near the food table, yakking on the phone, Pharaoh reared back and fired his blade. An instant later they heard a thud and a yelp of surprise, as the sounds echoed off the rafters.

The large mercenary shifted his eyes to Jacek. "That ought to get his attention."

Jacek was massaging his right temple as the larger man sat down in his chair. "Have I mentioned before that 'tact' is not your middle name?"

"Once or twice."

——

With the phone tucked at his shoulder, Cale poured a cup of coffee from the shiny chrome pot perched on the buffet table. He needed the caffeine. In the curved surface, he noted his reflection: the bleary eyes, the bruises and lacerations across his forehead, cheeks, jawline. And this was *after* his shower and shave. He could imagine how awful he'd looked forty minutes ago, when Cheetah had first wakened him.

"So, that's where we stand." Slink's voice reached him across the miles. "Green Bay's first public assassination—and you're off playing hooky."

"Anzio, Italy." Cale was staring across the dim-lit warehouse. He realized he could have been anywhere on the planet. "We're going over DHS intel as we speak. If Kinsella's fled back to Europe, maybe we'll get a bead on him. Flight records. A TSA tag. Something."

"And if he's back in Liberia?"

"Shit out of luck." Cale sighed. "Trust me, I'm not setting even a big toe back there again."

"And finding the girls? Any clue on a time frame?"

"I'll give it through the weekend. After that...like I said, I'm a one-trick pony on this."

"You've got to know when to pull the plug," said Slink evenly. "Europe's a pretty big haystack."

"One more thing..." Cale shifted topics. "I talked to Mags a minute or two last night. In the Naples airport—before we got cut off. Tell her I'm all right, would you?"

"Will do, kemosabe. Chloe and I are keeping her occupied. Working in shifts." Chloe Jeffers-Ravelle was Maggie's older sister.

Cale was silent for a beat. Then he asked, "About the other thing...you know? What you told me? Before I left?"

"Two words, Cale: *not now!*"

"Did she say anything? Or maybe tell Chloe?"

Slink's tone was curt. "No offense, but you've got too much on your plate at the moment. Killers, traffickers, missing victims. You can't be dwelling on problems on the home front."

Cale decided his partner's advice was on the money. Like it or not, he had to stay focused on his mission. "You're right," he said robotically. "Find the girls. Bring them home."

Yet at the same time, even this admission failed to silence the chiding voice in his head. The one firing questions in a playback loop: Was he the father? Or was the father the monster who had kidnapped and raped Maggie?

These torturous thoughts were interrupted by a slight breeze, which Cale felt a few feet beyond his left shoulder. Before he could turn, he heard the solid sound of a dull *thwuuk* close by.

He called out in surprise, but his voice was swallowed fast by the heavy walls of the warehouse.

Cale glanced over and saw the black-handled knife—with the weapon still quivering, it's killer blade embedded in the solid wood of an upright cabinet.

CHAPTER 4

Cale yanked the blade from the cabinet door and made his way back across the open warehouse.

"So where do we begin?" he asked, an edge to his voice as he approached the bank of computers in the warehouse's central section. His trio of companions remained busy, each concentrating on their monitors. Tapping Pharaoh on the shoulder, Cale scowled while handing the large mercenary his blade. After withdrawing it from the wooden cabinet, he had noted the knife was balanced, custom-designed for throwing, among other things.

The large man accepted his knife back without comment.

"Guy could lose an ear around this joint," Cale said, not kidding.

"Or get hit by a bus crossing the street, eh?" Jacek snickered over his shoulder. "Lighten up, Mr. Packer. We're just messing with you."

"I enjoy my ears. They're a matching set."

"*Pshee.*" The Czech waved a dismissive hand as he pointed to his computer screen. "Look. We are making headway, believe it or not."

"Slow but sure," added Cheetah, without looking up.

Cold meatball sandwich in hand, Cale observed the tables of sophisticated computer equipment. He leaned in and peered over Jacek's shoulder at an image frozen on the screen. Jacek was zooming in on what appeared to be a svelte Middle Eastern businessman in a Brooks Brothers suit.

"Remember our friend? Prince Mir Al-Sadar?" Jacek asked.

Cale studied the image. "The guy in the photo we saw the other day—meeting with Kinsella. The same guy Colonel Mabutu identified when we talked to him."

The man's appearance would match a thousand Wall Street clones, save for the sharp goatee and the pristine white *keffiyeh* he wore. The prince was strolling along a path beneath leafy shade trees and speaking—it appeared—to an elderly man in a brown fedora. Behind them lurked a set of suited men, wearing com-units and hundred-yard stares. Bodyguards.

On the folding chair beside Jacek, Pharaoh was cleaning a fingernail with his switchblade. The weapon (Cale had learned the day before) was called a "wasp" knife. Pharaoh pointed at Jacek's screen with the blade's sharp tip now, indicating something he spotted hidden in the background. Another bodyguard lurking near the tree line.

In a low voice, Jacek said, "The grounds appear to be well-defended." He added over his shoulder for Cale's benefit, "Agent Fronteer sent us these updates twenty minutes ago. Interesting intel from a château in Belgium, which your Homeland Security people have under surveillance due to potential arms-dealing activities."

Agent Amy Fronteer was stationed in Rome. Cale had met her when he'd arrived on Wednesday morning, two days earlier, before his fateful whirlwind journey to Liberia and back. The ICE agent had seemed capable and earnest, and well aware of what they were up against. She had shown them a series of surveillance photographs taken by Homeland Security—or it might have been Interpol, Cale couldn't remember—and allowed them to review the revealing pictures before they had departed on their journey.

"Decent of her to keep us in the loop," Cale said, his appreciation genuine. "A lot of Feds I've dealt with...they aren't so accommodating."

Cheetah was standing beside him, silent as a leaf-shadow. Cale was surprised. He'd neither sensed nor heard her move from her chair. "She seems good at her job," the petite mercenary said. "Concerned with trying to help."

"Long as she keeps sending us intel, it works fine for me." This from Jacek.

Cale checked his watch, glancing at Cheetah a moment later. "I have to drop off a package. Get it back to the States. ASAP." Arching an eyebrow at her. "I've got time, haven't I?"

"Overnight Air's delivery drop is eight blocks from here. Shouldn't be too busy on a Friday afternoon." Cheetah shrugged. "Twenty minutes more here, then I'll chauffeur you over there myself. We should have plenty of time."

Jacek interrupted them. "Cheetah, good friend, why don't you bring Cale up to speed on what we've got so far? I've got to make a few phone calls."

Jacek rose from his chair. Cale handed him back the phone he had borrowed. The Czech began punching in digits, walking away as he did.

Cale sat in Jacek's open chair, with Cheetah sitting beside him at her own monitor. She pointed out for his benefit a series of still photographs that sat frozen on both their screens. In her clipped British tone, she explained how the Interpol search for Kinsella had led to this new set of photos, pictures Agent Fronteer had received only yesterday.

On the screen, Cale spotted the previous Kinsella photo he'd become familiar with over the past days: the original of the man in deep conversation with Mir Al-Sadar, the Emer-Saud oil prince. They had learned that Emer-Saud was a small but powerful kingdom sandwiched between Bahrain and Qatar.

Cheetah worked the mouse, syncing their monitors.

Cale watched as downloads scrolled across his screen. They appeared to be updated shots of the same Prince Mir, a variety of images: here getting into a limousine, there outside a hotel in Bonn, Germany. Next, he was striding—head down, mobile phone at his ear—toward a private jet on an airport tarmac. Another series of photos showed him strolling the grounds of his opulent and spacious Belgian estate.

"Agent Fronteer is sifting through the prince's background," Cheetah explained, slender fingers poised on the mouse. "They're clarifying what Interpol and the other Euro intelligence agencies have on the guy. Determining how the prince's activities might connect back to Kinsella."

When Cale blinked at the screen, she added, "It turns out Prince Mir Al-Sadar's been on Interpol's human trafficking Watch List for some time now. They've been unable to tag him with solid evidence, however, indicating his involvement. He's rumored to run a high-end brothel in Brussels, along with having connections to arms and drug traffickers. His enormous wealth allows him to cover his tracks. Any suspicious activity is layered beneath a series of private dummy corporations or—"

"Subsidiary groups. Got it."

Cheetah added, "But as far as criminal charges go, thus far Prince Mir has remained untouchable."

Cale shook his head, frustrated. It came as no surprise. Guys like the prince would always be insulated by their money. "How about terrorist connections?" he asked. "You mentioned this guy might be into arms dealing. Even if he's not a direct player...born and raised in the Middle East, we can pretty much lay odds on where his sympathies lie."

"He showed up on DHS's radar as a weapons merchant. It's the reason they had him under surveillance."

Cale nodded, at once more interested in the prince than he had been.

"But we're staying away from all things political at the moment. Agent Fronteer wants to concentrate on the human-trafficking angle. Her primary focus. She doesn't want to wander too far afield."

Cale conceded the point with a nod. Agent Fronteer was correct, he understood. Any whiff of terrorism in this situation would overwhelm his small—by comparison—search for the pair of missing Wisconsin girls.

"What we have confirmed," Cheetah added, her tone crisp, "is that Prince Mir is the owner of a personal private harem. In residence at his Belgian château."

"Harem?" Cale felt his eyes widen and he blinked. "For real? The kind of 'harem' I'm thinking of?"

"Yes. That kind, Detective."

Wonderful, Cale thought. This mess keeps getting stranger by the minute.

CHAPTER 5

Cale's stare at Cheetah was tight. He snickered like an adolescent in a locker room, one told his teammates possessed photos of the cheerleading squad half-dressed.

"You want to maybe repeat the part about the harem?" Cale said, arching an eyebrow.

Alongside them, for Cale's benefit, Pharaoh began spelling out: "H-A-R—"

"Thanks, Pharaoh." Cale cut him off. "I got that much."

He continued to study Cheetah. "You mean like in the story books, right? Ali Baba and that band of thieves?"

It felt odd giving voice to the concept of a "harem" in a serious criminal discussion. Cale drew a mental picture of portly middle-aged sultans surrounded by nubile females wearing silk and gauzy veils. Something out of the sixteenth century.

"Indeed. A harem is a bevy of attractive concubines." Jacek reported this while waving his phone in the air, as he rejoined them. He grabbed an old wooden crate and slid it up to where they sat at the long computer station. "Kept on hand at the sultan's beck and call—"

"I understand what a harem is." Cale frowned at them all. "What I'm saying is: Didn't they go out of style with genies? Aladdin's lamp? Those goofy curl-toe slippers?"

"Storybooks," Jacek scoffed. "Harems continue to exist in our modern era. We're talking Middle Eastern royals here. Men with Fort Knox-type wealth."

"Always the money." Cale grunted the comment, conceding his frustration with a shake of his head.

"It's a cultural thing with them," Cheetah stated, no emotion. "They derive a perverse satisfaction by collecting females. The same way young boys collect trading cards, I suppose. Or toy soldiers."

"Or billionaires collect Maserati's," said Jacek.

Cale rubbed a hand over his face. He imagined Hugh Hefner or P. Diddy, guys who always seemed to have a gaggle of willing females around for their amusement. Didn't they also collect high-end automobiles? What was it with collecting cars and women? There had to be some phallic inadequacy issues at work. Or perhaps it was simpler: maybe they did it because they could?

"Wait." Cale held one hand up. "I thought we were focusing on human trafficking here. Not pricey high-end harems."

"Don't worry, Mr. Packer. We're coming to that." Jacek spoke like a college professor. "Just taking the scenic route." He opened his palms as if speaking to a challenged student.

"Ladies of a harem are well compensated," Cheetah explained further. "Whether with drugs, alcohol. Invitations to celeb parties; or even modeling or showbiz connections. There's a satisfactory quid pro quo involved."

Jacek said, "Prince Mir, however, is a tomcat of another breed."

"I'm afraid to ask."

Cale finished the last of his sandwich and noticed Pharaoh casting him a sideways glance. The large mercenary was not the warmest person in the world, and Cheetah had confessed the guy had dibs on the sandwich, if Cale hadn't woken up from his extended slumber. Tough luck, Pharaoh.

"He's what profilers call a 'preferential predator,'" Jacek said, sounding professorial. "It means he targets a specific *type* of victim. *Verstehe*?"

Cale narrowed his eyes at Jacek . He remained uncertain where they might be headed with all this mumbo jumbo. What the hell did any of it have to do with his hunt for two missing kidnapping victims? For Crenshaw's killer? Or for Kinsella?

Cheetah toyed the mouse with her fingertips, clicking a few times as the cursor jetted across her monitor. Cale couldn't help but notice her fingernails. The index and middle fingers and the thumb on each hand, he could see, had been chiseled into steel-hard points, lacquered until they'd become unbendable daggers. It was her favorite method of disabling an opponent. He'd seen Cheetah in action and could not imagine being on the receiving end of those sharpened blades. Something he hoped he'd never experience.

A series of new photographs popped onto her screen. Cale felt his eyes widen. The images were so startling he did a double take.

He was staring at photos of an array of females dressed in leather corsets, spike-heeled boots, thongs, bustiers. Some wore jodhpurs and leather vests and carried wicked-looking riding crops. Others wore feather masks or tight latex half-hoods. The pictures seemed similar to porn sites Cale recalled viewing during his days working vice. The costumes represented a variety of what he understood to be fetishes.

"He dresses his girls in these outfits," Cheetah stated, her tone robotic.

"'He, meaning this royal? This Prince Mir character?"

She bobbed her head. "He enters them in fetish competitions in different countries in Europe. One of which is scheduled"—she glanced in Jacek's direction—"for tomorrow afternoon. At his private château."

"A little shindig," Jacek added with a smirk, "they're calling the 'Belgian Fetish Festival.'"

They were silent for a beat, and Cale could distinguish the muted sound of an airplane flying overhead, headed north, hugging the coastline toward Rome, judging from the reverb echo.

"And this is all legal? This...this fetish crap?" he asked. While the others had seemed nonjudgmental, a note of sarcasm dripped from Cale's words.

Cheetah's accent sounded more clipped than usual. "As long as the females do so willingly, it's legal. Sweden, Norway, the Netherlands, Germany. It's considered tame by European standards, as far as vices go. Fetish enjoyment falls under the heading of adult entertainment." She sighed. "Besides, Prince Mir's females all appear to be over the age of consent."

"Most in their early twenties. No minors," Jacek added. "At least from the intel we're gathering."

Cale leaned in closer to Cheetah's monitor and studied the racy set of photographs. She backed away, giving him room, and at the same time seemed to guess what he was thinking. "Bottom line," she said, her tone more judgmental this time, "Prince Mir Al-Sadar is an a-number-one scumbag."

Cale said nothing.

"But there's always a rub, isn't there?" This was stated by Pharaoh, who until this time had remained mute. His sudden voice surprised Cale enough that he turned his head.

Cheetah added, her tone sober, "We're convinced the crimes are being committed at the prince's fancy château. We're not certain what *types* of illegality, but his behavior over these past few years fails to pass the smell test."

Jacek brought home the point by barking. "Proving it, proving it, *proving it!*" He sounded like a drill sergeant shouting the troop's mantra. "There's your rub for you!"

Cale shot a glance at his watch. He gave Cheetah a look that indicated he was ready to run his errand. He tipped his head, indicating the exit.

"One more thing, Detective, before we head out." Cheetah directed him toward her screen, and her slender fingers worked the mouse again. This time her monitor showed at least two dozen photographic headshots like the type modeling agencies use to advertise their "talent". But these weren't modeling agency photos, Cale decided. Although they weren't of the fetish variety, something about them seemed different than standard modeling photos. They appeared less polished, more natural and untouched—"rawer," if he had to choose a word.

"Where did these come from?" he asked.

Jacek said, "I obtained them through a personal contact, whom we agreed would remain nameless. It's a roster of call girls the prince—advertises. If that's the correct word."

Cale gazed at the pictures and stayed silent.

"As we now know, the Belgian authorities have been taking photos of Prince Mir's girl-toys over the past few months." Jacek spoke this like a TV anchor attempting to lure in viewers. "Agent Fronteer has begun cross-checking those with Interpol's Missing Person's database, specific for the age-range of your pair of kidnapped victims, Mr. Packer. The ones she informed them you're in search of."

Cale nodded. Maybe, at last, they were getting somewhere.

"See anyone you recognize?" Cheetah prompted him with a stare, indicating the screen with the business tip of one sharpened fingernail.

Cale focused on the bevy of feminine faces on the monitor. A few jittery saccadic movements later, his eyes landed on one particular blond-haired female. She had her honey-toned hair swept back in a tight bun.

"My God. I *do* recognize this one!"

He pointed at a photo in the seventh row, third from the right. Cale kept his eyes locked on the image, afraid if he glanced away for even an instant, she might vanish from the screen as fast as she'd appeared.

"You're certain?" Jacek shot a glance at Cheetah. "A lot of these blonde girls, they tend to look alike much of the time."

Pharaoh gave a snicker.

"Leslie Ann Dowd." Cale's voice sounded as dry as the walls surrounding them. "She's one of the women I'm searching for." Of course, he was certain. He'd been staring at her photo on their Missing Persons board every day for over the past year. He knew every contour of her face, right down to the singular dimple on her left cheek.

Cale fixed his gaze on the multiple faces, the rows of comely female pictures, one after the next. He was hoping to spot his second missing victim: Mary Jane Moore, also from Green Bay. He ran down the pictures, shot after shot, row after row, but failed to recognize her.

"Any idea when this photo was taken?" Cale looked at Cheetah.

"Can't say. They're taken off a website." She moved her eyes bac to the screen. "Interpol's best guess, maybe within the past three months."

"It means there's a good chance she's still alive, doesn't it?"

"Let's hope so."

Cale hadn't heard Jacek rise, but it was clear his friend was speaking into his phone as he walked, then stopped and turned. "Yes, that's correct. Positive confirmation." Jacek paused, listening before adding, "Affirmative. Full engagement."

Jacek snapped the phone closed. He addressed them in a firm voice. "Excellent. We're a green light from our end."

"A green light," Cheetah said with a nod.

With time running out on his mission, Cale decided this could only be a good thing.

CHAPTER 6

They strode across the open front area of the warehouse, headed in the direction of Jacek's van. The vehicle was parked near the tall exit doors. Cale carried a mid-sized cardboard box wrapped with electrical tape. Keys jingling from her slender fingers, Cheetah moved at his side, as silent as a flake of falling snow.

While they walked, Cale's mind replayed his earlier phone conversation with his partner, Slink Dooley. How ironic, it seemed, that although they were four thousand miles apart, their paths had meshed, and they were now working the same homicide case. Both in search of the Liberian hit man—Kinsella: Slink looking to book the man on a murder rap; and Cale hoping the (alleged) killer might lead him to his pair of missing abduction victims.

Nevertheless, while Jacek worked with Agent Fronteer to come up with a game plan, Cale's errand, at the moment, seemed just as necessary. If for nothing else than peace of mind.

He glanced down at the box in his hands. His thoughts returned to his earlier phone conversation with Slink. Cale had been holding the phone tucked against his shoulder, and while talking, he'd located the canvas sack containing the pair of African artifacts—sitting right where Cheetah said it would be—which he'd pilfered from Tazeki Mabutu, the Liberian military colonel.

"So, your suspicion is what, again?" Slink had asked, pointed and brusque. "That this Colonel Mabutu has ties to Kinsella? That they're involved in a trafficking ring together?"

"Just a theory. I've been wrong before."

Slink let it slide. "I still don't see how Tobias Crenshaw fits into the picture. Here? In Green Bay?" He'd paused. "What connection could he have to Liberia, of all places?"

"There has to be one. Otherwise, none of it makes any sense."

Both detectives had pondered the words silence. At last, Slink said, "Here's a bit of advice, Kemosabe. Next time you want a vacation, how about a relaxing shark cage dive?"

"Feels like I'm already on one—without the cage." Cale had exhaled. "Truth is, I thought about bagging this trip. Flying home early."

"Wouldn't be like you, man. You're a closer. It might take you twenty innings, but you get there eventually."

Cale worked the compliment over in his mind. "'Stubborn is a fancy word for stupid.'... It's what my old man used to say."

"No argument from this end."

While they'd been talking, Cale had discovered a few spools of tape and scissors and other packing supplies lying about. He transferred the pair of artifacts—the strange bronze-colored, ceramic statue of an evil-looking idol, along with the blond-haired, female shrunken head—into a mid-sized cardboard box. He bundled them tight, employing discarded Italian newspapers, then wrapped them in plastic bubble wrap. He'd stuffed the inner box tight, so the items couldn't shift. He sealed the carton with the thick electrical tape.

He'd set the box on the concrete floor of the warehouse and listened to Slink's theory on Green Bay's first public assassination.

The shooter, Slink had theorized, had known the precise time of Tobias Crenshaw's jail release. Disguised himself as a BET cameraman, hidden among the print and TV reporters. Used a modified camera disguised as a weapon. A preplanned hit. No doubt about it.

"Our guess is Kinsella—along with a partner, perhaps—drove up from Milwaukee. He dodged out of town after the shooting, while we still had our pants around our ankles."

Cale had massaged the bruises along his jawline. Courtesy of the man who'd tried to murder him the night before, in the Naples Military Airport. "Either way, it's on us. We should've done a better job protecting Citizen Crenshaw."

"Not many tears are being shed for the prick."

"Justice prevails." Cale's tone was macabre. "Or karma. Or whatever." His bandaged ribs complained as he'd swept away the packing mess from the table top. "So, this Kinsella. Where is he? This minute?"

"In the wind. A ghost. Over twenty-four hours now, since the shooting.

"You're saying he could be anywhere on the planet?"

"Sounds about right."

Great, Cale had thought. That narrowed it down. "Like I said, I've got three more days here. I'll see where it takes me." Across the warehouse, he could hear echoes of Jacek and his partners conversing at their computer stations.

"Watch your ass, Cale. I mean it." Slink's voice had tightened. "Sounds like those hombres over there are playing for keeps."

Cale had mumbled a response.

"One final message," his partner had said. "Maggie says, quote: 'Tell him to get his ass back here. In one piece—if he knows what's good for him.'"

"She's the boss."

"Never thought I'd hear you admit it."

"Admit what?"

It was an hour later now, as Cale climbed into the van's passenger seat. He positioned the large cardboard box on the floor at his feet. Cheetah keyed the ignition, and Cale could still hear Slink's warning ringing in his head:

These hombres were playing for keeps.

The van eased through the high doors of the warehouse. With their sunglasses shielding them from the harsh glare, the vehicle accelerated across the parking area. Cale's thoughts shifted once more. He couldn't stop thinking about what he'd witnessed on the computer screen ten minutes ago: the photo of one—just one—of his missing victims. He pondered the implications. Cale was a lead investigator, one who had worked his way up through the ranks. He was seasoned enough not to leap to obvious conclusions.

Yet the image he'd viewed of Leslie Dowd had jolted him. He prayed she was still alive. And hoped he could someday convey the good news to her parents and loved ones. As he'd informed Slink, however, his chances of locating her somewhere on the European continent...well, they were beyond Powerball odds. And his hourglass was flipped and running.

As Cheetah navigated them out onto the crowded boulevard, Cale's thoughts remained troubled. His mission hadn't changed: apprehend Kinsella, return him to the States to face charges. Make him reveal the whereabouts of the pair of missing victims.

And further, as grim as things appeared, Cale understood that Kinsella was not his solitary problem.

Somehow his search for the mysterious hit man had landed him in the crosshairs of Colonel Mabutu—a man who wanted, beyond any doubt, to murder him. Had tried three times already in the past twenty-four hours. And for what? For swiping a pair of insignificant items from the colonel's private collection? Stealing them only after he'd survived the man's first attempt on his life?

It seemed too far-fetched to believe. Or was there more to the man's apparent vendetta? More than Cale was seeing?

There had to be, he decided. But what? It remained a mystery. Unless, of course, the man was a card-carrying psychopath.

In light of these circumstances, Cale had calculated that his smartest move was to ship the pair of ill-gotten artifacts back home. They'd be safer there, out of reach, and he wouldn't have to worry about their safekeeping

The point? He could use them as leverage, something to bargain with—if ever he came face to face with Mabutu again. Not in this lifetime, Cale hoped. But on the outside chance he did run across the man, at least he'd have something to negotiate with. Items, so it seemed, that the colonel valued. The trick, in the meantime, was keeping the shrunken head and idol statue secure.

Cale had decided that shipping them out of the country was his best bet.

Out of sight, out of mind.

CHAPTER 7

Buses and cabs and open-air sightseeing trolleys—they all rolled past as if on parade, back and forth as the sun's sparkling rays glinted off windshields and hoods and fenders. Vans and SUVs were filled with tourists having trekked down the coast from Rome. These vehicles hummed together through the arid Anzio streets on a bleached Friday afternoon, and they were joined by the steady flow of smaller Italian, French, and German automobiles. Motorbikes, bicycles, mini-scooters—they wove in and out of traffic like persistent gnats. Strolling sightseers paraded the sidewalks on both sides of the wide central *viale*, moving in opposite directions like workers changing shifts in a factory.

Between the close-packed buildings the cerulean waters sparkled in the sunlight. Along the docks fishing boats were tied down, bobbing with the gentle sigh of waves. Too warm to fish this time of day, they'd venture out again with their nets when the sun began its downward arc. A few gulls cruised the air, searching for easy pickings where the sailors had discarded their offal into the water lapping at the wooden piers. The salty air smelled like brine, spiced with the tang of fresh octopus and seaweed.

Observing this all from the passenger seat of Jacek's dark van, Cale felt lulled by the warmth of the afternoon. He couldn't prevent his mind from drifting to more personal matters and wondered why he'd felt such an urgent need to ship the pilfered items—the shrunken head and the sinister-looking pewter idol— back home. He wondered why he'd taken the time to steal them in the first place. He'd done so over Jacek's protestations. Was it an effort at inflicting emotional pain on the man who'd attempted to snuff out their lives? Or was there some deeper reason? One Cale couldn't put his finger on just yet?

He shook away the troublesome questions and decided that making conversation with Cheetah seemed less taxing. He stared at her lacquered, unbreakable fingernails as her hands gripped the steering wheel.

Sensing his stare, Cheetah angled her head his way. "The girl on the screen?" she said in an earnest voice. "You're sure she's the one you're searching for?"

"Never been surer."

"Good. It means we're moving in the right direction."

"God, I hope so." Cale sighed. "Time's not my ally, you know."

He fingered the edges of the box at his feet, as if reminding himself it was still there. He felt revved, almost too antsy to discuss his positive ID of Leslie Dowd. He wanted to hop on a plane this instant, zip to Belgium, pound on the front door of Prince Mir Al-Sadar's pricey château, confront the man…and search the grounds to see where he was hiding Leslie and the rest of his "harem." Instead, Cale took a calming breath.

"So, how'd you get hooked up—business wise—with Jacek?" he asked, conversationally. "I mean, in the first place?"

Even her laugh sounded accented. "For real?"

"He's an interesting guy. I'm curious."

She paused as if arranging her memories, then said, "We were fighting in Angola. About eight years ago." She kept her eyes focused on the shifting traffic around them. "We both supported the rebel cause. We ended up trapped together, pinned in the jungle, separated from our units. Jacek asked me how many hostiles we were facing. 'At least twenty,' I told him, 'armed with Kalashnikovs, machetes, and hand grenades.'"

Cale studied her while she talked. Her cheekbones appeared sharp, as if they'd been sculpted from marble.

"You know what he said to me? Jacek?" Cheetah asked.

"Something noble, I'm sure."

"'Best odds I've faced in a year.' It's what he said." She flashed a too white smile. "We've been working together since. Trying to stay on Team Good Guys."

"Not always easy, I take it."

She shrugged. "People hire you. They claim they're fighting on the side of justice. Of freedom. The usual righteous causes, you know? Then, well, you find out later it's never as black and white as they made it out to be."

"Shades of gray. The story of my life."

Cheetah issued Cale a sidelong glance. She changed lanes, sliding the van ahead of a slow-moving Fiat. "My turn to ask something. Fair's fair, right, Detective?"

"Fair's fair."

"Your relationship? At home?" She kept her eyes focused forward. "I couldn't help overhearing you on the phone earlier. You sounded stressed. That what you mean by 'shades of gray'?"

Cale's brow furrowed. The directness of her inquiry gave him pause, and Cheetah was quick to add, "Jacek told us you're engaged to be married, so the cat's out, mind you."

Looking at her in the van's half-shadow, Cale decided she had the most curiously shaped ears he'd ever seen on a woman. They were angled back like those of an Egyptian cat, matching the perfect symmetry of her smooth jawline.

"I'm dealing with some personal...issues. Can we maybe leave it at that?"

Cheetah gave him a nod and stayed quiet.

"Fiancée issues, I guess you'd call them," he continued, ending the extended pause. "You know how it is—or maybe not." He toyed with the tape at the box's corner. "Guess I'll shut up now."

Cheetah cast her dark eyes in his direction, then back to the street ahead. "Trust me, I know." She exhaled. "So, are they big 'fiancée issues'? Or even bigger ones?"

Cale glanced out the van's window at the moving traffic on his right. At least fifty motor scooters were chugging along. He watched a bicyclist just miss a pair of college girls, then almost get clipped by a tourist van, himself.

Turning to Cheetah, he said, "Not easy to say, at the moment. But pass it along to Jacek—I don't let personal problems interfere with my work."

She stayed silent, intent on her driving.

Cale noted how Cheetah had mastered the art of being a good conversationalist, meaning she knew when to keep her mouth closed. Knew when not to pry beyond politeness. He continued to stare out the window at the homes, the buildings, the shaded trees along the wide boulevard. He could see the sand-colored houses on the distant hillside looking as if they'd risen straight from the ancient ground. He noted how each one seemed to gaze out at the sparkle of sun-drenched waters.

After a minute of silence, Cale eyed her where she sat. "That's it? No advice for the lovelorn?"

Cheetah seemed to ponder the question, before saying, "Best you can do is keep your mind off things you can't control." She lifted a bony shoulder. "Deal with the rest when you get back home."

He nodded. "So they keep telling me."

They rode the next six blocks in companionable silence. The lush trees bordering the busy *viale* flashed past. The creeping vines and crawlers climbed the archways and porticos of the buildings and homes, seeming to lash them to the landscape. The sandy, earth-toned structures—burnt orange, sage, sienna—with their high balconies and matching terra-cotta roofs seemed to stare back at them in dignified repose, a certain Italian aloofness.

"My fiancée." Cale broke the silence, his eyes staring out the van's windshield. "She's pregnant." He exhaled. "Maybe not by me."

"Ah. I see."

"Complicates things—somewhat. Guess you'd say."

"I suppose it would, wouldn't it." Not a question.

At the distant edge of the horizon the ocean was a mere hint below the high tufts of lavender cloud. A variety of boats floated on the water as if painted there. Closer to shore, Cale watched the sunlight as it splashed off the glitter of water near the breakers, and he allowed his mind to go blank while thinking of nothing until they arrived at the postal station.

———

Cheetah pulled the van into the familiar parking lot. Seconds later, she eased through the warehouse's dark and open doors, coaxing the van forward as if allowing it to be swallowed by some ancient behemoth. In the passenger seat, Cale felt immediate relief as they slipped inside the cool brick walls. He wondered, briefly, how people could dwell in this broiler of a climate. And it was still mid-May, for God's sake! He'd take the bruised gray clouds, the crisp January winds of a Wisconsin snowstorm, any day.

But no rain, please. At least not for a while. His memory of being trapped in the tedious downpour of Liberia's rainy season made his brain feel as soggy as a deep-sea sponge.

Mailing the box at the Overnight Air shipping service had gone off without a hitch. Cheetah functioned ably as an interpreter, helping Cale with the directions in Italian. He'd addressed the box back to Green Bay, payed the extra cost for "Next Day Air." It was understood, however, that because it was the weekend, it might take extra time to arrive. His package would be shipped that night, Friday, flying into Chicago very late due to the time change. It should arrive at Green Bay's Austin Straubel Airport sometime tomorrow—Saturday—they were guessing by late afternoon. There it would be stored in the airport security hold until he was able to pick it up on his return sometime next week.

It was the best estimate they could give, and Cale insisted there was no hurry.

"*Per favore, non c'e fretta,*" Cheetah told the clerk, who smiled and nodded.

Cale added, "*Grazie,*" as he pocketed the receipt, then made for the door. He wanted the objects out of his sight, wanted not to worry about their whereabouts. For this, he paid the express rate (triple the standard rate) and added flight insurance courtesy of his Visa card.

As the whole business—shipping the box containing the statue and shrunken head—might be related to the case, Cale wondered if Captain McBride would approve him for reimbursement, if he chose to submit the proper receipts to Accounting. The female shrunken head, after all, was potential evidence in a murder investigation. After pondering it further, he let the idea evaporate like morning mist. The odds of him getting his money back? About the same as his returning to Liberia for a fun-filled getaway weekend sometime in the future.

Cale decided Colonel Mabutu's precious items arriving safe at the Green Bay airport would be reward enough. "Antique collectables." That's how the contents were listed on the shipping invoice. He understood, further, that the objects would be x-rayed as they were processed through US Customs. He imagined the look on the scan operator's face as the evil little statuette, along with the smoke-eyes of the blond-haired shrunken head, looked back at them through the monitor.

Cale doubted any of the techs would run screaming from the building. But the thought amused him, nonetheless.

The trip to the shipping office, there and back, had taken thirty minutes. Striding across the cool cement floor of the warehouse now, footsteps echoing—his own, not Cheetah's—they made their way back to the long tables of the computer station. Jacek and Pharaoh were both working diligently. Jacek was on the phone. Pharaoh was downloading incoming encrypted information onto one of the hard drives.

As they approached, Jacek gave them a nod, raised his forefinger, and continued to speak in what Cale guessed was his native Czech. Maybe Hungarian. A few seconds later, Jacek ended his call. In English, he said, "Let's start packing up, guys. Personal necessities only."

"When's departure?" Cheetah asked, not missing a beat.

"We pack first. Then we'll have dinner, catch a few hours shut-eye. We'll be heading out sometime after midnight."

"Tonight?" Cale asked.

He received a narrow look from Jacek. "What, Mr. Packer? You want to wait for a written invitation by mail?"

Pharaoh rose and began lumbering off, not bothering to question their leader. Cheetah asked, "What's our heading?"

"We rendezvous with Agent Fronteer. In Rome." Jacek stated this in blunt fashion. "Then we cruise to Belgium on a predawn mission."

Cale said nothing. He was considering what this sudden change of plans meant. It was Cheetah who asked, "And our mission is what, exactly?"

"Search and rescue." Jacek aimed his firm chin toward Cale. "We're teaming up with Belgian military. They're assisting us. Full TAC squad."

"The target?"

"None other than the private residence of one Prince Mir Al-Sadar." Jacek gave them a knowing smirk. "For the extraction of Leslie Dowd and Cale's second victim, a Ms. Mary Jane Moore. That is, if we can manage to locate her."

When they gave him wide-eyed stares, Jacek added with a flourish: "Ladies and gentlemen, we are about to crash a Fetish Festival."

CHAPTER 8

Liberia, Africa

He needed his statue of Pazuzu back.

The loss of his prized possession would rob Colonel Tazeki Mabutu of his most potent powers. It would lead to his eventual demise. First his strength would fade; then his life-force would begin to ebb. Tazeki—a voodoo witch doctor, a powerful *botono* or *houngan*—understood the consequences. Instead of remaining a man filled with strength and vigor, he would age very fast, turning into a sallow sack of bones and leathered skin, drying, shriveling like a scraggy side of beef with the moisture cooked out. It was the price one paid for striking deals with demons.

He must get Pazuzu back in his grip. His control. The demon's evil power was imprisoned in the statuette.

Tazeki was a man accustomed to having things his own way, and the disappointment on his tongue formed a bitter taste. The elimination of Tobias Crenshaw, his old college roommate and minor flesh-pedaling partner, had gone off without a hitch. Kinsella had seen to that. But the Italian hit man he'd contracted with to eliminate the American detective had resulted in an amateurish failure. Nito Passetti was supposed to be a trained professional, and from all accounts, his ambush at the Naples airport should have been successful. And yet, here he stood— without his friend, Pazuzu. And without the satisfaction of knowing the American was dead. He was angry and frustrated.

But the game, Tazeki understood, was far from over.

Now the time had come—his urgency elevated, no doubt—to remove once and for all this American investigator who was the source of so much recent aggravation. He must destroy this puny irritant, this meddling amateur, and recover Pazuzu. As a team, he and his demon companion were undefeatable. First and foremost, their reign of supremacy must be maintained.

From the leather chair behind his massive desk, Tazeki gazed out across the gray dimpled waters off the Liberian coast. Despite the current drizzle, one of the veranda doors was propped open, and a copper-scented breeze flitted in, flapping the drapery, threatening to scatter some of the papers on his desk. The breeze was an imp, a ghost. It made him smile. Weren't ghosts, after all, the friends of every witch doctor?

It was Friday afternoon. If all went according to plan, he would have Pazuzu back in his hands by Sunday—at the latest. That was good enough. It would have to be. The status quo, he reminded himself...the status quo trumped all.

Fishing inside a lower desk drawer, he withdrew a disposable phone wrapped in cellophane. He unskinned the object and activated the power, punched in the desired numbers, and the ringer sounded twice. He closed the phone. The time was nearing three o'clock here in Liberia. They were two hours behind standard Belgian time. Thirty seconds later, the phone in his hand buzzed. It was Kinsella, of course, responding to his call.

"Report your status," Tazeki demanded impatiently.

Through the tall bank of windows, he could see the skies were dull and overcast. The sun, up there somewhere, remained hidden from view. The clouds were bruised battleships above the undulating steel-gray waters, which seemed to stretch forever toward the gloomy edge of the Earth.

"Just arrived at the château. As you requested. I'm on the front steps, heading to the dinner." Kinsella conveyed this with his usual efficiency.

The man-monster possessed a barrel-sized torso and the no-neck, bullet-shaped head of a human anaconda. His skull was shaved, and in his ear, a diamond stud. Kinsella always wore his sport coats a full size too small. He wore them with the sleeves smushed up to his elbows. The reason for his odd fashion statement, as far as Tazeki could determine, was two-fold: the jacket showed off his powerful physique to great effect, and the get-up conveyed to the world the man was in no way a slave to convention.

He could not care less how Kinsella presented himself. Why would he? The man was a psychopath and, much like Tazeki himself, enjoyed the taste of human flesh. They were Liberians, after all, and they were cannibals. What of it? Everything else was beside the fact. All he required of his right-hand man—his childhood best friend (called Nmanu back then)—was loyalty. He must do the witch doctor's bidding, and he must do so without question, without the slightest hint of hesitation.

Quite simple job requirements, all things considered.

Listening to his phone now, Tazeki could distinguish the murmur of voices in the background—the slam of car doors, tires crunching over the circular cobblestone driveway. There was even the nearby gurgle of the massive front fountain. He was quite familiar with the layout of Prince Mir Al-Sadar's lavish château.

"Give His Highness my regards," Tazeki said to Kinsella. "But listen, my friend, our priorities have shifted."

"No problems with the boat, I trust?"

He rotated in his high-backed chair. "None. The *Kwensana* set sail for the UK this morning. Two dozen fresh-faced virgins, ready as peaches to be plucked."

Kinsella gave no comment to the remark.

"Our shipment is *en route*, suffice it to say. But we still have a most annoying problem."

"What would you wish me to do, Botono?"

Tazeki felt his teeth grind. "This American detective...he escaped—somehow—from the eel pit. He murdered Kasim, and he stole Pazuzu. He was flown to Naples on a US military cargo, where the fuck-up, Nito Passetti, missed him. Once again."

"Ah. Pity."

Tazeki forced his jaw to relax. "The American is holed-up in Anzio. A secluded warehouse there."

"You want him terminated, I take it. With, as they say in the movies, with *extreme prejudice*."

"I want him terminated, all right. With extreme *pain*! Use your regular man. The one in Rome." Tazeki cast his eye across the room to the empty spot on the fireplace mantle. "This nuisance, this obscene gnat...this Van Waring... I want him eliminated. Tonight."

"I'll make the call at once, Botono."

"And Kinsella, promise you won't disappoint me like the rest of these incompetent fools."

"Obeah-mon—you know me, my brother. No worries. No worries at all."

Click.

Tazeki set the phone on his desk. He focused his eyes out the tall windows once more, as if mesmerized by the roll of waves massaging the rain-sodden beach with their foamy, kneading fingers. It was settled. Pazuzu would be returned with no evident harm.

"Soon. Very soon," he whispered to the wind, to the water, to himself. He felt the ghosts hovering just inside the open veranda door, and they graced him with thin and vacuous smiles.

Tonight, the colonel knew, he would sleep like a newborn babe. One just recovered from its first rude slap.

———

Château du Carthairs, Belgium

Inside the opulent château, Kinsella stood in a hallway outside the closed fifteen-foot tall doors, which shielded him from the inner dining hall. A half-dozen huge jungle ferns, leaves as broad as giant flat-screens, sprouted from colorful hand-painted urns. The carpeting was a swirl of gold on burgundy. The walls were painted with murals depicting Middle Eastern life of centuries past.

A servant in a crème-colored jacket stood at the far end of the lengthy hallway, out of earshot, waiting for him to conclude his telephone business.

Certain he could not be overheard, Kinsella punched in the numbers on his mobile. Tebbi Qa was stationed in Rome. It would take the man but a brief ride on the commuter train down to Anzio, shielded by the cover of evening darkness, a fitting disguise for a man whose skin was as black as the moonless waters of the Mediterranean.

Kinsella was garbed for the event in a too-snug black dinner jacket, one he had procured last minute at a clothier inside the Brussels International airport. When his old friend answered his phone, Kinsella smiled for the first time in months. In a discreet voice, he gave the hit man the address the botono had supplied him with.

"The method is my choice?" Tebbi Qa spoke with a Nairobian accent, deep and dry as sandpaper.

Kinsella kept his own tone modulated. "As long as it's quiet, mon. He's an American—a policeman. We don't want the local *carabinieri* nosing around like hungry raccoons."

"His sleep, then. Cyanide injection. Drop the naked carcass in the mile-deep waters beyond the drop-off."

"Fine. By the time he washes to shore in three days, they'll imagine another drunken tourist has drowned while pleasure boating."

"The payment?"

"Customary. Times three," Kinsella said, emphasizing the latter. "The Colonel is, need I say…serious."

It was settled. Flipping his phone closed, Kinsella gave the waiting man up the corridor the slightest of nods. The servant moved with haste down the carpeted hallway, his shiny jacket buttons glistening beneath the trio of crystal chandeliers. Quick as a mongoose, he opened one tall door to the dining hall and allowed his over-sized guest inside.

"*Danke schön*," murmured Kinsella, trying to be cute.

The servant's reply, if he made one, was trumped by the laughter and hum of dinner conversation, which swallowed Kinsella whole as he moved thuggishly into the room.

—————

Liberia, Africa

For the first time in three days Tazeki felt himself relax. His call to Kinsella filled him with a sense of relief. After all, he had the utmost faith his right-hand man would see to it the American detective was taken care of—removed from the picture, as it were. And Pazuzu would be returned to where he belonged: in his master's possession.

Tazeki rose from his chair, having decided to build a celebratory drink at the wet bar. But before he could take three steps, his desk phone began to flash. In better times, Kasim would have screened his calls, but his servant was no more. Besides, this

44

call was coming in on the "silver" line. It was a number only a handful of select business partners knew.

He picked up the receiver, announcing, "Colonel Mabutu here."

"Colonel, we've seen via satellite our shipment is in transit. The Corporation wishes to commend you for another job well done."

Tazeki's lips were tight. "Herr Berg. Allow me to say, it's a pleasure to work with your Corporation."

"Splendid, Colonel." The man had a little *knackwurst* in his voice, his accent just strong enough to be noticeable. "I won't bore you with platitudes. Your final payment will be deposited in your account upon arrival."

"The Bern account, if you please."

"*Ja. Wie du meinst.*" As you wish.

"Until next time then, Herr Berg," the witch doctor said. He heard a faint click, then pure silence.

Setting the receiver back in its cradle, with a smile he proceeded across the room to the mahogany and teak wet bar in the furthest corner. On the wall behind the bar hung a pair of long spears, feathers sprouting, crossed above a ceremonial mask carved from human bone. Although it was still early, he decided that rewarding himself with his drink was still in order.

Tazeki glanced across the room at the ghosts, who continued to hover inside the open veranda door. He spoke out loud to them:

"Better yet. I say we make it a double."

CHAPTER 9

In Western Africa, over two thousand years ago they were referred to as *juju*. They were little woven dolls or "poppets" strung together to create a personal talisman. Sometimes they were made of pieces of twine or twigs from bird nests, dried reeds from the riverbank, or roots, stones, or pieces of shell. Small chips of wood formed the eyes. Seven or nine or thirteen personal items—never an even number—were placed inside the poppet, which was then woven tight and closed. Doused with urine or semen or excrement to add *umbala*, a poppet could be employed to garner good health and wellbeing through the aid of the loa.

On the other hand, one could just as easily create a poppet of an enemy—either laboring alone or through a houngan or mambo or obeah man—or a dark botono (a witch doctor). The use of a poppet for evil would cast great bleakness over someone's life, plague them with untold hardship, constant pain, endless suffering. If left unchecked, these maladies would lead to a painful decline, followed by a bitter and withering death.

After the European invasion of the "cradle of humanity," the traditional poppet dolls evolved into small cloth sachets or pouches, which held these same personal items. These pouches were called *gris-gris*, and this is what botono Tazeki Mabutu preferred to use these days when he applied his magic. The pouches were easy to employ. They could be any size and be buried in the ground without worry from weather or predators. They protected the sacred objects within more effectively. They were also easier to dispose of once a ransom was paid or a debt resolved or if the spellbinder's desires, for whatever reason, happened to change.

His personal gris-gris, which Tazeki had implanted within the base of the statue of Pazuzu, contained the dark feather of a vulture, a leopard's eye, the dried anus of a goat, the Knight of Wands from his first tarot deck (*his card*), his dried semen, and the knucklebones of an albino infant. These were the first six items. The seventh—and most significant of all—was the weathered caul from his infancy, the remnant tissue membrane that had covered half his infant head at birth.

Tazeki Mabutu, grandson of the great botono Njada, had been born a caul baby.

Rumors spread from village to village when little Tazeki entered the world. The stories turned out—as rumors often do—to be true. A caul baby. In times when superstitions held more sway, an infant born with a membranous uterine attachment clinging to its skull was deemed a child blessed by the loa. At other times, the opposite: the baby was presumed to be destined for evil. Cain, the brother of Abel, was whispered to have been born in such a manner—as were Alexander the Great and Rasputin; and Benito Mussolini; and Judas Iscariot, as well, along with countless other notables down through the ages. The unofficial historical list was a lengthy one.

Tazeki's mother, he learned many years later, had been ecstatic. Her infant child, being born not merely the son of a botono (and grandson of the greatest wizard of his time), but also born with a caul...why, he would be destined for nothing short of greatness. He would grow up to be a man from whom kings would seek counsel. Or, perhaps, he might rise to become a great king himself.

A celebration had been held in the village. Tales were told of how the party continued unabated until the caul fell away on his fifth day in this world. As was the custom at the time, the women of the village went to great lengths to preserve the caul. It was dried and kept as part of the child's personal inheritance. In young Tazeki's case, it had been kept safe in his possession until the fateful day when he'd stood alone in the nighttime jungle and made his pact with the demon, Pazuzu, beneath the glow of a scarlet moon. His personal items were transferred to the demon's care as part of their pact. Inside the gris-gris, tucked within the statue's base, the objects had never been far from the botono's sight.

Until now, that is.

Tazeki sat alone in his study in silence, sipping his scotch. He pondered his grim situation. He understood how much he needed to locate his statuette. The American detective had stolen it from him. And until his sacred belongings—his caul most of all—were back in his possession, the rest of the world could be damned.

Much to his consternation, the wind ghosts inside the room began to snicker, to taunt him: *What if the foreigner no longer has the statue, Obeah-mon? Maybe he's discarded Pazuzu during his escape? Tossed him into the tall scrub brush? Perhaps thinking the idol a mere insignificant piece of bric-a-brac?"*

"Silence!"

Tazeki barked this to the air, the breeze, the patter of drizzle on the veranda outside the doors. Though the back of his neck felt heated, he blamed it on the whiskey.

The spirit voices had caused him to blanch with the bare uncertainty of it all. And doubt, of course, was an unfamiliar state for a powerful witch doctor. Reaching once again for his mobile, he punched in another number.

"Listen, Loba," Tazeki said stiffly, "you remember the Ualo woman? Yes. Her boy—little Chike—he should be, what, four months old by this time?"

He listened for a few seconds, before saying, "I want you to bring the tot to me. And, Loba...I want him still warm."

———

Château du Carthairs, Belgium

A canvas banner had been erected the day before. Set fifteen feet above the front entrance doors of the chateau, and stretching twenty feet across, it read:

WELCOME BELGIAN FETISH FESTIVAL

The banner, on display beneath the second story windows, looked down upon the curl of circular driveway, which rolled past the magnificent gurgling fountain and a dozen mature oak and willow trees.

On Friday, the arrivals had been steady all afternoon, keeping the valets hopping as they parked limousines and town cars and custom-designed SUVs. There was not a scooter or an electric or any ridiculous "hybrid" in the bunch. Prince Mir Al-Sadar had forbidden these. After all, he was descended from serious oil money. His veins ran thick with the stuff.

Now the rich summer sunset cast an amber glow across the horizon, and with twilight fast approaching it wouldn't be long before the Belgian countryside erupted in the usual cacophony of night sounds. Inside the château, in the luminous high-ceilinged dining hall, a variety of curiously garbed guests had seated themselves for the feast to follow.

Members of Prince Mir's private harem, his twenty prized females—each in a form-fitting dinner gown, each bedecked with glittering jewelry on loan from His Majesty's private vault—were seated ten to a room, divided among the guests in the adjacent pair of dining halls. Later, after the formal diner, the rooms' connecting doors would be opened and the two rooms transformed into a single celebration hall.

In the primary room at present, the one occupied by Prince Mir, Leslie Dowd couldn't prevent her eyes from shifting about. She eyed each of the seated guests. Leslie had been issued a position nine chairs down from His Highness (who was seated at the table's head, of course) and had presented herself just on time, short of breath.

Most of the guests had arrived before she happened on the scene and were already seated, so Leslie could only study them from the waist up. There was a mad-looking Hungarian man, his beard a forest, who wore a leather biker's vest over a long black tunic; there sat a petite, birdlike female dressed like a dark falcon, mask and all; a tall, slender Gambian man, wearing a colorful sari, had his face and shaved skull pierced with at least fifty silver studs and penny nails; and the rotund Englishman appeared to be a Savile Row tailor, until one peered closely enough to discern his suit was made of embroidered lizard skin. A goateed Spaniard wore a kangaroo-hide beret; and a pair of silver-haired Norwegian twins were garbed in some half-leather, half-spandex hybrid.

These and other colorful persons were the invited guests.

The theme of the event seemed clear: each guest appeared more outlandish than the next, and all were seated in the additional thirty chairs surrounding the length of the great table. The one constant, Leslie noted, was that each was in some way affiliated with the competition being held on the grounds tomorrow. And each, no doubt, was a fetish enthusiast.

Awash in their mellow heroin haze, the harem members at the table were on strict orders from the prince to behave themselves. They were to be polite, smile and nod, to laugh at every attempt at wit—no matter how banal—to comport themselves in genteel feminine fashion. Bottom line: be pleasant, and don't embarrass His Majesty.

Or suffer the consequences.

As she failed to recognize anyone resembling the German pony-girl contingent, at least not from her clichéd imaginings of what they might look like, Leslie felt her guard relax. None of the guests present would have the faintest clue she was the prince's team captain. She decided, further, that they could not have cared less. Once the girls were in their equine garb—eye-shields and halters, bits in their mouths, bushy tails and hooved boots—they all looked alike anyway. Wasn't it the point?

Beginning to grow more comfortable, her own narcotics blissfully kicking in, Leslie took a sip from her wine glass. A Bordeaux. Prince Mir had issued strict orders that team members be limited to a single glass this evening, before being shuffled off to an early bedtime on the eve of the contest. From where she sat now, Leslie could hear His Highness toss off a punch line and she smiled with the others, not having paid the slightest attention to the setup. Turning toward the table's head, she noticed for the first time the empty chair two spots down from the prince's right hand. Someone late for dinner? She prayed it wasn't one of the girls. The punishment would be stern and unrelenting.

As if on cue, a burly African man in an ill-fitting dark dinner jacket was ushered into the room by one of the servants. The man had a shaved head, no discernible neck, and a single glittery diamond stud in his right earlobe. The gem seemed more a nod to piracy than high fashion. He moved around the table with a certain bullish grace, acknowledging the prince with a bow, before easing his bulk into the vacant chair.

Leslie felt her blood turn to ice. Her heart began to gallop. This was the man of her nightmares. The devil she'd seen from time to

50

time standing beside the prince, watching their workouts and practice runs. He was the fiend who had captured her in the forest during her recent ill-fated escape attempt, the one who'd injected her with the knockout drug. This was the jackal who had tied her to the table in the basement dungeon, laughing like a sadist while threatening to slice away pieces of her flesh and consume them whole.

The man responsible for roasting her friend, Mary Jane Moore. The *cannibal*.

Leslie glared with seething eyes at the large African. Sensing her eyes on him, the bull rotated his boulder-sized head and grinned maliciously at her, recognition registering. His ivory teeth gleamed in the room's golden light, and he gave her a wink.

At once very ill, Leslie tossed her napkin on her plate. She rose, excused herself to those nearby, and rushed off through the back-kitchen doors of the dining hall.

CHAPTER 10

Anzio, Italy

Dinner had consisted of fresh vegetables and glazed scallops. Nothing too heavy, Jacek advised, as he was uncertain what all their mission might entail. They'd been seated on the outside deck at the same beachfront restaurant where they lunched before on Cale's first day in Italy. Jacek preferred the sanctity of familiarity and limited them to a single bottle of Moretti each. Cheetah had opted for mineral water.

They had returned back to the warehouse, with time to gather their gear for tomorrow's excursion, and capture a couple hours of sleep.

Inside his small sleeping room, having removed his combat clothes, Cale sat on the mattress in his socks and skivvies. He grabbed one of his heavy boots and used the heel to crush a roach-looking Italian insect crawling along the floor. It seemed to give off a metallic odor as it perished. Cale hoped this would be their final night in the tourist city of Anzio. If all went well during tomorrow's raid on the château, perhaps he'd be heading home by nightfall, his pair of rescued victims in tow.

He sure as hell hoped so.

Out in the central area of the warehouse, Cale could hear the others loading the gear for their late-night journey. They were leaving in four hours, sometime after midnight, and would be armed and ready for just about anything. It was the mercenary's normal state of existence: preparation twenty-four-seven. They were ready to chopper-off on a dime, prepared to eat on the run or to catch some filtered, one-eyed sleep on a forest floor. Whether called to invade a targeted cabin or cave, armed with knives, flash grenades, or AKs...to grapple with a hostile aggressor or rappel down a high building or off a cliff face, they were prepared to confront any challenge. It was high adrenaline, primo alert, kill or be killed. Cale doubted they had much of a 401k plan.

And if they did, how many were around to collect at age sixty-five? To him the answer seemed obvious.

When looking at it closer, he decided employment as a mercenary seemed to be the polar opposite of police work. In his everyday job, everything seemed to move at a snail's pace—interviews with potential witnesses, searching for minute clues, waiting for lab results, dealing with vague and disguised motivations on the part of offenders. It was always a waiting game: waiting for the DA's office to decide on charges, waiting for reluctant witnesses to come forth, waiting for a break in the case.

Prosecutors and their adversaries—the defense lawyers—seemed to be inverse specimens of the same predatory shark. They swam in sluggish, backed-up court waters, which were polluted by mounds of paperwork. And the paperwork proved a torture in and of itself. Things needed to be computerized, coded, logged, and filed without error. It was a never-ending morass of buttery slowness, everything working under the guise of due process. The pressure was always on—for the investigators anyway, who often handled five or six cases at a time—demanding the need to clear a case inside a five-week time frame.

Then it was on to another case.

Despite police work's frustrations, however, Cale decided he didn't envy his mercenary friends. He didn't relish dodging knives and bullets and explosions and sniper fire for a living. Although he was thankful for Jacek assisting him in his fish-out-of-water search for his missing victims, he'd be the first to admit—as things stood at present—he was pretty much along for the ride.

Jacek and his team led the way. Cale followed, as experience trumped novice. No complaints and no questions asked. It's how the world worked.

With a sigh, he removed his final sock. Homesickness for Green Bay gnawed at him, and he reached for the phone Jacek had loaned him. His own had been destroyed during their African adventure—drowned in the colonel's eel-infested grotto pool, the battery fried. He checked the time, calculated the conversion, punched in his home number. It was still light out in the Midwest.

Cale's last conversation with Maggie had bordered on surreal. No, strike that: it had been surreal. It was late last night, around four a.m. his time. He and Jacek had just arrived at the military airport terminal in Naples. Cale had called on a loaner phone and listened as she'd gushed about Tobias Crenshaw being shot in the head. Not even shot:

"Assassinated." Maggie's voice had exploded with emotion. "Shot and bleeding on the steps of the courthouse."

As if this bit of news hadn't been bizarre enough, with Cale being bone-sagging tired and almost unable to process what she was telling him, explosions had sounded inside the terminal. Seconds later, a hit man attempted to end his life by pithing the back of his neck with a razor-sharp blade. The key word here was "attempted."

"Crenshaw's lying in a hospital, not confirmed dead yet. He may still have the bullet lodged in his brain." This had been Maggie's gruesome report. Surreal? Yes. There was no other word that fit.

Maggie answered the phone with caution, unfamiliar (Cale understood) with Jacek's international mobile number.

"Hey, gorgeous," he said, playful. His voice sounded husky in the dimness, the confined space of his small sleeping quarters. "Got time for idle chit-chat?"

"Cale. Thank God." Her voice was thick with relief. "I was so worried. Slink told me you called earlier. You're all right, aren't you?"

"Fit as a pawnshop fiddle."

Maggie didn't laugh. Instead, she launched into a barrage of questions: Where was he? When would he be coming home? How much longer would his stupid trip take? On and on. Cale felt like a henpecked husband wandering home late on bowling night. And they weren't even *married* yet!

Or was there something else at play here? Maggie had never acted so—so emotional, so erratic—before. At least not since about six months ago, when she'd started dropping hints about their "future together". Questions about whether he was "in it for the long haul". After that, they'd had their disagreements, sure. What couple didn't? Had their little talks. All the general ups and downs of a normal relationship. But her tone sounded altogether different. Her grilling of him seemed to pour forth in a gush, as if she required but a solitary breath. He guessed she'd been holding it inside.

Pregnant?

The word summoned for Cale his own conflux of emotions. A voice in his head was goading him like a nasty high school bully, asking: "Hey, jackass! Don't you want to know who the *real* father is?"

"I'll be home, I don't know," he said, as if his words were disjointed. "Maybe by Tuesday? Or Wednesday? I'm hoping." His tone sounded modulated. "If everything goes according to plan."

Cale left it at that because he couldn't promise anything more. How could he? He was about to embark on a military rescue op against a troop of armed thugs who guarded a billionaire arms dealer.

Maggie was silent for an extended beat, as if a massive tsunami of thought might be approaching. Her silence sounded louder than if she were shouting at him.

"Mags, hey." He flavored his voice with concern. "You had a scare. I get it. But is everything all right?"

She remained silent, before at last stating: "*He is coming!* Or *it's coming*." She made this pronouncement like she might be sharing some state secret. "It's what Chloe says. It's a fact."

Chloe. Maggie's older sister. She was their resident psychic. Cale heard himself sigh. It figured.

He asked, "What's it supposed to mean? What's a fact?"

"I'm not certain. Okay? These things aren't exact."

Fantastic, Cale thought. He was nearly out on his feet—about to be dodging bullets again bright and early tomorrow morning—and she wanted him to play word games. "Maggie? Who's coming? Can you be a little more specific?"

"*He is coming!*" It was all she chose to say.

Who? The baby? Cale thought. Should he open that can of worms? At least maybe throw it out there? Attempt to clear a few things up before he arrived back home?

The simple answer was no. The cautionary voice inside him warned: Whatever you do, do NOT bring up marriage or babies, or who the father might be. You'll be walking through a dark door marked DISASTER.

Before he could utter another word, Cale heard her sob out loud, and the phone at his ear made a distinct sound:

Click.

He heard the disturbing silence and was aware the call had been disconnected. His impulse was to fling the phone against the wall, but guilt rushed him like a mugger, infusing him with some primal level of common sense. Cale wondered if he should call back. Try to continue the discussion despite being more fatigued than a man in a four-day life raft. There had to be some *Guy's Etiquette Manual* for how to handle situations such as this. Except Cale didn't have one. Never had.

Which was why he was still single, the bully in his head might tell him for the ten-thousandth time.

With a sigh, Cale rallied his reserves. He glanced at the button marked REDIAL. But before he could push it, the phone in his hand emitted a burpy half-ring.

CHAPTER 11

"Cale. Sorry. I'm a little stressed," Maggie said, sounding sincere. "The connection was fading, I don't know…"

"No problem. No big deal." He exhaled, fencing away the fatigue. "You sure you're all right?"

"What I was saying, about Chloe's vision." She paused, then continued, sounding theatrical. "A voice keeps telling her '*He is coming.*' All she can gather is it's some kind of monster, maybe? Headed our way?"

Cale steeled himself, choosing to stay silent. Don't throw gasoline on the fire, his inner-sense warned. He realized he was holding his breath.

"And she's also gotten images," Maggie continued, unfazed. "Of Leslie Dowd. Twice now. She's *alive.* I figured you'd want to know."

Cale felt his adrenaline ramp up, until he remembered they were talking about "psychic visions" here. Not some eyewitness account he could rely on. Nothing at all concrete, nothing tangible.

"Chloe's sure it was her? Leslie?"

"Of course." Maggie's tone was stiff. "They worked together in the same beauty salon for four years. But listen, Leslie's in danger. She's being held captive in a big house. Like a mansion of some sort. And she can't escape."

Cale pinched the bridge of his nose. He had to make sure his thoughts were coherent, and he was processing this information linearly. What Maggie was telling him fit his rescue narrative—at least somewhat—but still, they were talking about the visions of a psychic here. He had hours ago been staring at the photo of Leslie Dowd in, perhaps, a trafficker's line-up, with her staring back at him from Jacek's computer screen.

Indications seemed that she might be in the hands of a wealthy sadist named Prince Mir Al Sadar. A sicko who operated brothels; maybe even kept harems. And now Maggie, through her psychic sister Chloe, was informing him that Leslie was indeed alive.

The intel was not in any way verifiable, but at least it was another positive tick in his rescue mission.

After pondering the information, Cale decided he didn't need to hear all this from Chloe, herself. She received her visions, her "glimpses," and either you chose to believe them, or you didn't. He had to admit Chloe had come through for him the last time. She had "seen" Maggie trapped in the dangerous hands of Tobias Crenshaw. She'd seen enough to lead the authorities to the spot where her sister was being held captive.

Enough so they could rescue her and apprehend her abductor.

Cale took a moment to remind himself why he was in Europe in the first place. His mission was to locate the missing victims, bring them home to their families. To do this, he had to believe—at least in his heart—that they were alive. If Chloe was getting a vision of Leslie Dowd, her heart still beating, shouldn't he believe it at least plausible?

Besides, it confirmed what he'd hoped for all along: that he was on the right track.

For a moment, he considered the second victim: Mary Jane Moore. But he decided it didn't matter. If he located one girl, he'd be closer to the whereabouts of the other.

"We're frightened, Cale." Maggie's words jarred him from his reverie. "We feel so exposed. So...*vulnerable.*"

"I'm sure you're going—"

"Chloe insists something evil is coming. Something dangerous. You've got to get back here—please—as soon as you can."

Cale's shoulders were tight, his legs cramping as he sat on the mattress in his skivvies. He massaged his forehead, doing his best to will away his mental fatigue. He hadn't a clue what was in store for tomorrow's raid, but for the moment, he had to try his best to keep Maggie calm. He couldn't promise when he'd be back. How could he? He didn't know himself.

"It's going to be okay," he said, his voice soothing. "Thank Chloe for me. Tell her 'Good job!' Tell we're getting close to locating Leslie."

"For real?"

"We've got strong intel. In fact, we're headed there tomorrow." Cale shifted the phone to his opposite ear. "Like I said, when this is over, I'll be home as soon as I can."

She stayed silent.

"This has been hard on you, Mags—I get it. How are you feeling? You getting enough rest?"

"Just do what you have to. Then get back here." He heard her sigh. "And one more thing—this isn't the best time, I understand—but do you really want to start a family together? Or what?"

Silence.

The question slammed him like a punch to the sternum. Cale made no immediate reply. He was five-thousand-miles away, so perhaps the phone connection was fading. Might Maggie be drinking wine again? Was she stressed? Stoned on prenatal vitamins? All the above?

Might she be just as exhausted as he was? Cale considered all these possibilities in the span of three seconds.

Her voice echoed. "Cale? You still there?"

"A shaky connection...like you said. Not sure...heard...last part."

"We've talked about starting a family before." Maggie's tone was straightforward. "I'm curious, you know? Ballpark? A guess-timate?"

"Sure. Yeah. Uh, of course."

He was tripping over boulder-sized words. "Not *specifics*, I didn't think—did we? With all the wedding plans going on?" He pictured her running fingers through her hair.

"Look. I'm frazzled." She sighed. "Sorry. Chloe gets me going."

Cale wondered if he had dodged a bullet.

"She wants to hold an exorcism. Here. At the house."

Was it possible he hadn't heard right? His mouth was dry and he coughed, as Maggie continued: "She contacted Father Larchezi." This was stated matter-of-fact. "But—listen—let's talk about it when you get back. All right? Love you."

Click.

Cale stared at the phone with his mouth agape. Might he be dreaming? Babies...start a family...Chloe's visions...topped off by exorcism!

He doubted he could feel any worse than he had before the call, but realized he'd been wrong. Cale sat on his mattress like he was dead weight. He set the phone in its cradle charger on the floor. The room smelled stale, mixed with the faint scent of the squashed insect, whose remains—he imagined—still clung to the heel of his boot.

The door remained open a crack. Did that just happen? he asked himself. Did we have that talk? Cale massaged his forehead like a beat-up boxer, rubbing away cobwebs. *He is coming!* he thought, gloomily. Great. Just fucking wonderful.

A minute later, he wondered if Chloe's cryptic message might be about him? That he, Cale, was coming? As in coming home? Perhaps she got her psychic wires crossed? Was it possible? Deep inside, however, he understood the idea didn't wash. Wasn't that the problem with psychics? When they were correct one time, you gave them the benefit of the doubt for the next half-dozen times. Like a hot roller at a craps table.

"Something evil is coming. Something dangerous." Those had been Maggie's exact words.

At least she had the handgun he had given her. Cale shivered at the thought. In case some danger truly was headed their way.

The knowledge that Maggie could defend herself, however, failed to make him feel any better. Even though she'd been to the shooting range twice already; and even though Slink had taught her to at least handle the weapon.

Cale decided he'd better call Slink when he got the chance. Have him check on her. Make sure she wasn't having some sort of nervous breakdown.

He reminded himself that this was *not* what he needed at the moment.

He flicked off the room's small lamp. He dropped down on the mattress with one arm draped across his eyes. His muscles were still groaning from his African excursion—surviving the fall into the eel pit, the bumpy jeep ride across the treacherous landscape, the bullet-ridden helicopter escape. Followed by the lengthy flight back to Italy. Cale's ribs continued to throb. Even though he'd slept nine hours the night before, he felt exhausted. Not to mention having to kill the stupid bug. He didn't often admit it, but he hated insects. Despised them. Like a fraidy-cat ten-year-old who wouldn't sleep outdoors in a tent at night. Just knowing they were around, lurking somewhere inside the warehouse walls, crawling in silence, invisible, maybe mounting an attack.

None of this was helping his fragile peace of mind.

Cale lay in silence for the next two minutes. He wasn't sure it counted as praying—not real praying, anyway—but he thanked God for one small favor: whether it was the idea of having kids; or of crazed witch doctors running around trying to murder him; or even if a horde of insects was festering nearby, sizing him up for attack...he was simply too tired to care.

He felt his breathing slow. Perhaps these disjointed thoughts were something he had dreamed last night on the return flight from Africa. Some form of delirium-induced retro-hallucination. Maybe he was on the military plane even now, flying over the Dark Continent in the middle of the night.

Was any of it real?

But real or not, he seemed certain of one thing: It would all be clearer in the morning.

He drifted into a half-sleep. Was it a noise? The outside alley? Most likely the wind. In a tourist city full of revelers, down the coast from Rome, Anzio did not have the reputation as a "party" town. Still, the place had its moments. There would always be groups of college kids looking for a good time. There would be things going bump in the night.

Deciding he was not going to be spooked by strange sounds, not on this, his final—hopefully—night in Italy, Cale drifted off again. But not before wondering what the hell else could go wrong on this crazy trip.

Before his beleaguered brain could respond, he dropped into an echoless, yawning canyon of sleep.

CHAPTER 12

Château de Carthairs, Belgium

As Cale punched his ticket to dreamland, over seven hundred miles away Leslie was staring out her bedroom window on the château's second floor. Far below on the grounds, out across the thick bushes and trees of the surrounding forests, beyond the electrified fences, over the streams and ponds feeding the private lake, she could hear the steady thrum of night insects. The sky was a blanket of stars. It meant the weather tomorrow would be ideal for the race. Sunny and seventy was the forecast. Perfect.

Leslie swallowed two aspirin with a sip of water. She had a headache, no doubt caused by the presence of the evil Liberian killer, who had shown up at the dinner party. She loathed the...the *animal*—consumer of human flesh—with all her heart. There was no other soul on the planet she despised with more passion. There couldn't be. How much she hated the man they called Kinsella was beyond measure.

She wondered why Prince Mir tolerated the monster's unholy presence at the château. They were business partners on some level, Leslie understood, but still, if she could just once catch the giant ogre asleep in a chair in the study. If she had a sharp knife or letter opener or an ice pick in her hands, any pointed implement able to pierce a human heart—Ha! If he even had one—she would not hesitate to plunge the dagger home. No hesitation. This was key. With a single stroke it would be over. For her own peace and in revenge for her friend, Mary Jane Moore.

Leslie shrugged away these dark thoughts. Think positive, she reminded herself. Don't worry about things beyond your control.

And besides, in the larger picture, what did it matter anyway? Leslie understood she was a mere commodity here at the château: a pissant, a slave, little more than a fancy-dressed piece of meat, albeit one who could run very fast. Yet things being what they were, her opinions mattered little. What she could control, however, was how she performed on the racetrack tomorrow:

pulling the pony cart, leading her teammates. She remembered Prince Mir's bit of sage advice to her:

"Win the fucking race!"

That was it. Brief. Concise. To the point. How much more elementary a command could there be? Those were her orders, her ticket, he promised, to freedom.

Leslie sighed and let the thick drapes fall back into place. She moved from the window and set her water glass on the walnut bureau. It would make a moisture ring. Who cared? The housekeepers would buff it and add the lemon polish she could still detect in the room.

Turning back the blankets of her bed, she climbed in. She pulled the heavy quilt to her chin and tucked herself into its warmth. In the distance she could hear the vague thumping of music from the ballroom far below. Rising through the chateau's thick floorboards, it sounded grainy and scratched, as if an old Victrola was playing from the 1920s. The prince's party, she imagined, was kicking into gear. A gala she was supposed to be attending, standing there smiling and looking fetching in her slinky dress and heels.

"Screw him."

Leslie whispered the words inside the cocoon of her comforter. He had nineteen other girls who could stand around looking like vacuous mannequins. She, instead, was an athlete. She could not be replaced on the night before the big race—for no less than a fit of insubordination.

Sighing once more, Leslie flipped over onto her left side. She realized her eyes were clamped shut, her forehead furrowed, and she reminded herself to relax. She opened her mouth and allowed her jaw muscles to go slack. It will all be over soon, she told herself. Two days from now they will have won the race and secured for the prince his precious trophy. Some ridiculous fetish award, for God's sake! Along with whatever else he might have wagered on the event.

By this time next week, she'd be home. Back in Green Bay, where she'd been snatched over a year ago by the sick psycho who'd drugged her. She'd be reunited with her parents and sisters and friends, be able to sleep in her own house once more. Even back in her old bed.

Leslie felt her forehead furrow again. It's what Prince Mir had promised her—if she could just believe him for once.

"Win the fucking race." She planned to, she told herself. Her life depended on it.

——

Anzio, Italy

Moon over Italy. For an untold number of people this would be cause enough for romance: a starry boat ride on calm, silver-polished waters. Maybe a secret rendezvous beneath an awning of cypress trees. Or perhaps a violin-accompanied dinner on the *terrazzo* of some quaint restaurant. Though love was in the air for some fortunate souls, such was not the case for Tebbi Qa. This was no night for fun and games; this was, instead, a night for business. Tebbi had his orders. He would carry them out as dictated by Kinsella, a brutish thug whose temper Tebbi did not wish to agitate. He had witnessed firsthand the large Liberian's use of his ceremonial sword, applied to the flesh and bone of a human neck. Enough said.

From his spot across the street from the empty parking lot, the dark second floor window of a furniture store, Tebbi Qa had watched the van drive up. Watched it disappear inside the wide doors of the shadowed warehouse. One of the four people within was his target. He would wait for them to settle, then quiet as a cobra in the forest—with venom ten times as deadly—he would strike.

Now two hours had passed. Slipping like a black stain inside the darker shadows, Tebbi Qa crossed the street. There was little traffic. Anzio was subdued after ten p.m.

Moving in through an alley door, whose lock he had picked earlier this evening while the occupants were gone, he made his way down a long, lightless hallway. His shoes were silent as teardrops. No noise had issued from the inner warehouse for the past hour. The inhabitants, Tebbi Qa imagined, had turned in early. They'd be slumbering more sound than vampires in a daytime nest. If not—if he encountered any surprises—he would deal with them. Like Kinsella, he was a professional. It was the reason he'd been chosen for the task.

Employing a small penlight, Tebbi Qa slipped down a second shadowed corridor. He barely breathed, listening as he crept through the darkness. The penlight was held in his left hand. Inside his tight dark jacket, he fingered the cyanide-filled syringe in the right pocket. The plastic cap was secured over the needle on the outside chance he happened to misstep or was surprised in the dark. A needle-jab to the ribs, or anywhere else for that matter, would cause a human heart to stop in less than a minute.

Tebbi Qa paused again. He listened. Then he moved. Five cautious minutes later, the hallway merged into an opening, which proceeded to widen into the larger central area of the warehouse. This was perfect. The fewer doors he had to open and close, the quieter he could advance. Less chance for surprises.

He spotted a half-open office door that served as a sleeping room. Tebbi Qa stepped like a panther in the trees, listening, then moved into the room. He saw the figure's chest beneath a thin blanket, the rhythmic rise and fall. The breaths, however, were too faint. The form appeared too petite to be a grown man.

Back out in the wide central area he froze against one wall, merged into shadows darker than any eclipse. Tebbi Qa waited another full five minutes, making certain no one stirred. The clouds drifted above, and a spray of silver moonlight seeped in through a high, dusty skylight. It improved the visibility from his vantage point.

A second room was further down the wall, closer to the center of the warehouse. Like the first room, its door was cracked an inch. To the right of where he stood, Tebbi spotted an open area of floor where equipment—duffel bags and canvas satchels—had been set aside. They appeared ready to be moved. Perhaps at first light.

Tebbi Qa slipped into the second room. The man's breathing was steady, as if he might be trapped in the deathlike stupor of exhaustion. A phone sat in a charger near his right shoulder, not far from the mattress. Was he expecting an important call? The charger light sprayed the room with its delicate orange glow. Advancing, Tebbi Qa again fingered the syringe inside his pocket. He had memorized the form and facial features of his target, which he'd gotten off the Internet after Kinsella had revealed the man's identity. All Tebbi required was a brief flick of his penlight. The dark close-cropped hair, the firm chin, sunken cheeks, the nose.

Target verified.

The cobra was ready. He withdrew the syringe, twisted off the protective cap, exposing the sharp needle.

But Tebbi Qa was unprepared for the sudden sensation that seized his own neck. The pressure of a taut nylon cord—not letting up—pulled him upright. Feeling the large, looming presence behind him, Tebbi understood what was happening. He had one chance to survive: jabbing his aggressor with the needle before he, himself, succumbed to the garrote.

Most men would have been shocked into dropping the syringe. The urge to grab at the noose around their neck would be too great a survival instinct to suppress. Tebbi Qa was not most men. One chance was all he needed. Before he could stab the needle backward, however, he felt his opponent sidestep to his left, release the noose, and grasp Tebbi Qa by the chin and back of his head.

The echo in his ears was a hammer on steel and all went black.

——

Anzio, Italy – Later that night

Inside the warehouse, on the floor mattress in the office room, Cale sweats through a disturbing dream. Images dance in his head like twisted visions, erratic jumping, disturbing apparitions that feel like warnings, or even premonitions of his future. It is one of those too-real dreams, complete with night sweats, and faces distorted, all real and frightening—a dream where you try to break free and wake up, but you're frozen, unable to move.

Cale watches the nightmare take shape, and he feels the sadistic presence of Colonel Tazeki Mabutu—the Liberian witch doctor—lurking nearby, the same sorcerer who has entered his mind before.

"Keep your mind open, Detective," Mabutu commands, his rasping voice like wet sandpaper. "I will show you what your future holds."

At once the deep pain enters his brain like an ice pick through his skull, a piercing burn that doesn't let up. The pounding log drums punch the night inside his head, shakers rattling, a fire blazing in a jungle clearing. Painted dancers spinning and whirling, enthralled.

Cale has lost control of his mind and body. As if on acid, he lies frozen in place, mumbling incoherent words, gasping. And the sadistic killer Kinsella is coming at him with a long, curved blade. He is frozen on the ground. In a stupor, drugged, unable to move like a sacrifice...and he feels nothing as the giant Liberian runs the sharp blade deep across his throat.

The slice brings him back to the present. Escaping the nightmare, Cale lifts his body to a sitting position. He's gasping for air, clutching his throat. And the demonic laughter of the witch doctor cackles like an echo from deep in his brain:

"Our futures are not etched in stone, Detective. I just showed you but one thread of what might be," the unseen voice informs. "One mere thread...one possibility of millions."

Drums continue to pound in the background, softer this time. The witch doctor speaks again: "Another version is when I slice the fetus from Maggie's belly. And I stuff the mewling mass down your throat."

The cackling and demented laughter retreats, moving far, far away, as if sailing off into the ether of the universe.

Cale is wide awake now. He blinks his eyes, shaking himself free from the nightmare. He's sitting upright on the mattress, skin covered with sweat. The sinister voice of Mabutu has faded...and all he's left with is cold silence.

His wild eyes scan the room, seeing nothing but blackness, save for the tiny orange glow of the phone charger on the floor. He is disoriented, swampy with perspiration. And though he tries to resist, exhaustion wrestles him back to the lumpy mattress, where flat on his back, it takes only seconds for him to drop into a dreamless sleep.

CHAPTER 13

Liberia, Africa

The time was ripe for a magical trip.

Tazeki Mabutu removed from a satin pouch a large blue diamond, culled from the mines of Sierra Leone. It had been cut in Johannesburg. He had received the gift from a tribal chief some years ago for curing one of his sons of a green mamba bite. The sparkling stone, at times referred to as a "blood diamond"—when combined with an infant's fresh blood in a bowl made from the bark of the sacred iroko tree—had always been the botono's favored way of scrying the past, the present, the future.

Tazeki stood naked in his Blood Room, high on the third floor of the main house at his oceanfront compound. The sky was a deep purple bruise, the moon an amber afterthought behind the murky, rain-swollen clouds. Through the half-shuttered window, he watched a pair of his guards below. They were on patrol around the perimeter, the white walls high and fortress-like. Their flashlights probed the shadows, the heavy jungle brush, ever alert for a leopard or viper, a panther or rebel teen with an assault rifle.

Such were the perils of this land.

If Kasim—Tazeki's loyal and trustworthy servant of so many years—were here, he might assist the botono in this rite. But Kasim's services were no longer available, and the servant's absence lent a sobriety to the task at hand.

When younger, he had used goat milk as part of his scrying ritual. But after his pact with Pazuzu, the demon had demanded he use human blood. And not just any blood...but rather fresh bleed from an infant who had been sacrificed. This technique had made Tazeki's visions far more vivid and defined. Many times more intense.

The botono had never looked back.

The waves crashing against the rocks below sent arcs of foam three stories into the air, and the rain still fell in a somnolent drizzle. Tazeki moved from the window. Tonight, he wore a ceremonial mask. It had been crafted from human bone, sculpted, preserved. The bleak, hollow eyes gazed out at the world and beyond. The bone mask had been culled from victims of his grandfather—of which there had been many—and passed down to the Mabutu heirs: first to his father, and then to him.

To further add "character" to the starkness of the mask, drops of blood seeped from the eyes like tears, and the rictus bone lips were downturned into a permanent frown.

In the room's center stood a small table with eight-inch legs. Four lighted candles were set in the proper quadrants, causing the flicker of flames to dance across the bare walls. The elementals: they helped Tazeki attain the proper vision, helped guide his astral self both away and—more importantly—back into his body, when his tasks were complete.

Atop the low table sat his scrying bowl, and in the center was the diamond, clear, winking, reflective in the firelight. It was far beyond what any mere crystal might provide.

He slipped to his bare knees and took three deep calming breaths. From a pitcher he proceeded to pour a stream of the warm blood over the gem's faceted top and sides. Grasping the bowl with both hands, he began rolling it, causing the crimson fluid to swirl and pass around and over the twinkling gemstone.

A scent rose up raw and coppery and born of the jungle. And then, moments later:

Darkness. Complete, tarry, palpable. Darker than the edge of the universe, far beyond the reach of the last outer stars. Tazeki could feel an iron weight pressing down on him. Inside this desolate bleakness he was drifting, then flying, then soaring...and it didn't take him long—not long at all—to locate the ebony eyes of Pazuzu. They spoke telepathically:

"Ahh, there you are, my friend." The statuette was trapped in a confined space, dark and silent. He noted that his friend was unharmed, unblemished, and all was intact. The demon had been biding his time, patient, waiting for the obeah man to come to his aid.

"I am here, Botono," spoke the demon. "I am waiting, waiting."

"As am I, old one. I will come for you."

"So be it. Until then."

A moment later, Tazeki's astral persona became like that of a hawk, soaring high below the clouds. A roar—like the crash of waves pounding against the rocks, unrelenting and continuous—could be heard.

And then he was lowering into the light, and was in a city, hovering above a building. A moment later, he found himself dropped into a room, the way a raven lands without sound upon a tree branch.

Tazeki sat perched in a high corner, unseen, observing. His red eyes were aflame, disguised inside the bright and sun-filled room. He found himself spying down on a pair of females. They were in a modern-day living room, sitting cross-legged on a carpeted floor. A single, lavender-scented candle flickered in the narrow space between them.

Friday afternoon sunlight slipped in through the open blinds. It sketched a buttery outline on the carpet. The females—one dark-haired, attractive; the other with streaky red-blond hair and fuller of figure (sisters, Tazeki sensed)—were concentrating on a small piece of paper positioned on a silver tray. The older female was offering some low chant, and he could see the glistening rings on her fingers, the shiny bracelets, a medallion dangling from her neck. A necklace of silver...

A witch! A pair of witches?

He watched from his high vantage point. Tazeki's physical body added more blood to the scrying bowl, swaying his arms and shoulders to make it swirl again. His eyes were lizard-lidded, half-closed behind the bone mask as he knelt inside his special room, entranced, staring at the glimmer of reflections off the diamond's smooth surface.

Back in the witches' house again, he watched as the elder witch frowned. Her eyes closed. She paused in her intonation...and the skies, not dark yet, seemed to swell about them until her eyes blinked open, alert and alarmed, and she swung her pointing finger across the room to the precise spot where he was perched.

She shouted out: "There! There!"

"What are you— Where?"

"Right there!" cried the red-haired witch.

Behind her sounded a howling screech, and a sudden burst of commotion. The sound faded, and Tazeki's vision vanished as if a television had switched off.

Breaking his trance, lifting his eyes from the blood-coated diamond, he exhaled. He was back in the Red Room, back in his own body, his meager suit of human flesh. Slipping the bone mask from his face, the botono set it on the floor. While his scrying episode had been incomplete, the witch doctor nevertheless had learned two important things:

Pazuzu was being flown somewhere, encased in darkness. Perhaps inside a box. Or in a packed crate of some sort.

And the second thing, no doubt more troubling: the elder witch had sensed—perhaps even spotted—his sinister presence. Tazeki understood a new truth: From this point forward, he must be very, very careful of *that* one.

CHAPTER 14

Green Bay, Wisconsin

Hearing Hank's low-throated growl, Maggie swung her gaze around. She was startled to see the gray tabby's eyes wide and fur bristling. She heard him arch, howl, and leap frightened from the davenport cushion where he'd been perched, before sprinting out of the room.

"There! Right there!" Chloe's voice was shouting at the same instant.

Maggie had jumped up, eyes searching, then swung her attention back to her sister. Chloe was kneeling, staring up toward the room's far corner. Her right arm remained extended, her finger pointing in accusatory fashion across the room.

"Chloe! Jesus!" Maggie felt her heart return to its usual chamber in her chest.

"The ceiling. It was shimmering—I saw two red eyes." Chloe was insistent, her finger continuing to point. "Like a pair of laser beams."

They had been sitting Indian-style on the floor, opposite the scented candle. The candle Maggie had just about knocked over when Chloe shrieked, and Hank howled and fled. She continued to follow her sister's red-lacquered fingernail, which was still aimed across the family room.

"I don't see anything," Maggie said. Her eyes continued to search the walls and ceiling.

Chloe didn't look away. "You didn't feel the presence? See those crimson pinpricks?"

Maggie reached for her glass of merlot on the nearby coffee table. She was allowing herself one serving of wine per day during her pregnancy. She'd found new research in *So You're Pregnant!* a Swedish online quarterly that claimed a glass of vino per day was beneficial to both mother and fetus. Flavonoids—enriched antioxidants—if she remembered correctly. The key was limiting yourself to but a single glass of healthy red.

Maggie said, "If you're trying to make me not sleep tonight, you're doing a damn good job of it."

Hank eased his way into the room, slinking back to where they were. He rubbed his furry head against Maggie's bare leg, apologetic, and she stroked him. When the cat's tail swished too near the candle, she pushed him away.

"Sorry, pumpkin. We don't want Hank-flambé."

"You must've looked too late." Chloe frowned, thinking hard. She shifted her eyes to her sister. "You've got to become more *aware*, Mags."

"Aware." She repeated the word, unenthused. "Aware of what? Your hallucinations? During the daytime?"

"Not hallucinations: *visions*. You ought to know...how they come. At least to people with open minds."

Maggie blinked. Her eyes searched the room's corner once more. Then she shifted her gaze to the opposite corner. Again nothing. "Maybe it was reflected sunlight? Like off the wind chimes? A prism? Filtering in through the blinds?"

"It wasn't like that." Chloe didn't relax her frown.

"If you had just told me to look, instead of yelling like a maniac. Maybe I'd have seen it." She took a sip from her wine glass.

The sisters sat in pensive silence, until at last Maggie said, "So if something was there—"

"It was there."

"—do you think it's why Hank went flying from the room?"

Chloe issued her a narrow look. "Cats are *known* for their sixth sense."

Touché, Maggie thought, giving Hank a look. He met her eyes with a smug green stare.

"I just don't know what to think," Chloe said distantly.

She blew out the candle. Rising, she strode across the room to the suspicious corner and stared up at the blank space there. After examining the spot in question from several different angles, Chloe walked back to where Maggie remained sitting.

"What I do know, for someone to scry us like that, without my sensing his presence for who knows how long...to manifest visible points of light..."

Someone? Maggie thought, keeping silent.

"A very powerful sorcerer."

Chloe wrung her hands. She swung her gaze to the bank of windows on the room's western wall, peering outside across the green lawn and toward the high bushes and trees. Her eyes came back to Maggie. "We've got to start preparing. In case he decides to—"

"He?"

"Yes. He."

"Decides to what?"

Maggie held her wine glass frozen in space, her opposite hand holding her elbow. She realized it was close to the way she held her gun at the shooting range. Her gun. The police had confiscated the weapon right after the Tobias Crenshaw shooting, when she'd visited the station to volunteer her statement.

Damn. She needed to get her gun back. Just when she'd been getting good at hitting the practice targets. She better mention it to Slink. Again.

"Decides to pay us a return visit," Chloe said in a sober voice. She added, "Maybe in person next time?"

Maggie pinched the bridge of her nose and clamped her eyes shut. "Did you not hear my comment a minute ago? About not scaring me? I'm staying here all alone. Remember?"

"Sorry."

Maggie said nothing for a moment. When she glanced back up, Chloe was digging through her giant handbag, which had been sitting on the end table alongside the davenport. She withdrew a rose-patterned handkerchief, holding it up as if it were an antique heirloom.

"I found this—" Chloe chirped triumphantly, and a moment later she swayed and crumpled to the floor.

CHAPTER 15

Chateau de Carthairs, Belgium

The lavish bedroom in blue shades, organdy highlights, the curtains open, tall French quarter-pane windows... The moon set high in the purple night sky. You lie atop your quilted bed, gown discarded and flung to the floor, face buried in the feather pillows. The man in the goatee stands in the room's center, and you feel his presence.

"I'm not going back down to your party," you tell him.

"I'm not going to hurt you, Leslie," he replies. "I don't want you bruised for the race tomorrow."

"How very noble of you, Your Highness!" Sarcasm drips from your words. Sensing the man's tight expression in the dim light of the bedroom, you do not turn. It's a room where he has controlled you, whipped you, ridden you like an equine, hurt you. At his mercy, you do not wish to rile him. Rushing from his banquet table like a petulant teen, you have already caused him to lose face. Like most men of wealth, what frightens him most is public humiliation.

"Do you remember our bargain?" he asks, the question barbed. "You win tomorrow, I grant you your freedom." You remain silent. "Leslie, I am not interested in keeping a bird trapped in a gilded cage."

"Why don't I believe you?"

"Because you have always had difficulty trusting men."

You give him no response.

"No strings," he says, with practiced sincerity. "No questions asked. I will set you free. Why not? I can purchase ten more like you with the money I win on this race alone."

"You're such a liar." Turning your gaze his way, your eyes scald him. "You don't even know when you are lying. Do you?"

"As I told you: you have my word."

"Ah yes, the word of a sociopath."

His goateed smile is a smirk. "What choice do you have? To remain here like this, you will surely die."

"Yes. I will die."

"Then you will run tomorrow as you were trained. And you will win the race for me."

You hear the heavy door open, close. The click of the lock.

Soon, it will all be over. You will be free to return home. Free to see your family and friends once more.

But do you believe him, Leslie? Or is he playing games, his promises just more of his wicked, loathsome lies?

——

Chloe awoke with a couch pillow propped beneath her head. Where was she? Lying on a floor somewhere—Maggie's family room?—with her sister dabbing a cool washcloth to her forehead. Blinking, she asked, "How long was I out?"

"About five minutes." Concern caught in Maggie's soft brown eyes. "Are you feeling all right? Should I call an ambulance? Or Ed?"

Sitting up halfway, Chloe scanned the room. She spotted the rose-patterned handkerchief on the floor near the sofa. "No. I'm all right. I just had another—"

"Vision. Right."

Chloe stayed quiet, as if trying to remember the details of her dream.

"I figured," Maggie said. "Was it Leslie Dowd, again?"

The bedroom scene came back to Chloe in a rush. The girl cocooned in blankets on the high, plush bed; the stern, arrogant man with the trace scent of his velvety aftershave. "Yes. He's lying to her. She's in desperate trouble."

Maggie held her breath, kneeling on the floor. "Can you picture where she is? Can we do anything to help? Send the police? Or let Cale know?"

Chloe shook her head. "The man with her...I can never see his face."

"I told Cale she's alive, at least." Maggie frowned. "She is still alive, isn't she?"

"I think so. I hope so."

They were both silent for a beat.

"Don't worry about it, Clo," Maggie said, comforting her sister with a tender touch. "It will come to you—it always does." She rose and began moving across the room. "I'll get you some water."

"Wait!" Chloe rose to her elbows on the floor. "What time is it?"

"Coming up on four o'clock. Why?"

"My God! He's going to be here in a few minutes." Chloe was scrambling to her feet, a bit unsteady, causing Hank to stare at her strange behavior from a windowsill across the room.

"Who's coming? Who are you talking about?"

"Father Larchezi. Didn't I tell you?"

———

Father Ambrose Larchezi is the pastor at St. Phillip's, a Catholic parish on Green Bay's East Side, and has run the place like a battleship for the past fifteen years. His dusky skin is the color and texture of half-toasted bread. While this might frighten some small children, in his case, the kids all loved him. But no surprise there: children often skim the outer layers of a person and peer straight through to their hearts. And among his talents, diversified and many, Father Larchezi has been blessed with a very kind heart.

What many people don't realize about men of the cloth, is that each has a favorite hobby. Priests don't sit around all day studying the Bible, writing sermons, or memorizing scripture. Nor do they spend long hours in counseling sessions with faith-challenged parishioners. Some, of course, do. But Ambrose Larchezi is not one of those. He devotes the required time, it goes without saying, to the business of running his parish. The rest of his time, however— his private time—is spent steeped in his hobby: the study and practice of spiritual warfare. In other words, he is a man who enjoys doing battle with malevolent ghosts and demons.

If pinned down, Father Larchezi would define himself as a "soldier of St. Michael." He believes there is a continuous battle raging over the capture of men's souls, the age-old good-versus-evil thing—Satan's minions pitted against God's holy angels and archangels. The winning tally, it is understood, will be sorted out during Judgment's Final Days.

And thus…in light of these beliefs, it was no great surprise to learn that one of Father Larchezi's more interesting parishioners was the psychic, Chloe Jeffers-Ravelle. The same Ms. Ravelle, who had just weeks ago assisted the Green Bay police in the kidnapping investigation involving her sister, Maggie, along with six other females. The crime the press were referring to as "The Chemist Case."

Over the years, in fact, Father Larchezi and Chloe had shared numerous discussions regarding the nature of evil, as well as the presence of demonic entities. Real ones. Not the made-up media versions. Their views in this arena had decidedly overlapped.

And it was due to this long-standing friendship that prompted the priest to accept the phone call, when his secretary had buzzed his desk intercom that morning.

"Chloe Ravelle. Line two for you, Father."

"She say what she wants?" Father Larchezi had asked. He'd been busy jotting notes from a demonology text.

"A couple of questions for you. Something about performing…" She had paused, as if uncertain she should continue.

"Joyce. Spit it out, please."

"An *exorcism,* Father. That's what she's asking about."

"I see."

He had been in his study Friday morning, taking notes from his text, and peering at copies of Old Testament parchment through a magnifying glass.

Informing his secretary that of course he'd take the call, Father Larchezi had set down the magnifier. He picked up the phone, making certain the faithful Joyce had clicked off. Little pitchers had big ears, so the saying went.

"Chloe. What a pleasant surprise," the priest had said. "How can I help you?"

CHAPTER 16

By four p.m. that Friday afternoon, Father Larchezi was ready. He pulled his tan Kia hatchback into the Van Waring driveway and parked on the concrete apron. This was the first time he'd been at Chloe's sister Maggie's residence, though he'd met her several times after services, when she'd been in her sister's company. He hadn't had the pleasure of meeting Maggie's fiancé, Lieutenant Cale Van Waring, just yet.

Rumor had it the man was somewhat of a religious skeptic.

Extracting himself from his vehicle, Father Larchezi looked around. The lawn could use a good mowing. But otherwise the landscaping around the house appeared to be in decent shape. The shrubs and flowers were all well-tended. The same went for the flower beds adjacent to the outside deck, as well as those bordering the eastern edge of the property. There, four clusters of high bushes stood between a bracing of tall Dutch elms and served to isolate the yard from the neighboring property. A string of currant bushes attracted a half-dozen industrious honeybees. He could hear the distant sound of a lawn mower, cutting through the quiet of late-afternoon.

Father Larchezi took three paces in the direction of the high bushes. He stopped and spent a long moment studying the thick shrubbery. A good-sized animal or a standing person could lurk inside there for as long as he chose, and not be spotted. He shifted his attention back to the house. The high second-story windows were quarter-paned, gabled on the outside, as windows in older homes often are, the paint smooth and un-weathered. Through the windows he searched for movement, his trained eyes spotting nothing irregular: no shadows, no gauzy or misted faces peering back out at him from the shadows, or through the glass.

Chloe had sounded demanding on the phone that morning. Some evil was coming their way—she was certain of it. Due to their friendship, Father Larchezi had agreed to perform a house blessing. A purification. There was no need to provide this service on short notice, however. House blessings were seldom any sort of emergencies. Unlike, for instance, the need for a more urgent confrontation with evil—like the rite of demonic exorcism.

Father Larchezi continued to study the house, and as he did, he formed his impression. Yes. This was a warm house—well-tended and serene, in a middle-class neighborhood. While he wouldn't challenge Chloe's request for his presence, to Father Larchezi, this did not seem like a home in need of protection from the threat of evil.

Then again, wasn't this how the Great Deceiver worked? The Master of Lies and Illusion? Some of the most frightening homes he'd ever encountered had presented an outward appearance of normalcy. Like taking a bite of a shiny Red Delicious, only to discover you had a mouthful of mealy grub worms.

The backdoor swung open. Chloe exited, moving forward to greet him in a flowing khaki skirt. Her sister followed, hanging a few paces back as if uncertain about the situation. Maggie's dark hair was ponytailed back, held in place with an elastic band. It made her look like a college student.

"Father. Thank you for coming." Chloe extended her hand for a shake. A quartet of silver arm bracelets jangled. Her green eye shadow matched her blouse. "You remember Maggie?"

"Of course." The priest wrapped both hands around Maggie's. She was smiling, as well. He examined her countenance, making certain her expression was what it appeared to be. He reminded himself that one can never be too wary, when summoned to a domicile under attack by evil.

"Are you sure we'll have enough time, Father?" Chloe asked, sounding anxious. "To do this right? I know you've got confessions Friday evenings."

The priest nodded. "Thirty minutes tops to bless a house this size. And rest assured, most of our sinners don't dally when unloading their transgressions."

Maggie smiled again.

"But," Chloe persisted, "the entire place will be purified?"

Maggie's eyes twinkled at the priest. "She doesn't want the Costco special."

Father Larchezi gave them a smile.

"The whole place protected. Hello?" Chloe countered. "Is that too much to ask?"

The priest rummaged in the backseat of his Kia, before pulling out a gray canvas duffel bag. "I'm sure your home just needs a blessed touch," he announced. "Nothing more."

The women led the way toward the back entrance of the house.

"It's Cale's family home." Maggie shrugged as they entered. "His parents. I'm not sure what denomination they belong to."

"Ghosts are ghosts; evil is evil."

Chloe said, "He means that spirits don't play favorites."

Father Larchezi gave them a solemn nod as they stepped into the modest-sized kitchen. After looking around, moving forward towards the dining room, he said, "A pleasant home. Very bright." Pulling aside a curtain, he gazed out the window at the driveway. Turning back to the room, he said, "Like Chloe wants, we'll get straight to it, then."

Father Larchezi inhaled the fragrance of lemon furniture polish. Beneath the ceiling arch, which led into the wide, sun-filled living room, he spotted Hank lying atop a couch.

"And who do we have here?" The priest approached the tubby feline with caution. Cats were often leery of strange men garbed in black.

"This is Hank, Father." Maggie had shadowed the priest into the room, arms crossed over her chest. Hank didn't hiss or spit or run screeching from the room. He raised not a hackle in alarm but looked up at the priest with saucer-sized eyes.

Walking back to the dining room, Father Larchezi pulled one of the cushioned dining room chairs into the room's center. He placed his duffel bag on the chair and from inside it withdrew a purple stole, designed for healing. He kissed and draped it around his neck. His white collar-band remained visible. He extracted a plain wooden crucifix and, last of all, pulled out a fifth-sized bottle of holy water.

Eyeing the bottle, Maggie lifted an eyebrow.

"Grey Goose." Father Larchezi, said, and he held his stone face for a beat, before breaking into a chuckle. "Kidding, of course."

Chloe closed her eyes as if counting, before reopening them. "Father, please. As I told you, we're freaked out by this."

"Just lightening the mood. As you know, I take my ghosts and demons seriously." He studied them one to the next. "Now. Where would you like to begin?"

Chloe led him past the kitchen, down the long hallway and up the small set of steps, which led to the family room of the split-level home. Father Larchezi followed, with Maggie trailing behind like a reluctant third wheel on a date. They moved past an armchair and the wide flat-screen TV, and paused in the center of the room, to one side of the couch.

"This is where I spotted it. *Him*." Chloe was pointing up at the room's far corner, fifteen feet beyond the couch. "An hour ago. Two scarlet pinprick eyes."

———

Tazeki drifted through the ether of blackness, affected neither by time nor space. Like a shadow during an eclipse, he soared on invisible currents, propelled at thought-speed to whatever destination he selected. The edge of the universe, black, frozen, desolate, was his to explore if he chose. There he might waltz on a nail's head in the thunderous void of sound and gravity before yo-yoing back to the present faster than light could ever dream of speeding.

Spying on the pair of conspiring witches earlier, from his high loft in the room's corner, had intrigued him. He decided it would be interesting to pay them a return visit. It's where he was at present, perched inside the low corner of the large-screen Toshiba television. The same room he'd visited, so it seemed, mere seconds ago. Peering from his seclusion, Tazeki watched the silent parade as it progressed past. Here now! Here came the same pair of witches...but this time they were with what appeared to be a new player in the game: a solemn-faced man of the cloth. *Ah-ha.*

He watched in silence. Missing only were the incense and solemn chanting and lit candles, all carried single file by robed acolytes. What were they up to, these three? he wondered. *Let's watch and see.*

When it struck him, it landed like a clap to the back of his head. It took all his effort not to break into peals of laughter. These fools were performing a ritual! A rite of Catholic exorcism, or something of the sort. Tazeki considered materializing in front of them, forming himself into an incorporeal mist. The priest, startled, would no doubt shower him with his holy water. It would have little effect, however, on a master of African voodoo,—a powerful, full-fledged botono.

Instead he watched, silent as a spy.

The priest and witches (he enjoyed eyeing the cute brunette with the too-wide smile) appeared to study the room's far wall. He observed the man in black make the sign of the cross, heard his religious blathering: "St. Michael the Archangel, defend us in battle. Be our protector against the wickedness and snares of the Devil. Lord Almighty, bless and defend this room." Blah blah blah.

His holiness spritzed holy water from his holy bottle.

Then the somber parade turned and exited from the room. The trio progressed from one room to the next, moving throughout the house. Tazeki drifted behind them, an invisible ghost, watching, amused.

When they climbed the stairs leading up to the second floor, he decided he'd seen enough. He drifted past the kitchen and the dining room, moving into the sun-rich living room, where he cast no reflection in the mirrors. He gazed at the walls covered with framed photographs of the home's loving, laughing inhabitants— no children, he noted—deciding that the policeman, Van Waring, must be either ignorant, incompetent or impotent.

Perhaps all three.

Turning, Tazeki observed the feline lounging on the surface of the dining room table. Feeling playful, floating close, he allowed his eyes to glow. His face took on a misty form in front of the animal's damp nose. When the cat noticed him, at last, its green eyes grew far too large for its face.

He whispered, "Boo!"

The cat screeched and went scrambling, his padded paws slipping and sliding on the polished tabletop. Upon hitting the floor, he bolted from the room and sped down the length of hallway, up the six steps, where he disappeared into the hidden depths of the family room.

Like a proper spirit, Tazeki had already vanished. He'd allowed himself enough fun for the moment, hadn't he?

CHAPTER 17

The house was silent as they moved up the stairs. Maggie trailed behind Chloe and the priest. She recalled how uncomfortable she'd felt in the home for two full weeks after Tobias Crenshaw had abducted her from her bedroom. What had it been? Five, six weeks? After he'd been arrested, knowing her kidnapper was locked behind bars, living here had at last become palatable again.

Maggie was an attorney, after all. She understood crime was defined by actions and consequences. When the perpetrator was arrested and incarcerated, his crime spree was over. He was no longer a threat, could do her no further harm. Not after a five-million-dollar bail had been set.

Still, the phantoms of her abduction lingered.

In time, things would return to normal. The bad memories would fade. The ghosts would move on to haunt some other place. Maggie decided she would not allow herself to be a victim. She would not be afraid of living in her own home. This moment, however, she couldn't seem to summon her usual strong air of confidence.

Leave it to Chloe to stir things up, Seeing things—so she claimed—that were likely not there. Or worse yet, sensing things that were. At least Chloe's visions had nothing to do with Tobias Crenshaw. How could they? Maggie understood her tormentor was at present lying in a hospital bed, a nickel-sized dent in his forehead, a softball-sized section of skull blown out the back. She'd been in the crowd when it had happened. Seen the shooting at the courthouse firsthand, with her own eyes. Crenshaw was comatose. Brain-dead. A vegetable. So why was she feeling so uneasy? Why did she seem overwhelmed by what had happened to her here? Up these stairs? In this same bedroom where she slept every night?

Maggie decided it was because Cale was gone. She'd spent the past three nights sleeping by herself. Alone. Yet she wasn't certain that alone was it. Perhaps the quiet was getting to her. The isolation. Hank's presence only counted for so much. So yes, she was feeling alone and vulnerable. She doubted being pregnant was helping any. The hormones played tricks with your mind. It would help if she could get her gun back from the police.

"Mags? You okay?" Chloe was standing at the top of the stairs. She'd paused upon noticing Maggie dawdling like a five-year-old in a grocery store.

"Just a bit of nerves," she said.

Feeling a cool shudder creep up her back, Maggie climbed the remaining steps. Chloe wrapped an arm around her shoulder, gave her a hug. "It'll be all right, hon," Chloe whispered. "Breathe easy. No stress; no worries."

They still had the upstairs and basement to cleanse. Perhaps the garage, as well, though Maggie doubted any sort of spirit or demon or entity would travel from God-knows-where to spook them by hiding in the oily, foul-smelling garage.

Hovering outside the master bedroom, they stood together in the doorway, watching as Father Larchezi muttered his protective incantations. The priest spritzed the bedroom windows and room corners with holy water, before performing the same blessing to the upstairs bathroom and walk-in closets.

Watching him, Maggie's mind drifted back in time...

The broad and lengthy bedroom, the bed she slept in each night...this was where Tobias Crenshaw had drugged her. Where he'd trapped her. Where she'd first laid eyes on him silhouetted in the doorway, a sinister and shadowed figure. This is where the monster had hurt Hank. He'd kicked his small body against the far wall with such force that Hank had surely lost one of his nine lives that day. Then the bees had attacked and swarmed inside her head, and she'd collapsed, falling to the bed, frozen, drugged, unable to move, a victim of the Chemist.

Hank let out a sudden loud screech from below, and it caused their heads to turn. They were all confused, before panic touched Maggie. She heard Hank scampering down the hallway and up the family room steps. Arching an eyebrow, her worried eyes sought out her sister.

"He's just chasing a bird outside." Chloe said this in a flat voice, and the concern in her eyes seemed to belie her words.

"Cloe? Is everything all right?"

Chloe kept her lips pressed tight. She turned her attention back to the room, and Maggie followed her lead.

Father Larchezi paused at the foot of the bed and was staring towards the headboard. On the wall above the bed, Maggie had nailed a large jewel-encrusted crucifix, secured it to the wall with purpose. She'd done so two days after Tobias Crenshaw had attacked her here, after he'd been arrested, and she had returned home. Ready to get on with her life.

"What a beautiful gilded cross," the priest said, without turning their way. "The little inlaid stones. Splendid."

"It belonged to Cale's mother," Maggie reported. "She left it downstairs when they moved to Arizona." She wrung her hands. "She used to have it hanging in the dining room."

"So, Cale's family were believers growing up. After all."

"Maggie put it in here. Ever since the…you know…" Chloe said.

"I see." Father Larchezi lowered his head and sighed. Maggie knew what had happened to her was common knowledge. What her attacker had done, here, in this bedroom.

"What happened to Mr. Crenshaw," the priest said without remorse, "getting shot in the head the other day, well…" His voice trailed off.

"'Eye for an eye.' Like the Old Testament says." Chloe offered no hint of remorse. "Justice served, as far as I'm concerned."

"In mysterious ways, does work the Lord," recited Father Larchezi.

Maggie barely heard them. A frightening thought caused her face to drain of color. She looked hard at Chloe. "*He is coming!*" Maggie whispered the words. "You don't suppose it's Crenshaw, do you? Coming back to haunt us? Me? After he dies?"

Panic caused her voice to quaver.

Chloe shook her head. "No, Mags. Of course not." She reached for Maggie's hand in comfort. "It's not Crenshaw. Not at all. Or his—or his ghost."

"But you can't be sure. I mean…can you?"

"Trust me." Chloe gave her a heartfelt stare, meeting Maggie's moist brown eyes with confidence. "No way, José. I've seen things." She shifted her eyes to the priest, then back to her sister. "I'm *certain* of it."

Silence built between them until Maggie exhaled. She seemed to relax. She had to believe Chloe on this kind of stuff. The visions, the predictions, these were Chloe's turf. What other choice did she have?

"No need to worry anymore," said Father Larchezi solemnly, stepping away from the bed. "Your home is purified. Protected against whatever dark forces might try to enter."

The priest moved across the room and slipped past the women as they stepped aside. He marched down the hallway toward the stairs. Chloe followed him. Maggie began to trail them, then stopped and turned, taking a long look back inside the bedroom. Late afternoon shadows pooled in the corners. Once more she studied the ornate crucifix attached to the wall—it housed a relic of St. Anthony inside, so she'd been told—before turning and moving back through the doorway.

Maggie drifted out into the hallway, moving like a spirit, not quite feeling herself walking. She felt a chill as she trailed them both down the stairs.

———

Tazeki was having too much fun to return home just yet. Besides, he was in Green Bay, wasn't he? What better time to pay another astral visit to his old friend? His former partner in crime. His old college roommate.

In the time it took to consider the idea, he found himself, once again, inside the damp soggy folds of Tobias Crenshaw's brain. Here he discovered little activity, synapses fried, as dormant as daytime drunks in an alley.

"Hello, Tobias. Long time no see." Tazeki's singsong voice.

As if waking up from a dreamless sleep, he felt Tobias's mind pull itself to attention. Like a private caught dozing during five a.m. roll call. "Tazeki. What...where...?"

"Paying my old friend a visit. What? You want me to wait till you're moldering in your grave?" His laugh was a cackle. "Where's the fun in that?"

Inside the hospital room, Tobias's eye movements beneath his closed lids caused the soft palpebral flesh to twitch. The EKG unit showed an inconsequential hiccup in the steady rhythm of his heart rate. The EEG graph needle sighed. A bedside neuro-monitor, its screen a palette of patterned colors, revealed a soft orange tinge just off the red nucleus, located deep in the brain's cerebral cortex.

Other than that, Crenshaw's unconscious and unmoving body displayed no evidence of increased brain activity.

"Get out of my mind, you bastard. You've no right—"

"I have *every* right," Tazeki hissed, emphatic. "Without your sorry fuck-ups, I wouldn't need to be here at all. Flying bodiless around the ether. Searching for Pazuzu."

"I'm dreaming. This isn't happening. I'm—I'm going back to sleep."

"Tobias! I'm insulted. Don't feel like chewing the fat with your old friend? Don't feel like telling me about your event-filled time, since they let you leave your jail cell?"

"You set it up, didn't you? You hired—it was Kinsella who pulled the trigger, wasn't it?"

"How about it was you who betrayed us? Betrayed me? To the cops? Trying to save your own putrid hide?"

"You...you evil prick!"

Tobias lay in silence, like a man seething in his grave. His eyes were clamped shut, not a twitch beneath the closed lids. Tazeki guessed his friend had little going on brain-wise, most of the time; nothing he could recall, at any rate. He felt Tobias grit his mental teeth. The man was playing the victim here, feeling sorry for how much his life had been altered. He was also, no doubt, wondering why he was being tormented? Plagued further by the man responsible for his current situation?

A bleak thought rose within Tobias Crenshaw's core—perhaps his soul, if he had one—and Tazeki intercepted it. Crenshaw's mind flashed the question:

"Am I dead? Is this my place in hell?"

Tazeki modulated his reply to a low whisper. "You complained how bored you were with your life, Tobias. How mundane and tiresome it had become. So what's the big deal?"

When Tobias failed to respond, he couldn't resist needling: "By the way, I was meaning to ask: Remember our wager? From back in college? Remember when you predicted you'd design the perfect crime, someday?"

Tobias offered a mental sigh.

"My abductions were perfect," he said without speaking. "But when your psycho, that SOB—*Kinsella*—decided to dump the girl's headless body in the lake... That's what messed everything up."

Tazeki chuckled without humor. "All the crazy bets we used to make. Smoking weed in our dorm room. Who'd have guessed you'd take that BS seriously?"

Tobias stayed silent.

He decided he'd abused his old roommate enough. It was time to depart. Without a hint at goodbye, a millisecond later, Tazeki was gone.

The bedside EEG needle lifted so slight that a blink would've missed it. Statistical aberration. The heart monitor maintained its rhythm, steady as she goes. The vibrant colors across the mesh of neuro-monitors failed to change, and there was no electronic evidence of anyone having paid the comatose patient a visit.

Ghost or otherwise.

CHAPTER 18

Standing in the dining room, Maggie held the plain wooden crucifix the priest had used during his ritual. It was a gift Father Larchezi liked to bestow on the faithful after they'd participated in his house-blessing ceremony.

"Not as fancy as the one you've got hanging in your bedroom," he had quipped minutes ago, handing her the cross as a gift. "But it's blessed by the hand of God. That's all that matters."

"Thank you, Father." Maggie was comforted by the gesture.

"Can never have too many crucifixes in a house, can we?"

"I guess not."

Maggie handed the cross to Chloe for safekeeping. After all, her sister had orchestrated the event. Father Larchezi zipped up his duffel bag and headed through the kitchen, moving out the back door and into the fade of late-afternoon sunshine. The women trailed after him, escorting him across the driveway apron. As he paused at the Kia, Maggie thanked the priest again for coming on such short notice.

"Duty calls, Christ answers." His eyes twinkled as he entered his vehicle. "Perhaps I should license that?"

"Church. Tomorrow evening!" Chloe called, giving the priest a wave. They watched him execute a Y-turn and ease down the driveway. Father Larchezi still had confessions to hear, sins to absolve, his day far from finished.

As the Kia disappeared onto the street, the sisters began making their way back toward the house. Maggie stooped to pull a weed from beneath a pine shrub. Then another. Rising, she said, "A never-ending battle, isn't it?"

Chloe was staring at the crucifix in her hands. "You mean against evil?"

"No. Weeds."

Entering the house, Hank was there to greet them. It was time for his dinner. He meowed, curling his supple body around Maggie's ankle.

Chloe placed the crucifix atop the dining room table, near the flowered centerpiece. "I feel more relaxed. I think we'll both sleep better tonight."

"Hope so."

The electric can opener made a grinding sound. The pungent scent of chicken-parts filled the room. Chloe gathered her purse from the countertop, car keys, phone in hand. "At least we've got protection from whatever danger is headed our way."

Maggie set the food bowl on the floor and Hank dove in. She moved from the kitchen and leaned against the wall beneath the ceiling arch, which delineated the open dining room. "Whatever works, I suppose," she said, unenthused.

"You're thinking this was all a waste of time?"

Shaking her head, Maggie's ponytail swayed. She moved to a dining room chair and sat, hugging one knee to her chest. "Father Larchezi seems nice. And serious."

"But?" Chloe had her keys in one hand but didn't move.

"I just don't see...I don't get... Like I said, whatever works." Her fingers found the crucifix, lifted it from the table, studied it in the room's soft light. "I guess I'm still confused by what *He is coming* means."

"I told you. Simple. It means something evil this way comes."

Maggie frowned. "Couldn't it also mean Cale? He's coming home? Or maybe the baby—that the *baby's* coming?" She sighed. "Why does it always have to be something dark? An invader? A ghost? Or a demon? Something bad?"

"I'm not making all this up."

"It's just—we're different, you and me." Maggie chewed her lower lip. "Maybe it's...I don't know...my lawyer side. I believe in rules and laws and logic. I get that bad guys do bad things. But they're air-breathing bad guys; they're blood-bleeding. Not ghosts. And none of them have pinprick scarlet eyes in the corner of a room."

Chloe pondered her words. "You're like most people, Mags. Believe me, I get it. Myself? I understand there's more out there than the average person sees. Why? Because I see it in my mind. And then, even worse, it turns out to be real!"

"Thus, the presence of Father Larchezi. Here. At my house."

Chloe's forehead knotted. "It comes down to two choices: A or B. Safe or sorry." She made a move toward the backdoor and paused. "Call me crazy, but I'm choosing to bet on the safe side."

Maggie rose and followed as Chloe opened the door and stepped outside. "I hope to God I'm wrong," Chloe added as she walked in the direction of her car. "I hope it *is* about Cale. Or the baby. I'm happy to be wrong."

Her sister moved to her car, and Maggie chose not to follow, lingering instead on the narrow concrete pathway. A pair of starlings flitted through the nearby tree branches, playing tag. A lawnmower droned, the noise comforting on some level. It was an indication this was, indeed, a "safe" neighborhood, a place where people cared for each other.

Her eyes fell to the flower beds alongside the house. Maggie noticed a set of paw prints visible in the soft dirt. Not a rabbit, and too large for Hank's kitty prints. She hoped it wasn't a raccoon. They sometimes wandered up from the riverbank a quarter-mile away, searching for food or garbage. It was likely some animal out exploring during the night. It would move on, like they always did. Chloe was right.

The house was sanctified. She didn't have to worry any longer about invisible frightening things, the kind lurking outside at night, drooling over what they'd do once they got inside. Monsters like Tobias Crenshaw.

In the driveway, Chloe opened the blue Buick's door and slipped inside.

Maggie glanced over, about to call out something, when her house phone chirped. She could hear it through the open screen window. Her watch read 5:16 p.m. Without realizing it, she was calculating the time in Italy. "Might be Cale!" she called, rushing back into the house with a goodbye wave.

"Tell him *arrivederci* for me!" Chloe shouted through the open car window. Sliding the vehicle into gear, she swung around and navigated down the driveway.

Maggie rushed into the dining room, where the phone was chirping. Cops' home numbers were seldom listed for obvious reasons. It meant calls on the landline were infrequent. An insurance quote or a political ad. Did she want a new American Express card? The usual mundane crapola. The caller ID read "PRIVATE." She picked the receiver up.

It took a second to register, but the polished female voice sounded familiar: Renee Douglas, the local TV investigative reporter. The person who had assisted Cale during the Chemist case. Renee had pulled some strings, which had allowed Cale to conduct a live, on-air interview at her station. It became the ruse that flushed Tobias Crenshaw into the open.

She had met Renee a few times, at city fundraisers and charity events. After exchanging polite intros, Maggie said, "Renee. This isn't just a social call—I'm guessing."

"Can we get together and chat? Sometime soon?"

Journalists seldom call out of the blue. And not on Friday evenings at dinnertime. Maggie kept her radar on alert. "This is about Tobias Crenshaw, isn't it?"

She shouldn't have been surprised by the call. The news hounds would be trolling for storylines. A notorious criminal gunned down in public? Shot point-blank on the steps of the courthouse? As one of his victims, reporters would consider Maggie's opinion "newsworthy." She should have taken the damn phone off the hook.

Maggie shifted her brain into lawyer-mode. "I'm not a spokesperson for the victims' group. The Mothers of Missing Daughters? You get that, don't you?"

"Still, you must have some reaction," Renee said like a pro. "He was shot in the head, after all." She dangled the statement suggestively.

Inside her words, she heard: "Poor Maggie. We understand your pain. We all do. But our viewers have the right to know. The man who kidnapped and raped you? His life is dangling by a thread? How does that make you feel?"

Choosing her words with care, Maggie said, "I'd love to help, Renee. I would. But I've got to give it some thought."

"No worries. How about I call you next week?"

Maggie's brain snarked at what the reporter failed to add: "After he's dead. Given up the ghost. So, Maggie...can you share with us your reaction? About the man who scarred you for life? Oh, and by the way—rumor has it you're pregnant with his love child?"

Hanging up the phone, trembling inside, Maggie pulled out a dining room chair and plopped down unsteadily. She found herself staring at the simple wooden crucifix on the center of the table. She reached out and toyed with it, her thoughts a thousand miles away. Her eyes welled up and she closed them, as if to trap the salty tears inside.

When Hank leaped up on the table, she forced a fragile smile to her lips. Then she buried her face in his fur and began to sob like a teenager with a broken heart.

CHAPTER 19

A mile after departing Maggie's home, Chloe slowed her vehicle. She turned onto Hastings Street, a quiet residential neighborhood on the city's East Side. Older homes, mature trees, large backyards with separate garages, tomato gardens, and real rope clotheslines. After what she'd been through that afternoon at her sister's house—being spied upon by something sinister, then passing out and glimpsing another vision of poor Leslie Dowd—Chloe needed time to think. To organize her thoughts. She understood that once she got back home, with Ed and the kids demanding dinner and her attention, she'd become lost in the evening and forget a couple of the important details she needed to remember.

Chloe selected a spot halfway up the block. There was little activity early Friday evening. No cars were parked, no blader-kids on boards, no bicycles scooting up and down driveways. No Hot Wheels. She slid the Buick to the curb and cut the engine. The radiator pinged a few times as Chloe cast her gaze out the windshield.

Despite Father Larchezi's blessing of the house—and Maggie's skepticism—the facts of the matter hadn't changed: something evil was headed their way. Coming for them. Chloe didn't understand how the pinprick scarlet eyes were connected to its arrival, but she was damn sure they were. Still, she couldn't begin to guess what her visions of Leslie Dowd—imprisoned in the mansion by the sadistic, swarthy, goateed man—had to do with any of it. That part remained hidden in shadow. *He is coming.* It was the thing she was certain of. But who was he?

Try as she might, Chloe couldn't figure out any obvious connections.

Later that evening, she was scheduled to be interviewed on the *Mandy Daniels Radio Show.* It was a regional gabfest out of Kansas City, which featured a wide range of eclectic-type guests. The show was designed to focus on the supernatural, the unexplained, or on mysterious violent crimes that remained unsolved. As the most recent "psychic detective" in the news, bolstered by her assistance in the Chemist case, Chloe understood she should be more excited than she felt at the moment. If anything, she was frustrated. Blabbing about how she'd helped incarcerate Tobias Crenshaw—soon to be deceased—was not going to help her unlock the mystery surrounding Leslie Dowd's whereabouts. Not as far as Chloe could foresee.

Sitting in silence, she continued to stare out the Buick's windshield. Mature elm and ash trees on both sides of the street formed an arching leafy canopy overhead. A breeze swayed their uppermost branches, leaves twirling in the warmth of late-afternoon. Sprinkles of gold splashed across the hood of her car, though half the Buick's body remained in shadow. Just like her visions, Chloe decided. The answers often lurked in the penumbra just beyond the pale of light. It was up to her to coax them out of hiding, where they could be revealed.

She planned on doing just that.

Turning the ignition, Chloe eased from the curb and navigated up the tree-lined street. The leafy tunnel seemed to provide her with protection, like being wrapped in the loving folds of a mother's arms. When the tree cover ended, and she emerged at the intersection, she felt wide awake. She was determined to see this puzzle through. Leslie Dowd was in danger—the life-threatening kind of peril—and Chloe promised herself she'd do everything in her power to help the girl find her way back to the light.

———

Living in her small apartment, like a pearl in a sand-covered shell, Charity Tantram had a plan. Having a plan was the key to success in life, she'd always believed. And Charity's plan was simple: First, she'd win notoriety for her reporting, and for her book on the dark motivations of the criminal mind. This accomplished, she'd be asked to do national media radio interviews, and these would be followed, in turn, by live appearances. From there, who knew? There were always going to be criminals, and if anything, they seemed to be multiplying, as if feeding on one another's violence. Thus, as far as Charity was concerned, the sky was the limit to her endeavors.

At the moment, however, Charity's plan was still at the foundation level.

It was Friday evening, the sun casting longer shadows, and she was dressed in a pair of gray running shorts, a matching top, spotless white cross-trainers. She had her golden hair pulled back in a bun, pinned in place. After making certain her iPhone and iPad were interfaced, sitting upright on her couch, Charity keyed in the number.

The ringer trilled twice before a female voice answered with a tentative, "Hello."

Charity introduced herself as a professor at the local university. She indicated that she was trying to reach Maggie Jeffers and had already guessed what Maggie might be thinking: dinnertime, a stranger calling, the mention of the university likely meant the caller was soliciting a donation for one thing or another, and even over the phone line, Charity could feel Maggie stiffen.

"This is not alumni-related, Ms. Jeffers." Charity said this in her best authoritative tone. "A week ago, I conducted an interview with Tobias Crenshaw, before his release from the Brown County jail—and before the shooting. The topic was stalking and kidnapping."

"I'm sorry, Professor Tantram. I doubt I have anything to contribute."

"He brought your name up during our interview, Maggie. Specifically." Charity swept a loose strand of hair from her forehead.

Silence.

"I haven't published the interview on my blog, yet." She kept her tone neutral. "I wanted to speak to you first. Get your input, you know? Before I do?"

More silence, and Charity imagined the clammy perspiration forming on Maggie's lower back.

"Crenshaw's claiming that during your abduction, you two spent a lot of 'quality time' together. It's how he put it. *Quality time.*"

"Would you mind getting to the point, Professor?" Maggie said curtly.

"The point is..." Hold it, hold it, hold it... "He claims he's the father of your unborn baby."

Your. Unborn. Baby. Three stab wounds in the gut, Charity guessed. She added, "You're going to have to talk to someone, Maggie. As soon as...as all this stuff leaks out."

The woman let loose a guttural gasp, which to Charity didn't sound quite human. Then she heard the phone slam in her ear.

Charity stared at the silent iPhone in her hand. She couldn't blame Maggie Jeffers for hanging up on her. How could she? She'd blindsided the poor woman. Would she have done the same thing herself? Under the same circumstances? Hung up?

Charity pondered the question for a few seconds.

Okay. She had just informed a stranger that she, Charity, was about to reveal to the world that Maggie was pregnant. And the father of her child was the monster who had abducted, tortured, and raped her.

The answer—Charity decided—was simple. Of course, she'd have hung-up. She'd have slammed the phone down so fast it would have made the other person's ears pop. Enough said.

Still, she'd done what she needed. Despite the guilt she felt at the cold manner in which she'd operated, one thing was clear: Charity had opened the door to future communications. And that, after all, had been the purpose of her call.

It was part of her larger plan.

CHAPTER 20

Rome, Italy

The American Embassy in Rome housed the Department of Homeland Security/ICE offices inside the palatial, sand-colored building on Via Veneto. Special Agent in Charge Amy Fronteer ran her operation from a suite of small offices on the second floor—three secretaries, six field agents, eight analysts—where they monitored leads involving child-labor indiscretions and human-trafficking cases. That was an ongoing, worldwide area of concern, one that seemed to be worsening with the passage of every day, month, and year.

It was late night now, and chalk-gray clouds shielded the moon from view. There was not much breeze as Jacek's team, tucked inside the dark van, cleared security and was ushered into the private lot just south of the historic building. The three a.m. streets of Rome remained aglow, still inhabited by tourists on a Friday night in May. In the van's backseat, sitting next to Pharaoh, Cale's head was swimming from the amount of intelligence Agent Fronteer had supplied them with. The find-and-rescue operation seemed to be expanding by the minute.

ICE had gathered information on Kinsella, on Prince Mir Al-Sadar, and on active human-smuggling networks working inside Belgium, Germany, and the Netherlands. The UK was likewise a hot spot for the distribution of human sex and labor slaves. These individuals came from Eastern Bloc countries like Russia, Bulgaria, and Ukraine, as well as from Cambodia and Laos, North Korea and India, along with any number of poor African nations. The Sicilian mob was an active player, as were the Russian mafia, the Chinese Triads, and a variety of Jamaican gangs. Threads could be traced to both the Israeli and United Kingdom mobs. They all had their sordid fingers in the pie. It was a complex, international mess, one not remedied by national law enforcement agencies, each of whom dealt with the problem on their own local levels.

The human-trafficking dilemma, it was agreed by those in the field, could only be dealt with effectively on an international scope. Cale decided he wouldn't hold his breath: The United Nations couldn't even stop Japanese shark finning, yet alone the viral spread of forced human slavery.

Recognizing the futility of curing the world of its ills, Cale decided his best bet was to stick to the task at hand: to discover the whereabouts of the two kidnapped females he was searching for, return them home to their families. The newest photographs he'd ID'd of Leslie Dowd—taken, they were guessing, about six weeks earlier, on the grounds of Prince Mir's Belgian estate—had infused him with hope. It was the first glimmer he'd had since the flight across the Atlantic five days ago.

Why did it seem like five weeks? Five months, even?

Inside Agent Fronteer's office now, peering over the shoulders of one of the staff analysts, Cale studied the computer screen. It displayed the latest Interpol report on the involvement of a Basque kidnapping-terrorist group, concentrated in Spain and Portugal. Those country's young victims were at risk, as well. Each individual, Cale had learned, was worth upwards of seventy thousand dollars *per year* to their handlers. Multiply that number by ten females in an individual cell, times an approximate fifteen-year working life, and the results provided a glimpse into the hefty profits garnered in the sex-slave racket. Unlike narcotics, which were sold and used, each girl was a commodity to be used over and again, akin to a machine that kept on producing, cranking out cash for their handlers.

He cast his gaze toward Agent Fronteer's desk. The blond-haired SAC, wearing blue jeans and a blazer, appeared ready for action. Cale watched her typing on her desktop PC. Sensing his eyes, she glanced over at him, before returning her attention to her keyboard.

"They ID'd the hit man who attacked you in Naples," Agent Fronteer said with a hint of satisfaction, as if it was something that seldom occurred. "The Italian police confirmed him via airport surveillance tapes."

Moving toward her desk, Cale arched an eyebrow.

"Nito Passetti. A professional hit man for the *Napoli Camorra*. A notorious and ruthless bunch." Agent Fronteer exhaled. "Don't happen to recognize the name, do you?"

Cale shook his head. He peered over at Jacek, who was sitting five feet away with his elbows on his knees.

"Botched the job," Jacek said with a shrug. "He's no Carlos the Jackal."

"*Mafiosi?*" Cale's eyes widened. "What would they want with me?"

Agent Fronteer gave Jacek a pointed look. "Maybe not Carlos, but he's a professional. *Silenzioso assassino.* If Nito Passetti had wanted Cale dead, he wouldn't be sitting here right now."

"*Pshee.*" Jacek waved one hand. "Not so silent with his bombs going off in an airport."

The agent shifted her focus to Cale. "From the looks of things, the canvas sack you were carrying was more important to him than your life. Care to share?"

"Ha!" Jacek barked. "His precious little trinkets from Liberia."

Sitting across the room, Pharaoh sneezed. He rubbed his nose as if he'd just hit a line of cocaine. Cheetah, for her part, was paying little attention to them. Instead she chatted with the second analyst, who was also working the graveyard shift. They were studying a computer monitor together.

To Agent Fronteer, Cale said, "I grabbed a couple of items, okay? Artifacts. Like souvenirs."

He was aware that he'd smuggled the stolen possessions out of one country (Liberia) and into another (Italy). An international crime, to be sure, but not the end of the world. Besides, no one had seemed to care aboard the late-night military cargo plane he and Jacek had escaped in. What was done was done, at least in Cale's mind.

"These 'souvenirs' you swiped," Agent Fronteer said probingly, "they're of some relevance? Or worth anything?"

"To the man I borrowed them from—so it appears. Colonel Tazeki Mabutu."

Her stare was tight. "The Liberian the military head? The man in charge of their National Police?" Agent Fronteer frowned like a high school teacher Cale had once had, one who'd found neither his nor Slink Dooley's antics in her Civics class particularly amusing.

She continued, "The Italian authorities are speculating that Passetti was contracted to reacquire what was in the canvas sack you carried—i.e. the colonel's possessions. To return them back to him." After a sigh, she added, "It seems killing you would've just been icing on the cake."

Cale frowned. Her words were less than flattering.

Agent Fronteer ghosted a smile. "I hope these 'souvenirs' were worth risking your life over."

"They're gone." Cale shrugged. "I already shipped them to the States."

She shifted her eyes back to her computer screen and said nothing.

Cale was standing ten feet away from the agent's wide desk. The office was oversized with a lot of space between the desks and file cabinets, unlike the cramped quarters of his own homicide bullpen, where he worked every day. Agent Fronteer's workspace consisted of high windows facing west, and there was a twinkling view out over the lighted city.

Like a caged jungle cat, Cale felt unable to sit in his chair. Time, he supposed, would provide him with the answer about whether the artifacts he'd stolen were worth anything or not. But the two items he'd taken from Colonel Mabutu had to be of some significance. Why else would the man pursue them halfway across Liberia? And then, when that effort failed, send a hit man after him in Naples? It was unlikely that Mabutu would have risked such daring retribution—an attack in a military airport terminal, of all places—unless he had a very good reason.

By this time the Italian military and *carabinieri* would be on high alert. They'd have posted facial likenesses of Nito Passetti in every city, town, and village across the country. He was a wanted terrorist now. An airport bomber. The man would no doubt have disappeared deep underground.

Cale exhaled. Neither the demonic statue, nor female shrunken head, were in his possession any longer. They were already *en route* back to his home city—out of sight, out of mind. Colonel

Mabutu would have abandoned the pursuit by this time. It was simply too hot. Neither object was worth it, Cale reasoned, regardless of their personal sentiment.

It's what any sane man would do: cut his losses and move on.

Still, there remained a loose thread that bothered him. *Why?* Why had the man seemed so intent on recovering the items? Was it simple vengeance? Or the losing of face, perhaps? Cale had managed to survive the nasty eel pit, hadn't he? Might this be the reason? Or that they'd killed the colonel's favorite manservant— Kasim—the killer in the Nehru jacket?

The answer might be any of the above, or just as easily none of them. At this point, Cale decided it didn't matter. He no longer cared what the crazy colonel was up to. All that mattered was that he'd escaped Liberia with his ass intact. Barely. End of story.

CHAPTER 21

Cale watched the ICE agent's fingers clack across the computer keyboard. With a contrite look for the multitude of problems his mission seemed to be causing, he asked her, "Anything solid on Mabutu, yet? The connection between him and this Kinsella character?"

From the nearby chair, his legs extended, Jacek added, "The Colonel all but confessed to being a trafficker. In our presence." His tone was sarcastic. "Of course, he never guessed we'd survive to tell anyone about it." He glanced around the Homeland Security inner office as if noticing it for the first time.

Agent Fronteer wore her computer glasses perched on the end of her nose. She stopped typing and swept a strand of blonde hair behind her ear. She answered them without looking from her screen. "Sorry, but your Liberian friend seems a bit camera shy." She resumed typing. "We've managed some photos, black-and-white blow-ups of CC surveillance footage."

She stopped typing and spun the screen around for their benefit, pointing with the tip of her pen.

"The first photo here is Mabutu meeting with a Jewish gangster with known trafficking links. And this next one—he's with a Bosnian general, on a Copenhagen subway. The photo's a bit grainy. Best we could manage."

Jacek rose, joining Cale for a closer inspection. They peered at the images on the flat screen, like students studying a dissection in biology class.

"In other words, nothing substantial," Cale said in a frustrated tone. He'd been leaning in and now rose to his full height. "Nothing to prove actual criminal activity."

"Birds of a feather though, eh, Mr. Packer?" Jacek gave Cale a wink.

"Every circumstantial piece is a building block. As you're quite aware, Detective." Agent Fronteer leaned back in her chair. "What we need is a victim or two to step up. ID Mabutu specifically. His involvement in trafficking activity. Be willing to testify."

The men exchanged glances, feeling her words strike home.

"Not to mention needing an international indictment," Jacek said, judiciously. He eyed the ICE agent. "To actually prosecute. Issued by some world court. Correct?"

Agent Fronteer set aside her glasses and massaged the bridge of her nose.

"The U.N. has declared trafficking an international felony." Her voice was matter-of-fact. "Yet even when we do serve warrants, these people are up and gone—their victims shipped to God knows where. Often within a five-hour window. They've got multiple phony passports for each person in their 'employ.'" She made finger quotes. "They're mobile, besides. Enough so that prosecuting them is next to impossible."

"What about U.N. sanctions? Punish the countries harboring these animals?" Cale didn't disguise the edge in his voice. "In Liberia's case, maybe a food embargo? Couldn't you pressure them into policing their own trafficking mess?"

"You can't sanction every nation in the world." Cheetah's dose of reality hit them from across the room. She moved over to join them. "Besides, isn't your Colonel Mabutu, himself, a government official?"

"These are *individuals* committing the crimes." Agent Fronteer's voice sounded resigned. "Not nations. If you want my opinion, it boils down to a too liberal Euro world view."

"Animals by nature, eh," Jacek said pointedly. "Mix too much diversity together, this is what you get—human sex slavery."

Agent Fronteer opened her palms, as if to ask what-can-I-say? "As for Liberia—they've got far greater concerns than human trafficking. Poverty, disease, starvation. Lack of clean water, for God's sake." She ticked these off on her fingers.

"Okay. Let's set aside all the human rights bullshit!" Jacek roped them all with a stare. "And forget about Mabutu, for the time being."

He looked at Cale, who shrugged, staying silent.

"Our immediate concern," continued Jacek, "is Prince Mir, right? In Belgium? We find Cale's pair of Missings. And we break them out of the Prince's fancy prison."

"You mean his château?" Cheetah asked, arching her eyebrows.

"Call it what you like. When you're a prisoner, walls are walls."

None of them spoke.

"Jacek's right," Cale agreed, breaking the silence. "I only have a few days. We've got to stay on point."

Agent Fronteer studied her watch, then rose from her desk. She had an important phone call to make, she informed them, and protocol required she utilize an encrypted line. She left the room.

Cale shuffled over to a wooden chair and sat down. He felt out of sorts. Wearing the unfamiliar combat uniform once again didn't help, but like the others, he understood the need to be ready for action. Jacek was correct: You had to pick and choose your fights. Win the small battles. Forget about the greater war. It was a good way to avoid tilting at windmills. And the real battle, on this day, was with Prince Mir and his forces. That's where the focus should be: rescuing Leslie Dowd and Mary Jane Moore.

It was, after all, the purpose of his trip.

Ten minutes later, when the office door opened, they watched as the ICE agent strode into the room with a more determined step.

"All right, everyone," Agent Fronteer said, positioning herself in front of her cluttered desk. She waved an official-looking paper in the air. "We just cleared the final hurdle with the Belgian Minster of the Interior. We have an agency-sanctioned game plan here."

Jacek was alert at once. "We're heading out?"

"Transport time, door-to-door, is one hour and thirty-four minutes," she reported. "Your vests and gear, com-units and weapons, will be supplied courtesy of Uncle Sam. Chopper departs here in fifty-eight minutes."

"About time," mumbled Pharaoh, and no one disagreed with him.

———

The night was sultry. The Italian sky was filled with wisps of soot-colored clouds, set low against a lover's moon. Agent Fronteer had procured an agency helicopter to transport their group. When geared-up and ready, the craft lifted from a private, coastal airstrip just south of Rome.

Strapped in his narrow rumble seat in the rear section, Cale allowed his eyes to close, his mind to drift.

Without warning, the same futuristic movie-vision that Mabutu had shown him in the past, continued from where it had left off. Cale understood that it could not be real—it was impossible. Some sort of hallucination. Either that, or he was going crazy. He attempted to force himself awake, but found he was as paralyzed as a dog running it its sleep.

And as the images unfolded, Cale sensed the witch doctor's sinister presence lurking deep inside his mind once more. He attempted to scream: "Leave me the fuck alone!" But he was frozen, and no sound escaped his lips.

He heard only the throbbing drone of the propellers, which pushed them on toward a destiny that none of them might survive.

CHAPTER 22

Mons, Belgium

Outside the grimy windows of the arching building, the violet predawn foreshadowed the first early hints of daybreak. Through the corrugated metal walls of the old airplane hangar, through the drafty doors and windows, some half-open, Cale could distinguish the trill of a loon from a nearby marsh.

"Gentlemen, ladies," said the French-accented male voice, from the front of the gathered group. "This is your fair warning: today may prove a most challenging of days. And God willing, not one filled with bloodshed."

The speaker was Sergeant Luc Berceau. He was the man in charge of the military side of the joint operation.

The soldiers—in full tactical gear—had been assembled inside the rusted hangar building located just north of the town of Mons. The small airport appeared unused, its trio of narrow runways overgrown with weeds, grass, thistle, and purple wildflowers. It was a makeshift headquarters surrounded by farmlands and a grain factory to the west. Gathered within the hangar were two dozen members of the Belgian military, commanded by Sergeant Berceau.

Through the Department of Homeland Security, Agent Fronteer had requisitioned a handful of men from the US Army garrison, stationed at nearby Chievres Air Base. Along with Jacek and himself, and counting Pharaoh and Cheetah, they had a force of thirty-five soldiers. An ample team, Cale decided, to stage an effective daytime raid.

Château du Carthairs, here we come.

Taped to a bank of dusty metal shelves at the front of the area, where the sergeant now stood, were two dozen enlarged, high-detail GPS satellite photographs of the château's grounds. The soldiers used flashlights and a couple of erected power lamps to view the display, due to the dimness.

The photos showed an overview of the vast three-hundred acres of privately-owned property. And these generous and scenic acres sat alongside another six-hundred acres of adjacent forest land— federal property owned by the Belgian government. In total, it was an area just a bit larger than New York's Central Park.

Photos of the building structures on the estate showed the multiple garages, stables, various outbuildings, as well as spacious clipped-grass lawns. These would serve as picnic grounds and athletic fields. The private lake, streams, thick natural forests, and winding trails were a hiker's paradise.

At the epicenter of the property stood the expansive château itself: three magnificent stories, tall spires and high turrets, glazed French windows, balconies, and sloping cobbled rooftops.

It was a fairytale dwelling, Cale decided, studying the images of the buildings and surrounding wooded landscape. And like any good fairytale, the château was situated in a land inhabited by monsters. Only this time the trolls and ogres—and most terrifying of all, the evil prince—seemed truly to exist.

With a nod from the leader, Cale watched as Agent Fronteer joined Sergeant Berceau at the front of the group. She had changed outfits to suit the occasion. Like the rest of the soldiers, she wore a fitted, protective Kevlar vest over her street clothes—sweatshirt, slacks, sensible shoes—and she began by thanking the Belgian military for their assistance in the matter.

Agent Fronteer stared out at the wide eyes, the eager faces, and added, "By now, you all should have been briefed by your team leaders as to the nature of this operation. But to encapsulate the seriousness, think Marc Dutroux. Times ten."

This comment brought murmurs across the open area, the shuffle of military boots.

"We're dealing with human traffickers here," she continued soberly, "along with the likelihood of both drugs, as well as arms-smuggling ops." Agent Fronteer's eyes swept over the group, her words echoing off the arching metallic ceiling.

"While executing this incursion," she continued, speaking with authority, "let me remind you that at all times you are to proceed with extreme caution. The entire security staff and bodyguards on premises are professional mercenaries. They are armed, and they are dangerous. We are invaders on their turf—and they will not hesitate to engage us with deadly force."

Her stern words echoed off the hangar's ceiling and walls.

With a polite nod, Sergeant Berceau stepped forward again. He was a solid man, mid-forties, with eyes crinkled from too much time in the wind and sun. He wore a tight brown and green camo beret, dipped fashionably, as if he'd just stepped off a movie set with William Holden. The sergeant pulled his men forward, huddling them closer to the series of satellite blowups. Inside the team grouping, Berceau resumed highlighting the details his men would need to execute the mission.

Agent Fronteer had stepped aside, moving away from the pack. She strode toward the rear of the squadron, where Cale and the others stood waiting.

Turning to Jacek beside him, standing with his arms crossed, Cale asked, "Marc Dutroux?"

Jacek rubbed his jaw. "His name freezes every Belgian's blood. And for good reason: a decade ago, he was responsible for the disappearance and murder of over a dozen young victims. They only had proof of his guilt for four of them, but enough to convict him."

"A serial killer?"

"Worse. Serial *pedophile* killer. Kept his young victims locked up and starved. Used them as sex slaves.

"Jesus."

"Ties to the Russian and Israeli mobs," Jacek continued. "Some of the worst traffickers operating in the world today."

"He sounds like a wonderful human being."

"A real peach," Pharaoh said, his voice low. Cale understood that Dutroux must have been the scum of the earth to warrant such a reaction from Jacek's otherwise mute companion.

Agent Fronteer snapped her phone closed as she neared them. "I wasn't speaking metaphorically, mentioning Dutroux," she said, her eyes pulling them in. "We have new intel linking the man to Prince Mir. All the way back to '98. Surveillance photos of them together in Antwerp."

Cale gave her a narrow look. "Photos? Courtesy of Interpol, I'm guessing."

"Interpol is years ahead of our FBI on facial-rec and iris scans. And they've updated much of their backlogged data. Late last night, I requested a retro-search connecting Prince Mir with any known traffickers in Belgium. It came back a hit for Dutroux."

Jacek's nod was thoughtful. "Makes sense. Dutroux did his nasty work in this country. He became very wealthy, resulting in numerous political connections. So even if they never did business together, he and Prince Mir would have crossed paths."

"Furthermore," Agent Fronteer added, "the prince being expatriate royalty, we're not sure how many cronies he's got working inside the palace. Or inside the national government, for that matter. Belgium is still a monarchy, you understand."

"By 'cronies,' you mean partners?" Cale asked.

"I mean *connections*. Sad to say."

"How about Cale's guy? The Liberian, Kinsella?" Cheetah asked. "Anything come up connecting him with this Dutroux?"

"Negative. We've got little else on Kinsella. Other than the UK arrest on file, we've got essentially nothing." Agent Fronteer shook her head, frustrated. Her blond hair was pulled back tight and secured. "But this all changes nothing—we proceed with our incursion.

"Sergeant Berceau's finishing his briefing," she added. "Let's head to the transports."

CHAPTER 23

The predawn morning was advancing in indigo hues, becoming lighter, it seemed, by the minute. The spacious abandoned hangar remained cast in the muted haze. The mist lifted from the grassy swamps across the road, huddling low at the base of tree trunks. Not far away a morning bird screeched, the echo smothered by the damp air.

A moment later, the tall hangar doors were flung open like the swinging doors of a saloon, and the troop emerged into the crisp morning—vests over camo uniforms—moving like a pack of gunfighters. As Cale walked, he was thankful he'd consumed a pair of bagels on the flight from Rome to Chievrus Air Base. They would tide him over for a while.

Taking a closer look in the gauzy daylight, Cale noted that the outer shell of the hangar revealed patches of rust along it's husk of corrugated metal. As they walked across the cracked and weedy concrete of the tarmac, moving in the direction of the transport vehicles, Jacek said, "You doing all right, Mr. Packer? Your drawers seem a little snug."

Cale glanced at the mercenary. "Just some personal stuff."

"Not pregame jitters, I hope."

"No. But..." he paused. "Do you believe in psychics? Like tarot cards? Crystal balls? Gypsy kinds of things?"

Jacek offered him a smirk. "We're finally moving"—He lifted his chin toward the armed soldiers trailing behind them on both sides, the transport vehicles gassed-up and standing in wait— "and you're thinking about ghosts and goblins?"

"My phone call home last night..." Cale's voice sounded distant, and he cast his eyes over his shoulder. Beneath the shadowy overhang of the hangar's doors he caught a glimpse of a man in gray coveralls. A janitor of some sort. The man was positioned alongside the building, sweeping what appeared to be wood shavings with a push broom. He had puffy lips, and his face reminded Cale of old photos he'd seen of the famous mobster, Al Capone.

"Your house is haunted, eh? Is that the problem?" Jacek winked at Pharaoh.

"My sister-in-law. To be. She's a believer in this hoodoo stuff. Gets visions or premonitions—or whatever you want to call them."

Jacek shrugged. "My honest answer?"

"If it's not too much trouble."

"Okay. You see enough agony and death in the world, you wonder if there isn't something else out there. Something beyond human cruelty. Ghosts? Angels? Bogeymen? I'm not a believer *per se*, but I ask myself, why not?"

"My grandmother was a *mambo*." Cheetah reported this in her crisp tone. "The good kind of witch doctor. Protective spells, healing. Helping people find missing loved ones, or things they'd lost. Those sorts of things."

"Witch doctor?" The term summoned memories in Cale of his visit to Liberia three days earlier—the lush vegetation, the steady drizzle, the smarmy face of Tazeki Mabutu in his study filled with African tribal artifacts and old war photographs. The ceremonial bone-mask hanging on one wall. "You mean like voodoo? Painted faces? Bone in the nose?"

"Voodoo. Vodun," said Jacek dismissively. "All the same."

Cheetah gave them a consternated look. "FYI: for the past dozen centuries, everyone's tried to convert the people of Africa to one belief system or another. Yet voodoo remains the *unofficial* religion on the entire continent." Her look at them was telling. "It's the peoples' religion—despite anyone claiming otherwise. In fact, the loa we pray to are akin to the Catholic saints."

Cale noted how Cheetah used the "we" pronoun.

Feigning an accent, she sassily added, "And no, my gumma don't wear no bone in her nose."

They were silent as they walked, with the tromp of their boots adding a rhythm to their pace.

"'*Give me that old time religion…*'" sang Jacek, off key. His accent made the melody sound almost unrecognizable, and it caused them all to laugh.

In the ensuing quiet, they shifted their collective gaze to Pharaoh, who marched along in his usual brand of stoic silence.

After recognizing their eyes on him, the large mercenary pointed to his sidearm. "If it bleeds, I believe in it."

Cale learned Sergeant Berceau had already sent ahead a reconnaissance team, which consisted of a pair of soldiers dressed as bikers. The men wore black leather chaps and vests, and it was imagined they'd blend in with the gathering of fetish aficionados. The pair would travel to the château's outer grounds on their motorcycles, before moving inland. They would then proceed to infiltrate the festival gathering, reporting back via their phones, as the events on the grounds of the château unfolded.

Putting together an operation on such short notice had posed logistics concerns for both team leaders. Pooling their resources, Agent Fronteer decided Cale and Jacek would travel as a team in a rented bread truck, the back compartment emptied out. It would serve as the primary rescue vehicle, an essential part of their plan. The soldiers of both units, under Sergeant Berceau's command, would convoy in a larger transport truck. The sergeant and Agent Fronteer—along with Cheetah and Pharaoh and the ops communications coordinator—would travel in a separate SUV. It would serve as their base. The trio of vehicles would rendezvous at a point just outside the western perimeter of the château grounds.

As they moved across the weedy tarmac, the cracked and uneven cement of the runway, Cale headed toward the silent bread truck. Up on the high roof of the hangar, a pair of pigeons cooed. Maybe they were mourning doves. The truck remained ahead of them, standing in wait beside a brown SUV. Off to their right, the soldiers veered toward their larger transport vehicle and began climbing the ramp, disappearing into the back to seat themselves, weapons ready, quiet and serious in the pale light of the breaking day.

Earlier, it had been Cale's suggestion that perhaps the military men might dress in civilian attire. Wouldn't it be easier, he reasoned, to try and advance as covertly on the château as possible? Wouldn't it be simpler to infiltrate by blending in with the gathering?

His idea had been dismissed by Sergeant Berceau. His men, he informed them all, were soldiers, not spies. Besides, as the Belgian military was the final authority in the operation, they wanted to make their presence felt. The potential for resistance was considered high due to the nature of Prince Mir's private security force. The sergeant wanted his men prepared and in full gear, locked and loaded. "If this turns into a firefight," he'd said, his voice firm, "I want my people ready to defend themselves. Something they cannot accomplish while wearing Bermuda shorts and sunglasses."

"I hadn't meant dressed as bird watchers." Cale retorted this defensively.

"He means in leather chaps," said Jacek, kidding but maybe not. "Carrying whips and riding crops, showing off their pimply bare arses."

This had brought chuckles from the soldiers who'd overheard the exchange, the ones who understood English anyway, which proved to be most of them.

"*Ahem*." Sergeant Berceau had coughed, quieting his men. He arched an eyebrow in Cale's direction, inviting him to add any further comments. Cale kept his mouth closed, but when he glanced at Jacek, he could see the Czech and Pharaoh were both struggling to keep straight faces and not crack with laughter.

Cale decided Sergeant Berceau's plan made sense, after all. Once they abandoned the pretense of a stealth operation, why not go in with a show of force? Further, it might better play into the rescue plan they had devised. His main uncertainty concerned the leather fetish event itself. What the hell was that about, anyway?

"This fetish BS? It's for real?" Cale had asked Agent Fronteer the question when they'd been inside her office, back in Rome. He'd been gazing at the bizarre images on the wide computer screen. The photos were taken from a similar event held in Dusseldorf, Germany, over a year ago.

There seemed to be hundreds—maybe over a thousand—of men and women dressed in a variety of skintight garb and getups, parading around what appeared to be some medieval fairgrounds. The prevailing theme seemed simple: whether dressed as a slave-master, a quivering submissive, a feline or horse person, an eye-patched pirate, a biker gang member, or a fancy French swordsman, the common denominator was that the participants

116

did so in leather or shiny black outfits. Spandex and latex, or even rubber, so it appeared, were likewise allowed. Or just about any sort of combination thereof. Cale couldn't be sure.

To his own mind, nevertheless, perhaps the most eye-catching of the bunch were the pony girls: they were attractive, statuesque females (a few might be males) garbed in costume—mouth bits, harnesses, tail plumes, hooved shoes, arms bound behind them in laced-up leather binders—and made to pull carts or prance around half-naked, performing at the whim of their masters.

They were both fascinating and disturbing at once, he decided, depending on your point of view.

"It's for real all right, Detective," Agent Fronteer had said. "And it poses a major problem for us."

"By 'problem' you mean besides gunfire from the prince's security guards?" Jacek had asked this with his arms crossed, cocking his head to one side.

"The fetish thing amounts to one giant costume party—essentially." The ICE Agent had studied them, before turning back to her computer screen. "It makes things touchy when attempting a search-and-rescue op. Our targets might be dressed in jackbooted nuns' habits, for all might know."

"Or horse masks," agreed Cheetah, her tone belying her disgust at the concept.

"Or like wolves." This from Pharaoh, and when they looked at him, he'd shrugged one muscular shoulder.

They had continued to examine the fetish images on the screen. Jacek said, after a spell of silence: "Once we locate them, we're just going to have to rely on Cale to ID his two targets. It's all we've got to go on, sorry to say."

Cale had stared at the monitor: there a pant-less, hooded man was being crop-whipped across the back of his hairy legs by a woman in spike heels and leather corset. "Don't worry. If they're there, I'll find them."

He couldn't be certain if it was confidence or the curse of his policeman's bravado. But what did it matter? The bottom line was that he had to locate Leslie Dowd and Mary Jane Moore. And he would. This much Cale was certain of. Whether they were wearing spandex catsuits or garbed as Nazi seductresses, he would find them. Then he would gather each girl up and drag her the hell out of there. Away from the prince and his armed bodyguards. To safety. Then he'd fly them across the ocean, back to their homes in Green Bay, Wisconsin, where their families and friends would be waiting.

Just as he had promised.

Cale had come too far in this journey to fail. He'd been lied to, imprisoned, shot at, and nearly decapitated. Almost killed more than a few times. Thus failure, in his mind anyway, was not an acceptable option.

As they arrived at their vehicles, Cale paused, sizing up the bread truck for a long moment. It would have to do, he decided. Beggars couldn't be choosers. Especially when it came to a desperate rescue operation, one flung together at the last possible minute.

He watched as Agent Fronteer came toward them, talking on her mobile as she approached. Cale was pleased to see her no-nonsense attitude matched the seriousness he felt in his own gut. He wondered if the agent was as anxious to get on the road as he was, if she experienced the same pregame jitters all law enforcement felt, just before a raid went down.

Cale guessed she did. He could see it in the clear green hue of her eyes.

CHAPTER 24

Outside the abandoned hangar on the mottled stretch of concrete, which might loosely be called a tarmac, a pair of vehicles stood with engines running. The truck transporting the soldiers had driven off. The bread truck and SUV remained. The group was at last prepared to board.

Jacek stood next to Cheetah, his phone in one hand. His Walther 9mm was holstered at his side, and Cale tried to imagine what other sort of weaponry he had secreted on his person. Days earlier, trapped in Liberia, Jacek had saved both their lives by expelling a muriatic acid cocktail from a secret compartment inside his wristwatch. He'd sprayed the face of the assassin Kasim, whose intent was to kill them both. And the man would have succeeded, if not for Jacek's clever intervention.

The incident had provided Cale with a better understanding of his partner. While Jacek was a trained professional, a soldier through and through, he was also not above doing whatever was necessary to get the job done. If his methods happened to land outside the Marquis of Queensbury Rules, not to mention the dictates of the Geneva Convention, then so be it. In a world of survival, you had to kill or be killed—wasn't that the point? Therefore, the bottom line was evident: Cale would rather have Jacek Tumaj on his side than be locked in combat against the man. Any day of the week and twice...well, the old cliché went without saying.

Shifting his eyes past Jacek, Cale noted how Cheetah carried a sidearm, as well as a knife. He glanced at her fingernails, the ones that had been sharpened into steel-like points. He had witnessed her in action on the training mats in Anzio. Even if Cheetah had no visible weapon on her, she would be considered lethal—armed and dangerous in the law-enforcement vernacular.

A few steps behind them stood Pharaoh, who carried an assault rifle in a paw so large it made the weapon look like a child's toy. Pharaoh would intimidate most professional athletes with his bulk alone. The fact he was cat-quick and had the temperament of a cheesed-off rattlesnake, meant anyone choosing to cross the large man's path did so at their peril. Whether in a jungle firefight, a professional combat ring, or a sleazy Bangkok tavern filled with low-life gangsters…suffice it to say, Cale was pleased Pharaoh was wearing their team colors.

There was little doubt, he concluded, that these three could handle themselves in any sort of skirmish. And like a rookie at a table of poker hustlers, despite seventeen years on the police force, Cale accepted that he was the question mark in their foursome.

He pondered their mission now, as he stood near Jacek, just outside the clunky bread truck. He had been issued a familiar Glock 9mm, full ammo clip with six back-ups. Ensuring the safety was set, he tucked the weapon in the leather holster at his hip.

"Here's an idea, Mr. Packer." Jacek turned to him without smiling. "This panty raid of ours goes as planned, I know a quaint little restaurant in Brussels. They serve a fine *eel* parmesan."

Cale grimaced at their private joke. "Kind of you. Think I'll pass."

With the sun just peeking over the horizon, the small Belgian village took on an amber glow, as if it might be auditioning as a movie set.

Agent Fronteer's phone chirped, and Cale listened as the agent spoke. "Affirmative. I'm on it." She flipped the mobile closed and faced them all. "We just received another trump card. A potential inside informant."

"Inside the château?" Cale asked.

She nodded.

"Does your informant know about the targets? The ones I'm searching for?" Cale felt excited for the first time in days, as if a new ray of hope might be glimmering down on him. He watched Jacek head for the truck's passenger door, recognizing that he'd been elected to drive.

"We'll find out soon enough, Detective," Agent Fronteer said. "We'll do an assessment interview on the way. Follow the SUV. I'll brief you when we arrive at the contact point."

"Who's the informant?"

"As you guessed, a man inside the château." She flipped her sunglasses back over her eyes. "If we manage to turn him into an asset, it's a huge coup for us."

Five minutes later, their two-unit convoy had crossed through the northern edge of town, having motored past homes and storefronts, warehouses and ornate, russet-brick and white-painted clapboard churches. They were on the road to a village called Casteau. NATO's SHAPE (Supreme Headquarters Allied Powers of Europe) military command was located there. Cale understood—all things considered—that the Allied powers didn't give two shits about their mission to rescue a pair of missing American females, who were innocent victims in the war on human trafficking.

Despite NATO's altruistic intentions, Cale remained a skeptic concerning the international organization. In his mind they specialized in two things: political bluster and cronyism. Three, if you counted wasting American taxpayer dollars. And this being the case, he accepted that he and his team were little but buzzing gnats in NATO's ever-expanding world universe.

Following the chocolate-brown SUV, Cale watched it slow to a crawl as they moved through the heart of the village. He glanced at Jacek in the passenger seat. The man had his eyes closed, as if catching a quick catnap. Cale's phone buzzed. Agent Fronteer was calling from twenty yards ahead of them.

"See the wooden feed warehouse? On the left? Cobbled roof?" she asked.

Through the side window Cale noted where she meant. There was a large sign on the adjacent building that read: CORN FEED: FRESH. He wondered why it was written in English rather than Walloon or French or some other local dialect. "Affirmative. Got it."

"Our home-point. Post pickup. Where we'll rendezvous with the packages after the extraction."

"Copy that," Cale said, keeping with the lingo. He watched as the SUV accelerated ahead of them, moving up a morning street as scenic as a holiday postcard. The warehouse, he told himself: memorize it. It might be their last life raft in a storm, hours from now, if the excursion went south and they were fleeing for their lives.

Dawn had risen in full as the vehicles crossed a small bridge and moved beyond the final outcropping of buildings and storage sheds. Minutes later, free of the village, they were cruising through the countryside on the flat, two-lane ribbon of asphalt. There was little traffic to speak of—a morning delivery vehicle here or there, or a pickup truck running errands. These, plus a couple of cars and a semi-cab without the trailer, headlights still on, which Cale imagined were searching for the nearest petrol station.

The bread truck's brakes squealed at a four-way stop. Other than the rumble of the tires over the cracked asphalt, it was the only sound the new morning revealed.

As he drove Cale spotted the black speck of a hawk cruising overhead, searching for her morning meal in the alfalfa fields below. The sky gave off an orange blush in the east, and Cale allowed his mind to absorb the splendor of the rural Belgian scenery as it settled over them, pretty as a Monet watercolor.

His inner voice reminded him to enjoy it while he could. Once the bullets started to fly, the next time he passed this way, he and his friends might be dodging hot bursts of lead

Cale wondered, hypothetically, if this image might not be some dark premonition of his own.

PART TWO:

THE BARCELONA TWIST

CHAPTER 25

Belgian Countryside

They swung onto a country road and headed northeast. At the wheel of the bread truck, Cale paid close attention to the SUV ahead of them. Jacek roused from his meditation after a bit and he gazed out the windshield, content at studying the stretch of bare asphalt ahead. A pair of farmhouses was set back far on the right, with feed sheds, a few grain silos, summer crops of barley and corn already planted. The terrain was fast becoming a series of rolling fields, interrupted by distant hillocks and copses of conifer pines, which served as barriers against the winds.

Turning to Cale, Jacek said, bluntly, "You had an intruder in your room last night."

"Yeah. The little bastard—I smashed him with my boot heel."

Jacek explained how Cale had slumbered during the assassin's attempt on his life. The man slipped through their defenses and reached Cale's sleeping room, planning to inject him with potassium cyanide. Pharaoh, on night watch, had disposed of the trained killer.

"For real?"

"Real as it gets, Mr. Packer." Jacek added in Czech, "*Tichy vrah*."

Cale didn't need an interpreter to understand he meant "silent assassin." Cale swiped his nose with his sleeve and looked at Jacek. "I didn't hear a damn thing. Out like a light, I guess." A shiver climbed his spine, though he attempted to feign nonchalance.

Jacek had relayed the event as if it were a common occurrence. He withdrew his sidearm and freed the ammo clip, inspecting it the way a butcher studies a veal cutlet. He said, "A permanent light—just about." Jacek slid the clip back into the weapon. "Good thing we sleep in shifts." With the safety locked, he holstered the 9mm.

When Cale glanced over, his partner had closed his eyes to resume his cat nap. He shifted in truck seat and stayed quiet.

Deciding to thank Pharaoh when he had the chance, Cale found himself suddenly wide awake. The knowledge that he shouldn't be alive—not just for the second or third day, but the fourth straight day, as well—had a way of sobering you. It brought to mind a saying he and Slink sometimes shared, after a few beers, how "God protects babies and drunks." He decided he could add "fools" to the list and John Hancock it himself.

Jacek's revelation, however, summoned an even more troubling question: Who would want him dead badly enough to send a professional hit man a second straight night? Not just the assassin at the Naples airport but a second man? To Anzio? Less than twenty-four hours after the first attempt had failed?

Only one suspect came to mind: Colonel Tazeki Mabutu.

Ever since Cale had escaped the colonel's eel pit, the man seemed to have a personal vendetta against him. He had placed him atop his People-To-Kill-ASAP list. No doubt about it, the Liberian military man wanted Cale's head on a platter.

But why go to such extremes? First the eels. Then the Naples airport. And now a nighttime attack in a fortified warehouse. Cale thought about it harder. Was it possible Mabutu might be tracking his whereabouts? GPS-ing him somehow? How else could his henchmen locate him so readily? Unless, of course, he was using a crystal ball. He was about to snicker at the idea, label in farcical, until a voice in his head cautioned: "He's a witch doctor, isn't he?"

This frightened Cale even more. Was it possible that his nightmares the past few nights had been real? That the voodoo man had truly been inside his mind? That his threats of violence against Cale and his family, the dire future predictions, had been real? And not just crazy dreams?

The idea turned his blood to ice. Yet perhaps he was simply being paranoia? His body reacting what Jacek had told him—the nighttime assassin?

Cale decided to shake it all away. He had more important things to dwell on at the moment: namely, his rescue mission. And besides—he could ill afford wasting time on things he couldn't control.

He would deal with Colonel Mabutu, if he still had to, when the time was right. When his rescue mission was concluded.

With both hands gripping the steering wheel, Cale focused on the SUV moving ahead of them. Yet with Jacek still snoozing, it didn't take long for the image of the insane witch doctor to return to his thoughts.

Like every investigation he'd worked, Cale understood that the solution always boiled down to *Why?* What was motivating the colonel's actions? He decided he must have gotten too close to something. A secret the man couldn't risk having exposed.

Cale's mind ran through the options:

Might it be his mission of rescuing the two kidnapped girls? Or was it his pursuit of the man's accomplice, Kinsella? Or perhaps the threat of exposing Prince Mir Al-Sadar? His connection to Colonel Mabutu? Or was it something even closer to Mabutu's black heart? Something that threatened the man's very existence?

Cale considered the pair of items he'd stolen: A) the sinister little statuette. It wasn't worth—in his opinion—much more than some prize at a county fair. That left B) the female shrunken head. But weren't they sold for a buck a bushel in Africa? On display at flea markets everywhere? The real ones, as well as the kind manufactured on assembly lines in Beijing?

The puzzle remained. One with too many missing pieces to solve at the moment. Cale decided his best bet was to set it aside, ignore the fist-sized knot in the middle of his chest, and get on with the more important business at hand.

With his hands steady on the wheel, he followed the SUV ahead of them. They moved along the narrow strip of asphalt road, progressing through the pristine Belgian countryside. Their two-vehicle caravan remained locked on a northeast heading. The farm fields soon gave way to the thicker woods, which seemed to narrow closer to the roadway like enemies sneaking closer.

Without warning, the SUV flipped on its blinker. It swung a left onto an even more secluded road. The bread truck shadowed behind, and a minute later, they cornered again, this time the opposite way. It didn't take long before they found themselves navigating along a furrowed, one-lane track, which jarred them with as many dips and bumps as a cow pasture.

Jacek awoke from his meditation with a start. "If I'd wanted a ride like this, Mr. Packer, I'd have joined the rodeo."

"Maybe you missed your calling."

Cale kept the truck a safe distance back, easing along, with the engine protesting every twenty or thirty meters. Not long after another turn, a rustic farmhouse appeared in the center of a wide clearing in the woods. It rose before them as if conjured by some wizard of the forest.

"This isn't the fancy château I was picturing." Jacek rotated his neck, before making certain his weapons were secure and holstered.

"Just following the lead horse," Cale said evenly. "I'm curious to get a look at our inside man."

"You've worked your share of informants, Detective. As you're aware, they come in all shapes and sizes."

Pulling to a halt on the weed-strewn grass, both vehicles cut their engines. Sergeant Berceau was speaking into his mobile as he exited the SUV's passenger side. Agent Fronteer and Cheetah emerged from the rear seats, advancing into the morning light. Morning jays chirped from the trees, and the air smelled of pine and tangy currant bushes. A squirrel paused, inquisitive, staring at them from beneath a high chestnut. Willows stood like stoic sentries, arm-locked against the encroaching forest.

It was dank and musty inside the country house. They opened the windows to invite in the morning air. A few minutes later, a husky-limbed man appeared at the front door. He was the janitor Cale had noticed outside the airplane hangar, the man sweeping sawdust: Al Capone-face.

The man knocked on the door and entered without ceremony.

"This is Claude Dierckx," said Agent Fronteer, acknowledging the visitor's entry. The man wiped the dew off his work boots. "He's a ground man working for Belgian Secret Service." Dierckx nodded to them all, and the agent continued: "Claude's helping us with our informant—our contact asset inside the château."

While they waited, Sergeant Berceau stayed glued to his phone, listening to update reports. Sitting on a too-soft couch, Agent Fronteer booted her laptop. She was speaking on her phone, having some sort of document prepared, from what Cale could gather.

The rest of them settled into the place. Cale chose to stand in the smallish country kitchen, leaning against an oaken countertop, too anxious to sit. He glanced at his watch every sixty seconds.

A few minutes later, Claude Dierckx turned from his chair at the kitchen table. He glanced over at the American and lowered his eyes, before Cale shifted his attention full-on, eyebrows arched above a stare.

"I apologize," Dierckx said, looking his way again. "But are you by chance a Belgian? You have a familiar look."

"Sorry. Wisconsin, born and raised. U-S-of-A."

From a nearby chair, Jacek snorted. "Belgian? He wouldn't know a waffle from a bowl of booyah."

Before Cale could comment, they were interrupted by the approach of a vehicle outside. It was a light blue pickup truck and the squeal of brakes sounded like the sharp call of a blue jay. A car door closed. Moments later, they watched a diminutive man in a brown fedora as he approached the wooden front porch steps with caution.

Agent Fronteer opened the door and greeted the visitor. She beamed a welcoming smile. Once inside the dim and rustic house, the elderly man looked around with the darting eyes of someone uncertain whether he should remain or turn and sprint back out the door.

"Everyone," announced Agent Fronteer, easing closed the door behind their guest. "This is Mr. Ernst Anselm." The visitor removed his hat and eyed them, his nerves showing. She added: "He will—we are *hoping,* anyway—be assisting us today."

——

Château du Carthairs, Belgium

Inside the multi-floored, spacious château, in Prince Mir's private first-floor library, with the strangely-garbed guests beginning to appear outside the beveled, double-height windows, Kinsella dialed Tebbi Qa's mobile. The hit man had been ordered to call him or to leave a confirming message when the American detective was disposed of. No word had come late last night. No word as of yet this morning. Radio silence, in Kinsella's tight world, was seldom a positive.

Now the bulky Liberian was becoming even more concerned. He had to report back to the botono today, inform him the mission had been accomplished. Inform him that the nuisance—the pesky American detective—was no longer a problem, that he'd been eradicated like a bothersome beetle.

Kinsella had hoped to report, further, on how the colonel's precious personal items had been recovered undisturbed. How they were safely back in their possession. But as things stood, with no message from the hit man he'd hired for the task, Kinsella could make no such proclamations.

He listened to the unanswered mobile's annoying trill. Then the message prompt, then the sandpaper-scratch announcement. "Tebbi Qa." An extended silence was next, followed by an equally annoying beep.

Kinsella spoke gruffly. "Get back to me, Tebbi Qa. ASAP." He rang off.

He understood the botono—all seeing, all knowing—did not require his phone call to understand how things stood. Still, it was protocol. Kinsella, a man called many things during his life, and most of them not so complimentary, was nothing if not loyal to the colonel's cause.

He would of course make the call. But not until hearing from his assassin. It was better to be tardy with good news, he told himself, than too hasty with bad.

CHAPTER 26

The Belgian countryside was an artist's palette of pastels. Church bells sounded from a far-off chapel, and deep in the valley a speed-train cut through the pristine acres, its whistle echoing through the woods and over grassy knolls and hillocks and farm fields and meadows of purple wildflowers. Beyond the tall spires of the Château du Carthairs, a pair of hawks soared in the eastern sky.

Two men in dark clothing—knit shirts, black tactical pants, matching boots—stood on the château's extended rear patio sharing a cigarette. Each wore a Swiss-made MP-9 assault pistol strapped across his shoulder, standard carry for all twenty men in Prince Mir's security force.

The entire troop would be on patrol for the Fetish Festival, the invitation-only event hosted by the prince. For the uninitiated, the affair might appear little more than a freak show. And there was, admittedly, no shortage of odd characters. One couldn't toss a stone in any direction without striking some leather-clad butt boy or latex-strapped minx with a riding crop. Fetish enthusiasts from more than three dozen countries were on the private invite list. The limit, however, was four hundred guests. As far as these sorts of events went, Prince Mir's gala was considered first-rate.

Booths were ready to hawk the latest in upscale fetish fashion. A Belgian beer-chugging contest was scheduled for late Saturday afternoon. Leather-clad musicians—today's group was a quartet of fag hags called The Mod Starlings—jugglers, clowns, gigolos, patrons in zippered latex horse heads, body paint, feathers, stiletto heels...all things imaginable were on display. And yet, beyond any doubt, the highlight of the day's events would be the four-hundred-meter pony-girl race.

Five times prior, either the German or Swiss teams had captured the event. This time, however, with the prince having hired a professional equine trainer to stack the deck in his favor, the Belgian contingent was cast by oddsmakers as a six-to-five favorite. In fact, so confident was Prince Mir of the outcome, that he'd wagered three times last night: against the Germans, against the braggadocio-filled Italians, and against the enigmatic Chinese team owners. One million American dollars *each*. The money, of course, was of little consequence to a man of Prince Mir's vast wealth. But still, in the heat of competition, winning the pony-girl contest would give him bragging rights across all of Europe and Asia.

For the next year, at any rate.

The pair of security guards now stared out across the forested grounds, past the massive oak trees and tall conifers, beyond the hedge maze and gazebo and flower gardens in full summer blossom. Content to smoke in peace, they did not speak. Ever vigilant, they were relaxing for these few minutes. It was early, a little after eight a.m., but already a few costumed participants were beginning to trickle out onto the main courtyard and fairgrounds situated on the south lawns of the château. A pair of giant striped hot air balloons were tied to moorings beyond the grassy playing fields. The bandstand stood ready, empty but for a trio of technicians running sound checks. Canvas tents had been set up to provide relief from the sun: wearing snug leather or latex on a heated day in May can dehydrate a person at an accelerated rate. Ample water bottles and beverages of all types were supplied, courtesy of Prince Mir. An on-site medical station was ready to provide assistance, if required.

By quarter past eight, the two guards had strolled back around the château and were entering the security outbuilding adjacent to the multiple garages. One side of the building was devoted to ordinance stockpiles, arms and munitions, enough firepower to equip a small army. On the opposite side of the security center was the electronic surveillance core. This oversized room consisted of multilayered banks of CCTV monitors, over a hundred in all. The cameras were set in strategic locales and hidden throughout the grounds of the estate. There were over six hundred individual camera units, disguised high up in trees or secured to low-lying stumps and logs. Every corner, every nook and cranny—from stables to main house, to garages and the outbuildings; across the lake, streams, forests, rooftops, and every entryway of the château itself—all these were covered by cameras. It required a half-dozen full-time technicians just to maintain the intricate surveillance setup.

Of course, everyone was aware blind spots existed. Three hundred acres of château grounds proper—and double that of the surrounding adjacent forests—proved far too substantial to cover completely. Nonetheless, the closed-circuit cameras went a long way to monitor against unwanted intrusions. One thing could be said of Prince Mir: when it came to protecting his valued assets, he was a man who left little to chance.

Inside the security building now, just as the pair of guards entered, they were greeted with flashing red alert lights and the shrill cry of a persistent, whistling alarm. They rushed to the surveillance room.

"We've got a breach. Sector forty-two," one of the video techs informed the guards.

"What kind of breach?" The men hurried to the monitors to see for themselves.

Another tech was pointing halfway up the video bank at a quartet of black-and-white screens. "A pair of bikers. Rolled up together, covered their bikes with brush. Right here...can you see them? There. They're moving through the woods. Headed our way."

Guard One spoke into the com-unit on his wrist. "Gamma three, this is base. You've got intruders entering the southwest quadrant. Respond. Proceed with caution."

"Copy, base," came the response in his ear.

The entire security detail was put on alert. The men in the surveillance room remained huddled before the monitors. As they watched with keen eyes, an even greater security threat appeared on the screens. A parade of two trucks and an SUV made its way along the tree-lined road across the outer perimeter of the grounds, an estimated mile-and-a-half from the rear gates. The vehicles slowed to a halt in the shade just off the road. Armed military personnel began pouring from the larger truck and SUV.

Again, into his com-unit, Guard One barked, "Delta and Joust teams, we've got a second perimeter breach. Quadrant north, Olde Hill Road. Appears to be a military unit. Respond STAT. We're in contact with the prince as we speak."

While the others watched the monitors, awaiting the response of their comrades to the intruders, Guard Two was already calling Prince Mir's private line. He informed His Majesty what was transpiring on the outer grounds. The prince seemed—as one might expect—none too pleased.

"Local police?" asked the royal, his tone revealing his irritation.

"Belgian military. From the looks of it."

"Tell our men to detain and hold. I don't want any aggressive action taken until we confirm what this is about."

"As you wish, Your Highness."

"And tell your team leader I'm on the way. We'll clear this up on the spot."

———

In his private quarters on the second floor of the château, Prince Mir adjusted his headpiece in front of the full-length mirror. He'd decided to wear the white *keffiyeh* to confront these interlopers: it added an emphatic point, letting these knuckle-draggers know with whom they were dealing with. While news of the Belgian military gathering on the edge of the château's grounds was distressing, it was by no means the end of the world. A simple phone call should remedy the situation. Besides, the Emer-Saud royal decided, today was far too important to waste it being angry at meddling fools.

Plucking the cordless from his desk top, he dialed a number he was quite familiar with. The prince waited, smoothing his goatee with two fingers, until a secretary answered in clipped French.

"Prince Mir, here," he said crisply. "This is urgent. I need to speak to His Royal Majesty, at once."

CHAPTER 27

Cale had been driving the cleaned-out bread truck for fifteen minutes, foregoing idle chitchat, content to follow the SUV at a comfortable distance. The leafy forest canopy was thicker here, and with each passing kilometer it seemed poised to close in on them in earnest. Jacek was quiet once again in the passenger seat, and Cale imagined he was thinking about the mission, or rather of all the things that could go awry.

Despite the apprehension consuming him—on this entire overseas trip, truth be told—Cale couldn't stop his mind from wandering. Maybe it was the hypnotic rolling of the tires beneath them. Or perhaps it was Jacek, who remained trapped once again in the quiet cocoon of his own internal musings. Whatever the reason, Cale couldn't prevent his thoughts from drifting to Maggie: What was she doing right now? Where was she? How was she holding up?

How was she dealing with the pregnancy?

Cale could not allow himself to consider the topic at the moment. It would drive him crazy. Instead, he shifted his thoughts to the warning Chloe had revealed to her sister, which Maggie had in turn passed along to him: *He is coming.*

At once his inner voice chided him: Was that any better than thinking about pregnancy? He decided it was. At least it was more abstract—and therefore safer.

He wondered what Chloe's premonition could mean. Who *"He"* might be, Cale didn't have a clue. What he did understand, was how accurate her visions had been in the past and that he'd be a fool not to take her warning seriously. Still, what could he do about it? He was four thousand miles away. The answer came simple and concrete: he could do nothing. At least not until he had more information.

The bread truck rumbled through a curve, then up a slope, staying beneath the high arch of trees. Slanting arrows of sunlight shot down through the branches as if fired from the heavens. The SUV cruised ahead at a modest clip. They were driving in silence.

Cale kept the radio off in case Agent Fronteer called on the mobile. A warning sign flashed past, announcing an upcoming dip in the road, and Cale glanced at Jacek, who still had his eyes closed. After clearing the slight down-drop, reducing speed, he allowed his thoughts to drift even further back into his past.

He remembered his first two years in college, long before he and Maggie had met. There had been his first true girlfriend, Mary, way back then. Their relationship had ended in senseless tragedy. Cale seldom thought about the incident, having locked it in an emotional vault deep within his core. There it remained buried inside a tight little box he seldom opened. But it was always there, lying in wait on moonless nights when he had difficulty drifting off to sleep.

He blamed himself for Mary's death. Even though he'd been just twenty years old at the time—college kids not being known for their decision-making sagacity—Cale had had trouble getting past it. He'd acted careless and irrational when confronted by a youthful armed robber. If he'd handed over his wallet that day, the kid would have fled like a startled deer. The robbery would've been over in under a minute. Instead, youthful Cale had gone for the assailant's hand—the one gripping the gun. In the ensuing struggle, the weapon discharged. A .38-caliber slug had ripped through Mary's chest.

An accident. A fluke. Of course, it was. Nevertheless, the memory still caused his guts to wrench, and every time he remembered the incident the bitter taste of bile would rise in the back of his throat.

Cale realized the tragedy—like it or not—was the underlying reason behind his current mission. On the night he'd arrested Tobias Crenshaw, over six weeks ago, the man had goaded him about Mary's death. The Chemist had ripped the scab off his deepest emotional wound. He responded in primal fashion, fighting pain with pain. He'd fired a 9mm round into Crenshaw's thigh, dropping the bastard unceremoniously on the slick wet lawn near his house of horrors. Careless once again? Yes. Irrational? Of course.

In front of a dozen witnesses didn't help.

Despite what the Internal Investigations Board had ruled—the shooting of the suspect deemed "justifiable"—in his heart, Cale understood if he hadn't shot Crenshaw, he would not have been suspended for the two weeks. He therefore would not be where he was at the moment: a couple of continents away from home, dressed in military gear, about to face-off against a troop of armed mercenaries.

Still, he reasoned, it was how the world worked. Sometimes you choose the mission; sometimes the mission chooses you.

Cale's clammy hands gripped the steering wheel. He couldn't prevent the question from rising in his mind: What if the accident years ago with Mary had never happened? What if he hadn't gone for the robber's weapon? What if Mary hadn't been mortally wounded that day? There was little doubt his life would have turned out differently. Would he even have met Maggie? Let alone be contemplating marriage to her? The answer came swift: perhaps not. And with such being the case, Cale couldn't help wondering if it wasn't the real reason behind his indecision in their relationship over the past three months, dragging his heels about making a long-term commitment.

How can he tell Maggie he loved her—in all honesty—when if fate hadn't intervened, he likely be married to someone else?

Cale was no shrink. Furthest from it. But armed with what he did understand about human nature, and with these old demons bottled inside him...well, it did make for some frustrating nights, at times.

All right, then. He warned his mind to stop reminiscing. It was what it was. Content with his robot-like trailing of the SUV ahead, Cale spent a long moment gathering his thoughts: So where did it all leave him? Right here? Right now?

Truth be told, he was still cursing Slink for having revealed Maggie's pregnancy, just before he had departed on his European excursion. Couldn't Slink have waited until he returned home? Before dropping such a bombshell on him? Considering the situation at hand...weighing pros and cons... No. Slink had been right. Cale would have wanted to know. In fact, he knew he would have done the same thing if he'd been in Slink's shoes.

Knowledge was power, he understood. No matter how much it hurt. It was better to have the facts than not have them.

And besides, hadn't Slink's revelation served another purpose? Knowing Maggie was pregnant was forcing him to face the Big Question. The one Cale continued to wrestle with: how he might be using the pregnancy as a reason—perhaps an *excuse* even—for considering calling off the marriage?

If it was another man's child, was it wrong to walk away?

Cale sighed. Sloughing these troubling thoughts from his mind, he decided it best to table the discussion for now. Like Cheetah had suggested: Best to keep your mind off things you couldn't control. He had to stay focused on the task at hand. Forget about all the ifs and what-ifs. Forget about the Big Question.

The SUV was forty yards ahead. Cale pressed his boot on the accelerator and shortened the distance. Turning to Jacek, he noted how the man remained mute in the opposite seat. Very un-Jacek like. He guessed his partner was meditating in the fashion of some Buddhist monk, hashing and rehashing the game plan of the upcoming mission. It was Jacek's style.

Nevertheless, with their destination approaching in less than ten miles, Cale decided it was as good a time as any to reel his partner back to the present. He gave the steering wheel a slight tug, and the truck swerved across the road's centerline.

Jacek's eyes sprang open like a man who realized his shirt had caught fire.

CHAPTER 28

"Whoa! Hey! What the—"

Cale's sudden cry and the jerk of the bread truck across the narrow roadway made Jacek bolt upright in his seat. His pupils were wide as nickels. Cale eased his foot off the accelerator and maneuvered the vehicle back into the proper right-hand lane. "A raccoon, maybe," he offered. "Or could have been a deer."

Jacek snorted and settled back into the seat. He closed his eyes again.

"For a second, I thought you were going to call me an asshole."

"Arsehole," said Jacek.

Cale drove on in silence, following the twisty road through the arching tree-tunnel, trailing the brown SUV the way a newborn puppy shadows its mama. It had been a bullshit thing to do, jarring Jacek from his quiet space. Yet he could feel an anger brewing at his core, and it seemed to be warming like a cauldron over a fire. He understood the root cause: it was what the horse trainer had revealed in the cabin—that Mary Jane Moore had been killed. Butchered by sadists.

Not now. Cale's his inner voice warned. He needed to stay focused on the task at hand.

More kilometers slipped past, and he decided to break the silence. "So, what's your crystal ball telling you?" he asked out loud, half-kidding. "Is this thing going to play out like we're planning?"

Jacek flicked open his eyes. "Every mission holds a surprise. You know this, Mr. Packer."

The truck's inner space held the lingering odor of yeast, which Cale guessed was typical of bread trucks, whether full or empty. "Maybe our surprise is we catch a break. We find our target; we get the hell out of Dodge in one piece."

Awake now, Jacek rolled his neck and shoulders, cracked the knuckles of one hand. "Americans. You want to rescue the girl, ride off into the sunset. Like John Wayne."

"I love John Wayne," Cale confessed. He glanced at his partner, keeping one eye trained on the road ahead. "You know what's pissing me off? For real?" His question caused Jacek to turn his head. "First, I feel sick about what Anselm—the horse trainer—told us back there at the cottage."

Jacek remained silent.

"Second"—Cale's voice dropped—"I've got problems on the home front. Things I need to...deal with. When I get back."

His partner narrowed his eyes at him. "Not ghosts, I hope. Not voodoo or witch doctors."

"I'm not joking." Cale gave a humorless laugh. "Believe me, I wish it were that simple." The cauldron was bubbling inside him, causing his guts to churn. He forced down the taste of bile.

They drove a minute in silence, until Jacek said, "Cheetah told me—about the situation."

"It's a word. You can say it."

"The *pregnancy*, then."

Both men were silent.

When Cale spoke, his lips stayed tight. "I was so wrapped up in a case, six weeks ago. In a manhunt. We knew who he was. We were closing in."

Jacek kept his earnest eyes on the road ahead.

"The bad guy we were chasing, he found out about Maggie, where we lived," Cale continued, his voice hitching. "He drugged her. Took her away. He had her for over five hours, for Christ's sake."

"It wasn't your fault. How could you have known?" Jacek pulled his weapon from its holster, ejected the clip, inspected it.

"I *should* have known. It's why it's...I should've been..." Cale's voice trailed off. He was gripping the steering wheel, his knuckles pale, bloodless.

Jacek holstered his weapon. "No blame, no shame. Let it go. Before it eats you up inside."

"Let it go?" Cale asked. "The constant—reminder. How do you live with something like that?"

A churchlike quiet engulfed the truck cabin.

"You love her?" Looking at Cale, Jacek's eyes didn't blink. "Your Maggie?"

"She's hurt. It was my fault. She suffered pain. Rape. Other—"

"That's not what I asked."

Cale flicked his eyes at Jacek's profile, then back to the road ahead. He said in a low voice, "More than—Jesus. More than I realized."

"You've got two choices then. You slide it in a box, bury it, like we do when our memories get too heavy. Or—"

"Or it eats me alive." Cale's lips were dry.

Jacek cast his eyes out the windshield, a far-off stare. "Cops as a breed aren't very romantic. Can't afford it. Like lifelong soldiers, you learn to internalize, shield yourself against it all."

"We feel, though; we still feel. Just because we don't show it."

Jacek continued to examine the heavy foliage out the window. "Things will work out, Mr. Packer. If you want them to." He cracked the knuckles of his other hand. "But it's on you. You carry guilt for too long, it gets heavy as an anvil."

"What about the guilt, the eating away…? From the inside?"

"Let it go. You didn't do anything wrong." Jacek closed his eyes, as if meditating. "Pain. Heaviness. No matter—the cure's the same." His smile was faint. "Like they say in Paris. *Ce sera magnifique.*"

Cale was peering at the reflective back windshield of the SUV ahead of them. He watched as the vehicle disappeared around a bend in the road. "Psychologist, Jacek? Missed your calling. But I suppose you're right."

"A regular Siggy Freud, aren't I? But much better with an AK."

Cale gave him knowing look.

Ten seconds later the SUV was back in sight, and they rolled along with the flickering sun and shade and the sway of the upper tree branches in the breeze. Without turning, Cale said, "Changing the subject, how about you and Cheetah? She cares about you— even Ray Charles can see that."

"Mr. Charles is deceased, I believe."

"A metaphor."

Jacek looked his way again. "Cheetah and me." He gave his head a shake. "Let's just say one of us might be crazy. But which one, eh?"

"Do I get a vote?" After a smirk from Jacek, Cale shrugged a shoulder. "*Ce sera magnifique?*"

Jacek's grin at him was crooked.

CHAPTER 29

The rendezvous point was a quarter mile beyond a crossroads, deep in the forest, just outside the expansive estate's known perimeter. The vehicles had all GPS'd the location. The transport truck pulled into a clearing beneath the canopy of high leafy trees and the soldiers, having arrived earlier, were already exiting through the back.

Slowing their speed had served to arouse Jacek's intensity. He peered around now, gathering his bearings, watching as Cale eased the bread truck into the shade beside Agent Fronteer's SUV.

Now that his partner was back in form, Cale realized that during the drive he'd been holding another dark pain inside. Thinking about it, he felt his stomach tighten. The cause? It was the information Ernst Anselm had revealed back at the cabin. Disturbing was one word. Sick, sadistic, unhuman were others. Though he'd seen a lot of bad things in his law enforcement career, Cale was having trouble wrapping his head around the concept.

He silenced the engine, leaving the keys where they were. He shifted his eyes to Jacek. "The second girl—Mary Jane Moore. The horse trainer said they butchered her."

"Put it out of your mind, Mr. Packer. You need to stay locked on the here, the now."

"But cannibals. For God's sake!" He slammed the heel of his hand on the steering wheel. "Erase it from my mind?"

"Focus on the mission. Our purpose. *Verstehe*?"

"And ignore something...something like that?"

"It's how we stay alive. Ourselves."

Even as he spoke, Cale recognized his error. It was he, himself, who had back-burnered the gruesome revelation. He'd put it out of his mind as if it were too grotesque to process. His thoughts while driving, instead, had shifted to his situation with Maggie. How was that for irony? the voice in his head needled. It took a story of flesh-eating cannibals to force you to consider your own relationship issues.

Cale admitted Jacek was right. Pondering the fate of Mary Jane Moore would best be saved for a later date, when they had proper time to analyze it. "Maybe it's not even true," he lamented, hopefully. "Just some rumor to frighten them all? Cow them into submission?"

"True or not, there's nothing we can do about it," said Jacek. "Not right now."

"The old man, Mr. Anselm. He's headed back to the château, right?"

"Yes. With all the excitement going on, it's doubtful his absence will have been noticed."

"You're sure about that?"

Dismissive, Jacek said, "He runs errands for the stable every day. Why would anyone suspect him in the least?"

They had removed their protective vests during the drive, discarding them on the floor of the bread truck. Exiting the vehicle now, Cale and Jacek put the vests back on, before joining the others.

They were assembled in a loose pack, tense, anticipating action, awaiting orders from Sergeant Berceau. Birds called from the branches in protest of their presence. The smell of adrenaline and gun oil was mixed with the musty loam of the woods. Sunlight sprayed down through the leafy overhang and cast tawny pools of warmth across the needle-laden floor of the forest.

Addressing his troops, the sergeant cleared his voice.

"Listen up," he said in a firm tone. "This is our entry point, people. We move off in two-man units. I want a wide sweep around the lake. We should make the fairgrounds by"—he glanced at his watch—"ten-hundred hours. Calibrate your watches, com-units on. Com-command stays here with Corporal Lux." The sergeant shifted his eyes toward a diminutive, dark-haired man with glasses, who had set up his equipment in the SUV's open rear cargo space.

Agent Fronteer added, "Remember, everyone, this is a rescue mission. No fire unless fired upon. We rendezvous at the rear steps of the château. No civilian casualties, understood?"

Helmets nodded. Ammo clips were checked, assault rifles locked, loaded.

"All right, then," Sergeant Berceau proclaimed. "Let's move out."

Just as they crossed the road, prepared to enter the thicker forest, the sound of approaching vehicles interrupted their advance. Engines whined, coming nearer by the second. The sergeant held his hand up, halting the troop's progress.

All heads spun in the direction he was looking.

"Shit!" said Agent Fronteer.

"Double that," agreed Jacek.

Appearing down the tree-lined road was an open military jeep. Four dark-garbed men were riding front and back, hands gripping the roll bar, weapons held at the ready. To the left, back the way they had come, over the small crest in the road came a second jeep—like the first.

Standing frozen, Cale felt a tugging at his shirtsleeve. Cheetah had him by the elbow, pulling him toward the thicker vegetation. Backing away from the group of soldiers, he followed her, slipping away from the road. Together they scampered through the leaves and the dense underbrush and made two dozen long strides into the forest before they stopped. Cheetah crouched low, putting a finger to her lips as Cale shadowed her movements. They were shielded by the trunks of a group of angular box elders. Back on the road, both jeeps pulled to sliding halts in the center.

Nudging closer to her, Cale watched as the leader of the security guards exited the first jeep and began speaking in a stern voice and thick French accent to Sergeant Berceau, who had stepped forward. The guard waved his arms in the air.

Moments later, their exchange was interrupted by the fast approach of a third vehicle. It was an oversized, black luxury SUV. Prince Mir Al-Sadar's private transport, Cale guessed.

"Lower your weapons," barked Sergeant Berceau to his men. The soldiers complied. They all waited in silence for the large SUV to ease itself to a stop thirty feet away, positioned in the middle of the road behind the first jeep.

From their secluded spot in the forest, Cale shifted his eyes off to his right. He could detect the outline of a man lying on the ground near an oversized, moss-covered stump, blended into the landscape of the forest. Pharaoh. In their mad scurry to escape into the sanctity of the trees, Cale had neither seen nor heard the man moving behind them. And Jacek? Cale's eyes scanned the gathered mix of guards and soldiers, but his bodyguard was nowhere in sight.

Had Jacek disappeared silently into the woods, as well?

Back on the road, the security team leader and Sergeant Berceau both stood with their eyes glued to the gleaming black SUV. High off in the trees somewhere, a woodpecker knocked, breaking the tense silence. From the SUV's rear door emerged a slick man in a dark business suit. Cale recognized the sharp goatee from the photos they had earlier studied: Prince Mir Al-Sadar. The prince approached the military men and handed his phone to Sergeant Berceau.

Placing the phone to his ear, the sergeant listened attentively for at least a minute. He said a few words before turning quiet, lips pressed together. Then, with an angry single nod, he handed the mobile back to Prince Mir, who spun on his heel and strode back to his waiting vehicle.

With a slam of the rear door, the SUV spun in a tight circle and accelerated away, heading back the way it had come.

Sergeant Berceau elbowed past his men and stepped toward the military trucks. He barked an order to the others, and with their shoulders drooped, the soldiers started filing back into their transport vehicles.

Cale squinted, shielding his eyes one-handed like a cavalry scout. He watched Agent Fronteer take a quick survey of the forest before ducking inside her SUV. A soldier climbed aboard the empty bread truck—where Cale had left the keys in the ignition— and the parade of all three vehicles turned around and drove off in the direction they'd arrived from.

They were headed back to town.

———

The pair of security jeeps departed as fast as they had arrived, each heading off in opposite directions. They waited a full two minutes before Cale whispered to Cheetah, "You happen to catch any of that? What they were saying?"

"Too far away." Cheetah rose, dusting the knees of her camo pants, picking at twigs and stray bits of leaf. He protective vest fit like a fashion accessory. "Whomever the prince had on the phone, he trumped any orders from the military."

Cale accepted this, exhaling in silence. He peered back through the forest, where streams of sunlight highlighted the uppermost tree branches. The leaves swayed and shimmied in the dancing breeze. The woodpecker knocked again.

"Now what?" he asked.

"Plan Z," said a low voice behind them. Turning, they saw Pharaoh standing beside the large trunk of a sentinel elm.

Cale noted the matching width of their torsos. He wondered out loud, "Any word from Jacek?"

No one spoke, and Cale could detect the smell of pine in the air around them. Leaves and thick, twisted, broken tree limbs, rocks and ferns and a variety of bracken, these all covered the forest floor and impeded their path in every direction. Cheetah and Pharaoh remained silent. No one had seen their leader slip away during the roadside confrontation.

"Plan Z it is, then," said Cheetah, moving into the thicker woods as if only she could discern an uneven path forward. Without speaking, the men trudged along behind her.

———

Roots and fallen tree limbs and underbrush seemed to grab at their booted ankles. Cale felt perspiration on his brow and along his lower back. The earlier adrenaline rush had worn away, followed now by monotony. They had been weaving their way through the woods for over thirty minutes.

As if on cue, Colonel Mabutu's voice again invaded his mind: *"Time is an illusion, Detective. Infinite points of chance on a linear continuum."*

Was the voice even real? Cale wondered. Could he be suffering from PTSD? He pondered the possibilities. Had he hit his head on the rocks when falling into the colonel's eel pit days ago? Hallucinations were one of many side-effects of a nasty concussion. It was the brain's way of recalibrating itself. Might he be imagining the witch doctor's voice in his head? An illusion concocted by his stressed mind?

Real or not, Cale understood he had to fight it. Otherwise, the vision would drive him to sanity's brink. Yet he had to remain silent, walking with his partners. He couldn't allow them to see he was under some form of...*psychic* attack.

The colonel's wry chuckle. Cale couldn't shake the sensation of being eavesdropped upon. And the ice pick migraine was growing in his skull. Making it worse, he could detect the faint thumping of skin drums once again, rising to further torment him.

"I'm showing you what will happen, Detective," came the witch doctor's voice once more. *"If you manage—however unlikely—to survive my attack on your family."*

"What attack? You bastard... *When?"*

Cale's mind shouted the questions, receiving no response. The unanswered questions looped through his brain, repeating like knife thrusts. He forced his subconscious to go blank. Yet the vision unfolded once more behind his half-closed eyelids, playing on the movie screen of his mind.

CHAPTER 30

Château du Carthairs, Belgium

With a dark-suited bodyguard on each flank, Prince Mir moved through the massive front foyer of the château. He dipped his head to a handful of guests as he passed, pausing to shake hands with a German lady in black spike heels and a nylon cat suit.

"Good luck today, *meine liebe Dame*," the prince said, his voice dripping syrup.

"*Danke schön*," she replied. "And to you, Your Highness."

Inside the first-floor study, the prince waved away his bodyguards. At the wet bar he poured two fingers of brandy. He needed to steady his nerves. The hasty call to King Alfonse, followed by the confrontation with the Belgian National Guard unit on the road, had served to rattle his confidence. He seldom lost his composure, so he blamed his bout of apprehension on nervousness regarding today's big race. Not big, he corrected himself: Huge, huge, *Huge!*

He sipped the brandy and reminded himself to stay focused. Eyes on the prize. He stared down at the auburn liquor as if he could read the future in the swirls.

"Anything I should know about?" asked a thick voice from the doorway.

The prince turned, watching the bull Kinsella stride into the room. The man wore his customary sports jacket, two sizes too small. "Personal business," said Prince Mir, aloof. When the Liberian's stare didn't let up, he added, "A couple of brush fires. Our security team squelched them."

"I heard. Belgian military."

"I called in a chit. Last we'll hear from them."

Prince Mir slugged down his drink and reached for the brandy decanter once more. Three fingers this time. He lifted an eyebrow at his guest, who declined. "King Alfonse uses my ladies on a regular basis," the prince explained. "He issued an order to the military. Poof!" He snapped his fingers, watching the invisible problem dissolve in the air.

Plopping his bulk in a Queen Anne wingback, Kinsella crossed one thick leg at the knee. "Something is up—too much coincidence. Where I come from, the cautious panther lives to see his coat turn gray."

"Where you come from," the prince shot back, "witch doctors still butcher albinos."

Kinsella said nothing, watching Prince Mir sip the amber liquid from his tumbler.

"Anything else on your mind?"

"Your horse trainer," Kinsella said, after a pause. "His eyes are beady. I don't trust him."

"You've said the same a hundred times."

"A hundred and one, now. I'm keeping an eye on him today."

Silence for a long beat. Through the heavy chateau walls, they could hear the muted sounds of the band tuning up. Someone tested a microphone, producing a high squeal of reverb, which was carried on the playful southerly breeze.

"Keep your eyes focused on the race, instead. You're a judge—remember?"

"As a favor to you. And to the Colonel—the botono."

"This isn't the jungle, Kinsella. You're on my turf here."

The large brute gave the man a narrow look, and he pushed one of his sleeves to the elbow.

Prince Mir changed the subject. "I just came from Security. We also shooed away a pair of drunken bikers, who seemed intent on crashing the party. So. Our monitors are now clear. No sign of intruders."

"Tell your men to keep their eyes peeled. A lot of distractions out there today." Kinsella repeated, his voice a deep bass. "Lots of distractions."

The muscular man rose and exited the room.

Prince Mir finished his brandy. He looked out a double-height window at the pair of colorful hot air balloons, which tugged at their tethers in the distant field. If he studied them long enough, he could detect the slightest sway of their moorings. He wondered if that was what the psychopath Liberian had been doing with him—testing his moorings.

Well, so be it.

———

On the château's vacant back patio, Kinsella stabbed at his phone. He checked for messages. Nothing yet from Tebbi Qa. He ended the call, whispering to himself: "Tebbi Qa. You are beginning to make me nervous. Very nervous."

He spotted the pony girls beginning to exit from the stables, milling about in their dark and shiny equine garb. Kinsella lumbered down the steps and strode over the clipped lawn, headed in their direction.

———

They were silent as they moved through the morning forest, ever on the lookout, the silvery dew clinging damp to their boots. They heard the occasional rustle of deer, along with small mammals foraging for food beneath the ferns and thick underbrush. Another woodpecker's knock echoed hollowly through the trees, and two blackbirds trilled back-and-forth. They caught flashes of aqua sky between the uppermost branches, and monitored the time by the sun's ascending arc, as it slipped behind thin tufts of cloud.

Cale's demented vision had disappeared as fast as it had come. He was left wondering if it had even happened, or if he'd dreamt the entire thing. His headache was gone, and so was the sound of thumping log drums. He shot sidelong glances at his partners— nothing seemed amiss. Neither seemed suspicious. Neither had noticed he'd been mentally absent for a full five minutes.

Cale's phone felt heavy in the pocket of his camo pants. He considered calling Jacek's mobile, getting a read on the man's whereabouts. Or at the least sending him an abbreviated text message. But he guessed that wherever their leader was, he'd let them know when he was ready.

He whispered to Cheetah: "Shouldn't we try contacting Agent Fronteer? Get a status update, at least?"

Cheetah shook her head. "We're too close to the château grounds. We best stay dark. As things stand, we're lucky to still be operational."

"How about calling com-command? At least we could learn if we've got alternate backup."

Pharaoh spoke in a low voice. "The château's security places a premium on surveillance. Transmission sensors will alert them if a mobile signal emanates from these woods."

Cale eyed the larger man as if he'd spoken in Swahili. It was the most he'd ever heard Pharaoh speak since they'd met.

"Like Cheetah says," the large man added, "we stay dark."

Cale frowned at them. "This is some sicko sex gathering we're about to rain on. I didn't know we were dealing with the Russian High Command, here."

"You caught a glimpse of the prince's guards," Cheetah said, her tone remaining firm. "They're high-tech equipped. We can't underestimate them."

Pharaoh added, "Prince Mir's playing with unlimited oil money for his toys. He's got more gadgets than your CIA."

"For some bullshit fetish party..." Cale's words trailed off with a shake of his head.

They tromped another twenty yards through the woods, kicking through underbrush, navigating over and around fallen tree trunks.

"You're not so cute when you pout, Detective." Cheetah put a final stamp on it. "We must assume we're on our own."

After hiking what Cale guessed was another half-mile inside the perimeter of the forest, they came, at last, to a clearing. Pharaoh motioned them to a stop inside the tree line. He pointed across the way. They spied a leaf-colored CCTV camera hidden among the bordering trees, mounted halfway up the trunk of an ash, tucked among the lower limbs. Had they had not been moving with caution they would have blundered straight into the camera's field of view.

Having taken measure of the angle of the lens, Pharaoh kept them secured in the shadows. They moved around the wide, open clearing—filled with blossoming wildflowers, yellow lilies, cattails, lilac bushes with honeybees flitting about—watchful for more cameras.

They trudged on through the warming air of mid-morning. Staying silent. Ever alert.

Some good distance later, on the opposite side of another clearing, they came to a running stream and halted in the shade of a cluster of high trees. Pharaoh's keen eyes swept the area. They could hear music far beyond their sightline. Occasional bursts of laughter and voices reached them, floating on the gentle breeze like cotton puffs.

"Mind telling me what Plan Z is?" Cale kept his voice low. He was afraid to ask, as if he might be the only one not in on a joke.

"Not much off from our original plan," Cheetah whispered back, somewhat obtusely. "Procure a vehicle. Locate your target."

Cale noted how she didn't use the plural, in light of the veteran trainer's confirmation that Mary Jane Moore was deceased. "We create a diversion and steal her away," Cheetah added. "Then we head back to the warehouse in Casteau. Like we planned."

It sounded simple enough. But Cale also knew, as things stood, there was no way this elementary strategy could play out in the manner they'd first hoped. First, they had lost their element of surprise. Second, they no longer had military backup. They were on their own against an armed professional security force. They were undermanned, had far less firepower, and they were deep inside enemy territory.

"We procure a vehicle." Cheetah had voiced this without as much as a blink of concern.

Cale guessed Jacek's partners were each adept at hot-wiring a car or truck in under thirty seconds. But what about the third, fourth, and fifth problems, which with even the most precise planning, were certain to arise? With hidden cameras concealed throughout the landscape, weren't their chances of being spotted increasing, as they crept nearer to the chateau?

Not to mention that they'd lose much of their cover. The odds against being spotted ahead of time were not in their favor. Cale told himself: Plan Z? We might as well be planning a lunar launch.

The original strategy had seemed functional, if not a bit simplistic. It had called for Cale and Jacek to drive the bread truck up to the delivery entrance. Another truck amid the cluster of caterers would not seem out of place. Then, while Cale dithered with the guard at the gate, Jacek would slip from the truck's rear doors and soundlessly—it was hoped—disable any other security guards within the vicinity.

Trainer Ernst Anselm, for his part, was to tip off Leslie Dowd of an escape plan in the works. That she was about to be rescued. He was doing so, Cale had learned earlier, in exchange for the Belgian government dropping all back-tax penalties he owed for excessive gambling earnings. It was a sweet deal for Mr. Anselm. But only if he could escape the prince's clutches with his hide intact.

"What about the second girl?" Cale had asked the seasoned trainer, moments after the man had signed Agent's Fronteer's agreement. "Is there another American girl? Inside the château? Her name is Mary Jane Moore."

"Eliminated, I'm afraid. She was—" The man lowered his eyes.

"Are you saying she's dead?"

"She had some sort of...of mental breakdown." Ernst Anselm had removed his brown fedora, mopped his brow with a handkerchief. "The prince purchased both American females from the Liberians. A large, rough-looking man—goes by the name of Kinsella. He's the one who *consumed* the poor girl."

"Consumed?" Cale repeated.

"As in—yes. Cannibals."

Silence had held the room.

"This man, this Kinsella, is he—"

"If you're going to call him a *sadist*," interrupted Mr. Anselm, "that would sum it to a T, sir."

Cale had slammed his frustrated fist on a coffee table. It would fall on him, he understood, to break the devastating news to her parents. In how much detail, he wasn't yet sure of. He didn't look forward to the task, but it was part of his job. It went with the territory.

As he stared off now in the direction of the chateau's grounds, where the festival was beginning to commence in earnest, all he could do was curse beneath his breath. Kinsella. With any luck, he hoped to get a chance to repay the debt. To avenge the poor girl's death. For the moment, however, it was the business at hand.

Plan Z.

Rescuing one person, he reasoned, was better than rescuing none at all.

——

In the quaint Belgian village of Casteau stood the old wooden feed warehouse. It was the location they had planned as their escape rendezvous point. The two leaders were huddled there now, inside the dusty inner office, a space they had designated as their temporary headquarters.

ICE Agent Amy Fronteer stood with her phone at her ear, her voice animated.

Sergeant Berceau stood across the room with his arms crossed, annoyed, listening as they awaited their forthcoming instructions. Half his men were congregated out in the greater warehouse, milling about, grousing about their lack of activity. The other half—along with the Americans—had been driven back to their home bases via the large transport trucks. It left the remaining dozen men at Casteau with three jeeps, along with the empty bread truck and brown SUV. Their invasion had been thwarted, their mission dismantled.

The entire affair, as far as Sergeant Berceau was concerned, was dead in the water.

"The king of Belgium? King Alfonse?" Agent Fronteer said this into her phone, while shooting the sergeant a furtive glance. "I thought he was a figurehead, for the most part." She listened and issued a deep sigh. "All right. Yes sir. I suppose it will have to do."

Ending the call, Agent Fronteer shifted her eyes across the room at Sergeant Berceau. She was frustrated as much as he was. "Your king, I've just learned, controls all the country's ministers. He also happens to be a personal friend of Prince Mir Al-Sadar."

Sergeant Berceau's mouth was a tight slash above his jutting jaw. "BOHICA," the man said without humor.

"Sorry?"

He smirked. "Apparently, Agent Fronteer, you were not a member of the American military. It means—"

"Bend Over. Here It Comes Again," she interrupted. With a shake of her head, she added, "I don't need a military handbook to understand we've just been fucked!"

"You're a fast learner, Agent," replied the sergeant, with no smirk this time.

CHAPTER 31

From inside the pony stables, there came a flurry of activity. The ponies were being prepared in their individual stalls. Grooms rushed about with purpose, busy and stressed. Assistant trainers prepared the specialized human/equine equipment: bridles, halters and bits, saddles and blinkers, high-boots and arm binders. All four teams participating in the four-hundred-meter pony-girl race were prepped and testing their gear. Anticipation filled the air. Though the participants tried their best to feign confidence, none seemed quite able to pull it off.

This same apprehension was evident, as well, for the lead pony of Prince Mir's favored Belgium team.

Instead of feeling frisky, Leslie felt more nervous than she had ever been in her life. Although she'd run upwards of fifty track and cross-country meets back in high school and college, none had seemed as stressful as this one. But then again, in none of those races had her life been on the line.

As the grooms were readying Leslie's equipment inside her private stall, Mr. Anselm approached. He shooed the flunkies away. Expecting some last-minute words of encouragement, she could not have been more surprised when he leaned in close and said in a low voice, "There is a man, Leslie. An American detective. He's here to rescue you. To take us both away—right after the race."

Her eyes widened with immediate concern, Leslie's initial reaction was to protest. Mr. Anselm, however, silenced her with a tender finger to her lips. "First off, we need to win this contest." He had stated the obvious.

Uncertain that she was hearing him correctly, Leslie had no immediate response. It was as if her favorite uncle was telling an off-color joke, and she must wait cringingly for the punch line. A groom walked past, carrying a half-sized saddle. The scents of leather and saddle soap filled the air around them. A pair of the Chinese team ponies slipped past on the lawn, walking in unison, as if attached at the hip.

"I met with them this morning." Mr. Anselm kept his voice low, making certain no one could overhear. Leslie started to speak, but he held up his hand, saying, "They have a plan to get us out of here. To safety. Both of us."

"But the prince—"

"Forget the sadistic bastard." The trainer frowned. "You must do as I say, Leslie. Trust me. Right after the race, the prince and his bodyguards will be celebrating. They'll be distracted, laughing and swilling champagne, paying no attention. They will never miss us."

"But what about—"

"No buts. This is our one chance. Do you understand?"

Confused more than anything, Leslie focused her eyes on him in silence.

He exited the stall and began striding away, but only five steps later, Mr. Anselm froze. Around the corner of the stables stepped the man-monster, Kinsella. His black eyes performed a quick survey of the grooming area.

"Is there a problem?" Mr. Anselm asked. Turning, he saw Leslie was hovering at the open stall door. "We were going over our prerace strategy."

Kinsella looked the diminutive trainer in the eye, before shifting to Leslie, where his gaze seemed to feast on her latex-clad body. Leslie couldn't tell if it was simple male lust, or if he was picturing her the way a hungry man stares at a glazed pork chop. She shivered.

"I've got my eye on you both." The Liberian shot them a hard frown. The creases between the overhang of his thick brow ridge formed like river branches on a map. He moved in closer, until he was a mere yard away. His thick biceps beneath the tight sport coat seemed to flex of their own accord.

"A message from the Prince," Kinsella said with a growl, "His Highness says: 'Win the fucking race!'"

Mr. Anselm appeared shaken but stuck out a defiant chin. "Of course. We always...we intend to."

"And quit dicking about here." The large man glared at Leslie, before barking at the trainer, "You! Come with me." Grabbing Mr. Anselm by the scruff of his neck, he steered the smaller man away from the stables. "The Prince Mir wants to have a word with you, *mon*—you bloody little wanker."

Leslie watched in horror as the bulky thug frog-marched the trainer along the path, which led back up to the château.

———

They were gathered outside the stable's high double doors. The scent of clipped grass blended with the heady tang of adrenaline and leather polish. The "ponies" from all four teams were in full race gear now. They were also in character. It meant they could no longer speak, could make no human sounds at all—only whinnies, snorts, or the occasional huff.

Leslie recalled Mr. Anselm's words, playing them over in her mind for the fiftieth time. "They have a plan to get us out of here. To safety. Both of us." My God! A thousand questions had stung her brain: First off, who on earth were they ? Something about an "American detective." But the trainer's other words kept tripping over themselves in her mind. Mr. Anselm had not specifically said "him," Leslie remembered—but instead had specified "they." More than one. A group.

So, who were *they,* exactly? Soldiers? Police? Enemies of Prince Mir? And how many were there? Enough to take on the prince's armed security force? There had to be at least twenty guards. Maybe more, for all she knew.

"An American detective..."

Was he with the FBI? she wondered. He couldn't be someone from Green Bay, could he? Someone sent by her father? Sent to rescue her? Flying all the way to Europe? To Belgium? It made no sense.

No one even knew she was here.

Leslie felt her stomach knot. The words of the prince rose from the recesses of her mind—his promise: "If you win this race, Leslie, I will set you free. You have my word on it. I have no desire to keep you trapped here like a bird in a gilded cage."

Last night up in her bedroom she had made him repeat his promise. He had spoken the sentiment with sincerity, claiming his heart ached, and how she did not believe him—how she did not, in fact, trust him. Isn't this what practiced liars did? Feigned "victimhood" when you didn't fall for their act?

In her heart, Leslie understood that the freedom Prince Mir offered her was, indeed, a long shot. Maybe even a mirage. He was a goddamned sociopath, for Christ's sake!

On the other hand, Mr. Anselm's tone had seemed genuine. No doubt desperate. He reminded her of her grandfather, and she had found no occasion over the past year of his tutelage to not fully trust him.

But trust him with her life?

The grooms were now approaching, ready to lead her and the rest of the ponies down to the running track. There they would begin their pre-race, loosening up exercises. Leslie's thoughts drifted back to her friend from Green Bay, Mary Jane Moore. The girl who'd been sold to the prince along with her over a year ago. Poor Mary Jane never had a chance. Now she was gone. Dead. Her life ended because she would not cooperate. She had refused the nightly shots of "vitamins" (heroin). She had declined to partake in the prince's sordid little games.

Now he was offering Leslie her freedom. Would Prince Mir honestly allow her to depart the château after the race? Would he pat her on the back, hand her a one-way ticket home? Maybe offer her a courtesy ride to Brussels International Airport?

Or was it more likely she'd wind up on the sadistic African cannibal's dinner plate?

Just like Mary Jane Moore.

The question remained: whom should she trust?

Leslie shook the jumbled thoughts from her mind. Focus, Leslie. Focus! Only one thing mattered now:

Win the fucking race.

———

Glancing at his watch, Jacek could hear the far-off sounds of a band kicking into gear. From his perch behind a broad chestnut tree, he consumed an energy bar that tasted like chewy, honey-flavored cardboard. He'd learned long ago to grab nourishment at any chance he could find. High above him, the overhang formed a leafy ceiling that allowed glimmers of sunlight to pour down.

Jacek peered around the tree trunk. He picked out the small CCTV camera he had spotted a minute ago. The seventh one he'd seen since beginning his trek through the forest. How many had he missed? This was the larger question.

Was it time, Jacek wondered, to risk communication with their support team?

Despite the canopy of leaves, he guessed his phone would function without much problem. He swallowed the last of his nourishment and withdrew the phone from the thigh pocket of his camo pants. Jacek punched in the number and held the phone aloft. Agent Fronteer answered on the second ring. Without wasting time, he explained his plan and issued his request.

"I need a GPS uplink to my current position."

"I'll get it to you straight away," she said, with no hesitation. "Just let me tag your coordinates."

Thirty seconds later, his mobile purred. Agent Fronteer gave him a status update. "I'm going by the surveillance photos," Jacek said, his voice modulated. "We avoid the electrified fence by circling the lake's northern border, right?"

"Affirmative. There's a twelve-foot fenceless gap. A delivery path. But heads-up on the CC cameras."

"Right about that. They're thick as flies on a dead mule's ass."

After receiving the information, Jacek silenced and pocketed his phone. He inched his head around the base of the tree's thick trunk. Then he cupped his hands over his mouth, fluted his fingers, and blew out a familiar trill.

CHAPTER 32

"You hear that?" Pharaoh whispered to Cale. He was crouched a yard away, alert now, listening with the intensity of a fox creeping out of its den.

"Hear what?"

Cale glanced across the way at Cheetah, who was hidden behind a clump of elderberry bushes. She was peering through the low bristles of a pine tree, employing a pocket scope, studying the oval racetrack in the far distance. The costumed revelers were gathering, it appeared, for some sort of event. Though he was fifteen feet behind her, kneeling in the waist-high weeds outside a cove of trees, Cale could catch glimpses of the running track from his elevated position. With the main contestants still absent from view, he guessed the crowd was gathering for prelims of some sort.

These would lead—so the horse trainer had informed them—up to the day's main event: the pony-girl race. And if this was the case, they were running out of time.

"The loon. It's Jacek." Pharaoh's eyes searched through the trees at the thicker forest. "He'll be joining us here in a minute."

Cale frowned. He declined to comment, deciding it best to take Pharaoh at his word. "Oh, hey, before I forget..." He spoke hesitantly, aware he was shifting topics. Pharaoh shifted a granite-like stare his way. "I wanted to thank you, you know? For last night? The intruder? Jacek told me."

"It's why we sleep in shifts."

It was all the man said before he swung his eyes back to the woods. Cale decided to drop the topic. He had thanked Pharaoh for merely doing his duty. That was enough, apparently. The large man was declining any praise for what to him was routine, was part of the job.

Cale trailed Pharaoh back inside the tree cover. The muscular mercenary proved correct. Ninety seconds later, Jacek stepped from behind the trunk of a golden maple and joined his team. He blessed them with his familiar lopsided grin.

"So, here's the pressing question. How much have you missed me?" Jacek's voice was a mischievous whisper.

"Where the hell were you?" Cale's voice was an octave higher, and Jacek held a finger to his lips. Cheetah slipped over and joined them where they crouched inside the trees. Cale whispered this time: "How the hell did you find us?"

"Find you?" A smirk. "The same way a blind tiger tracks three drunken pachyderms in the jungle."

Pharaoh snorted, not buying it.

Withdrawing his phone, pulling them all close like boy scouts around a dead raccoon, Jacek flicked on the power, punched a few keys. Immediately the satellite images were revealed on the small, colorful screen of his mobile.

"This is the delivery area," he reported, pointing to a small quadrant on the western side of the château.

"With thirty different delivery trucks, and caterers coming and going," added Cheetah with a nod.

"Correct. This is where we'll strike."

———

Prince Mir sat in his private box in the center of the bleachers. He had removed his *keffiyeh* earlier, and his hair was slicked back with styling gel. Someone unfamiliar with the man might guess he was Greek, or even perhaps an actor from Spain. And as he stared down at the oval track, he caressed his sharp goatee, a nervous habit.

Although he had a companion on each side of him—a monied French count and Grunwald, his personal banker—as well as a pair of his suited bodyguards at the door, His Highness felt a quiet calm about him. He took a long moment to cast his eyes across the splendor of the event, savoring the moment. It was happening at last. His festival was proving to be a success. A smile crept across Prince Mir's lips as he surveyed the surroundings: the racing track, the pristine lawns of the infield and adjacent hillside, the throng of satisfied enthusiasts. His was the knowing grin every event host has experienced at one time or another: the sly and satisfied expression of a man who has pulled it off.

Still, Prince Mir reminded himself, it was all just the tense calm before the storm.

On the manicured, emerald-hued south lawns, sometimes used for polo or cricket matches, a huge oval racetrack had been constructed nine months earlier. It was similar to a running track around a football pitch. The distance around the oval was exactly four-hundred-meters. It had been overlaid with a smooth, all-weather polyurethane surface, designed to allow the wheels of the sulkies to roll unencumbered. The ponies wore custom designed footwear to ensure that their heels made no contact with the ground. These were firm, rubber-soled pony boots. They were geared toward perfect traction and to negate the potential for even a fraction of slippage.

Adjacent to the competition track on one side stood a series of modest bleachers. In their center sat eight private viewing boxes, constructed of mahogany and forest pine, protective awnings overhead for comfort from the wind and sun. These were designated for the judges, or for the privileged. On the opposite side of the track, at the top of a grassy, sloping hill, stood a copse of mature fir and maple trees. Beyond these, further past their sturdy trunks, loomed the high southern walls of the château.

The twang of rock music, thumping bass and steady drumbeat, echoed through the giant speakers and swept out across the open acres. The smell of frying sausages and Belgian waffles and pies, *kolaches*, French fries and sweetmeats, drifted in the fragrant air.

The fairgrounds were already teeming with male and female enthusiasts garbed in a variety of leather and latex and dark spandex outfits. For the fetish crowd, these were not once-a-year Halloween costumes, but rather a way of life. A few ponies pranced past on the track, put through their paces by their masters, mistresses, or trainers, who kept them in check with leather riding crops or quirts. A pair of sulkies rolled along on the outer oval, the charges putting in a practice run, getting their "lather" up, as it were.

Beneath the oversized band shell near the refreshment tents, where colorful balloons drifted, and feathers, pennants, and streamers twitched in the gentle breeze, the band had drawn a good-sized gathering. Fifty or sixty guests were clapping and dancing, swaying to the rhythm of the Mod Starlings, who were playing 90's retro with a heady backbeat. Guests held cups of varied beverages, liquid refreshment against the bleached midday sun.

It was indeed a carnival atmosphere.

At one o'clock the band's music halted. This came on cue from a mini-skirted, ginger-haired woman with a clipboard: the events coordinator. From up the hill across the track, medieval trumpeters wearing traditional Belgian red, black, and yellow-striped royal guards' uniforms, raised their long horns and began to blow the announcement heralding the event of the day: the pony-girl contest. With the judges and honored guests already seated in their private bleacher boxes, the remainder of the revelers moved with haste to ring the oval track.

Prancing, cantering in their stylistic fashion, the ponies worked in teams of four as they pulled their sulkies, moving at a warm-up pace. They wore shiny latex helmets with matching blinkers, mouth bits, bridles, and halters, arms encased by behind-the-back arm-binders. All wore colorful tail or helmet plumes; all had thick rubber-hooved boots, which forced their steps into an equine facsimile.

As Prince Mir's prized team slipped past the bleachers, the ponies broke into a sudden choreographed prance, heads held high, knees pumping up to their waists while they slid along in perfect unison. The crowd applauded. Appreciation for the precision on display by the unit. It hurt not at all that each of the prince's pony girls was a statuesque blonde, equipped with, so it seemed, self-supporting breasts.

His team having passed inspection, Prince Mir cast a fleeting glance at the judges' box. He noted the lusty expression on Kinsella's face as the man watched the Belgian pony team in retreat. Knowing he had at least one of the judges in his hip pocket was comforting. Still, what mattered most to His Highness was not this crass display of costumed fancy. Anyone could win the Appearance Trophy. What mattered many, many times more—in fact three-million American dollars more—was winning the four-hundred-meter team race. That's where the true accolades lay.

Along with the bragging rights.

At this moment, little else mattered to Prince Mir Al-Sadar.

CHAPTER 33

Green Bay, Wisconsin

Saturday morning and Maggie had a full day planned. Her first stop was the downtown Farmers' Market. She was eating for two, so she decided she'd better try and eat as healthy as possible. Afterwards, she planned to weed the old flower beds along the fence line. Then maybe mow the lawn, if she could rally her ambition.

She would do these things while awaiting Cale's call. She couldn't remember where he said he would be today. Belgium, she thought. But the way his trip was going, she could not rule out Italy or Africa or Morocco. Maybe even China. Wherever he was—and it truly didn't matter, as there was little that she could do about it anyway—he promised he'd be home sometime next week. Tuesday maybe. Or Wednesday at the latest. He was due back at work Thursday morning, the end of his two-week suspension.

She could wait until then to hear the gritty details firsthand.

Instead of her best-laid plans, however, Maggie had spent the first twenty minutes that morning kneeling in the bathroom. Morning sickness. Again. Last night, lying in bed and still spooked from Chloe's "glowing red eyes" episode—not to mention Father Larchezi's sprinkling holy water throughout the house, protecting them from invading ghosts and demons—she wondered why her knees had felt so sore. Now she understood: it was from worshipping the porcelain goddess day after day. When would it let up? She hoped today. She prayed this would be the last of the torment.

She dry heaved again.

Fifteen minutes later, after showering and brushing her teeth— twice—Maggie went downstairs wearing a pair of navy cotton sweat pants and a sleeveless T-shirt. She couldn't risk putting on real clothes. Not if she might go rushing off to the bathroom again at any moment.

In the kitchen she poured Hank a bowl of dry cat food, deciding she was unable to stomach the odor of his canned stuff. Hank would have to suffer, eating like a peasant for the time being. The toaster popped. Skip the butter. In fact, she was eating no better than a peasant herself these days. Maggie was aware that, instead of gaining five pregnancy pounds, she had—if she had to venture a guess—lost as much over the past two weeks.

Her phone chirped. The readout said it was Chloe, calling from work.

"You sleep okay?" her sister asked.

"'Glowing red eyes? He's coming!' How do you think I slept?"

A blow-dryer sounded in the background along with the conversational hum of voices, and Maggie sensed Chloe turning her back to block the sound.

"Not fair." Her sister sounded put out. "Can I help it if I see things? I'm only trying to help, you know."

"I know. Sorry."

Without realizing it, tears had begun welling up in Maggie's eyes. Her voice sounded raspy, and she suddenly felt frazzled and overwhelmed by her lack of restorative sleep.

Sensing her sister's mood, Chloe said, "Aw, Mags. It's not about the baby, is it?"

"No." She lied.

How could it not be about the baby inside her? The whole Who's-the-father ordeal was driving her crazy.

Last night, between fits and jerks of troubled dozing, she had dreamed about the time she'd spent in the hands of her kidnapper: Tobias Crenshaw. Despite her efforts to suppress them, vague and disturbing images had filtered into her consciousness. Maggie had imagined that if she paid them no heed, they would fade from her memory like a scary childhood nightmare.

She was wrong.

The images had not faded. She did not want to remember her experience with the Chemist. Yet try as she might, her mind kept flinging the awful flashbacks at her—taunting her, forcing disturbing visuals into her consciousness.

"What then? Cale's not in any trouble, is he?" Chloe's tone expressed her concern.

"No—I don't know. It's just, you know, all of it!"

Maggie exhaled, adding: "Crenshaw getting shot in the head. Poor Cynthia Hulbreth being accused—Jesus! What her parents must be going through."

"You can't beat yourself—"

"Add in the missing girls. Their families not knowing what's become of them. Reporters calling...me not knowing who the baby's father even is!"

Chloe made a cooing sound, like how you'd talk to a child with a skinned knee. "I'll come over later. Check on you. Soon as I finish up here, okay?"

"Call first," was all Maggie said, before hanging up. And as she did, a sad realization washed over her. This damned uncertain-unwanted-*unplanned* pregnancy...it was causing the single thing she feared most in life: she was losing her sense of humor!

Just as fast, she abandoned the thought. *Here we go again.*

She hopscotched Hank, lying in the middle of the hallway, to make her way to the downstairs bathroom. After retching her insides dry, she began to cry again. Yesterday, she had asked Cale point-blank about starting a family. She had shot him straight in the guts with the question. No subtlety there. It had been unfair, she knew, but that's how she'd played it.

Maggie decided now that he must hate her. Or perhaps even despised her. He had to suspect—he was a detective, wasn't he— it was Tobias Crenshaw's baby. Cale was probably figuring out how to let her down easy. That's why it was taking him so long to return home. He was allowing her time to stew in her own juices, allowing her space to figure things out.

Cale, she irrationally reasoned, wanted her to recognize things weren't working out between them. That they might never work out. He would advise her to end planning their wedding. How could they get married? She was carrying another man's child, for God's sake!

"Better face reality, Maggie," her inner voice lectured, sounding like her father's stern voice when she'd been young. "This is how life works."

It mattered little that the father of the baby was her rapist. Facts were facts. This was the sad way of the world, one of life's sadistic curveballs. Maggie understood she was not the first girl who'd been jilted over in a similar—and unfair—situation.

Blame Cale? Of course not. The sorry truth was, she'd be more surprised if he *did* still want to marry her.

Perhaps she was cursed. Maybe she wasn't even carrying a normal baby. Maybe it was some demon child. Whatever the case might be, she was getting what she deserved.

Hank meowed outside the half-closed door. She used her foot to swing it open and the plump tabby tiptoed inside. Hank, no doubt, felt the same way as Cale. All the men in her life hated her. Why should he be any different? The one person not mad at her was Tobias Crenshaw, hooked on life-support in ICU, a brain-dead vegetable.

Maggie felt torn in half. Like God had taken a scissors to a cloth doll, snip-snip-snip. This should be the happiest time of her life, shouldn't it? Yet here she was alone, puking her guts out. She had wanted to get married, begin a family. It would make things perfect in their lives. Instead, she had a demon baby growing inside her. Was it unholy? Malignant?

Was it forcing this sickness on her?

"Morning sickness. Nothing more," Chloe had informed. "Don't worry, sweetie. It's all normal."

But was it?

How did she know her sister hadn't called Father Larchezi—not to exorcise the house—but to exorcise her? Soiled and unclean Maggie. The holy water? Add in the Latin mumbo-jumbo?

Maggie closed her eyes and coughed. A string of drool dripped down her chin and into the toilet bowl.

After the break-up with Cale, perhaps she could move in with Chloe and her family. At least until she could get her own place. Maybe they'd convert the empty spare bedroom into a nursery for her and the baby. A DNA paternity test—called a CVS—could not be performed until at least ten weeks in utero. She recalled this from paternity cases she had handled in court. It meant she could not confirm the father for at least another month. God! Maggie doubted she could wait another hour without knowing for sure.

As things now stood, only God knew who the true father was. But everyone—all their friends and family alike—would damn sure know a demon baby when they saw one. And giving birth to such a child would not just alter her life forever, but it was a recipe for lifelong disaster. For both her and the baby.

She had to stop thinking like this. Had to stop torturing herself.

Hank brushed his soft forehead against the clammy skin of her calf. Maggie gave him a heartfelt look. Then she turned her head and vomited again.

——

Chateau du Carthairs, Belgium

Cale knelt behind a thick clump of bushes. Jacek was positioned a few yards ahead, concealed by the trunk of a mature ash. An airplane cruised overhead against the Belgian sky. The rear wall of the massive chateau stretched high, its gray, lichen-covered stone roughened by over a century of changing weather. The air smelled sweet with lilacs and an undercurrent of charcoal. Cale studied Jacek's broad back while a rook chirped in a high branch. They were awaiting Cheetah's signal to advance.

The sudden voice in his head caused Cale to nearly jump from his skin.

"I slipped inside your feeble brain," Colonel Mabutu's voice said, in his head again without warning. *"Back in my study...the first time we met."* Cale attempted to will the voice to silence. It couldn't be real, could it? It had to be an auditory illusion, like a hallucination, some sort of parlor trick.

The voice in his head hissed. *"The clock is ticking, Detective. I am coming to slaughter your family. And to reclaim the items you stole from me."*

Cale felt the rage swell inside him. He wanted to ram a knife through the colonel's evil heart. This was the bastard who had dropped him into the eel pit, the same prick who'd sent a hit man to try and sever his spinal cord. Cale gritted his teeth. Though seething with hate, there was no corporeal body to lash out at.

Try as he might, he could do nothing to prevent the migraine-like pain from rising and the dream-vision from spinning again in his mind. A dark image of the witch doctor emerging from the mouth of a mountain cave headed straight at him, sturdy, determined...blood-eyes staring out at him from his frightening mask of human bone.

CHAPTER 34

Château du Carthairs, Belgium

In the judges' box, four spots down from Prince Mir's shaded, private compartment, Kinsella was conversing with a silver-haired Austrian judge in a biker's leather vest and chaps. The man had an inch-long chrome T-bar stud in his nose and a single solid streak of ebony running through his hair. It lent him a rather skunkish appearance. Kinsella's mobile buzzed twice before going silent. He rose and stepped a few paces away, up to the top of the bleachers.

There he hit the redial on his phone, and Colonel Mabutu answered on the second ring.

"The American detective? He floats beneath the cool Italian waves by now?" the colonel asked wryly.

"No word yet from Tebbi Qa." Kinsella's unease was galloping neck-and-neck with his heart rate, faster than any of the sulkies who would soon be rolling breakneck around the track. "I left three messages."

"I'm flying to the States. The Canadian jet service I use. I've located Pazuzu." The colonel's annoyance came through in his tone. "I will be most displeased if I don't learn of the American's demise by the time I land."

"I'll go to Rome myself, Botono. Soon as Prince Mir's, uh, contest here is over." Kinsella cleared his throat.

"Bring your ceremonial sword, my friend." Mabutu advised this with a hint of dark irony. "I seem to have an open space for a new head on my mantle."

Kinsella understood the implication. The American girl's shrunken head remained missing, along with the witch doctor's precious little ogre. "I'll make certain of it, Botono."

He closed his phone and made his way back down to the judges' box. Out on the track, the sulkies were easing their way up to the starting line. *At least they circle the track just once*, Kinsella thought, awash with relief.

171

Prince Mir glanced across the nearby stands as the large Liberian thug returned to his spot in the judges' box. He wondered why Kinsella still had on his sports jacket in the warm afternoon sun. Why the man didn't find a proper-fitted one, he would never know. The too-tight coat he wore made him appear buffoonish. A muscle-bound oaf.

The prince shifted his attention back to the track. Mr. Anselm was down on the edge of the infield, issuing last-minute instructions to his charges. He would be ensuring the sulky was properly hooked-up, and further, he'd be making certain their driver was true to the task. Ready to guide the ponies on their four-hundred-meter orbit.

The key to the race, Prince Mir understood, was not which ponies ran fastest. The trick lay in the rhythm, the teamwork. Each of the ponies must move in unison. They had to match one another stride for stride, moving as a well-honed machine. It was the reason Leslie Dowd—his alpha leader—was so integral to their success. She was the perfect team captain: athletic, purposeful and disciplined. Like a work of art, a previously undiscovered gem. Purchasing her from Colonel Mabutu had been the prince's "steal" of a lifetime.

And she is mine, thought Prince Mir, a knowing grin playing inside his tight goatee.

The crowd now grew hushed with anticipation. The four sulkies were lined up at the starting post. All the trainers and handlers had backed away onto the infield grass. In the entertainment tents, a loud air horn sounded. All wagering was halted; and the betting windows were shuttered. The spectators in the bleachers rose to their feet, tension mounting as each second ticked away. The starting judge raised his pistol in the afternoon air.

And fired.

———

Moving in paired units, they slipped past the parade of tall leafy trees, which lined the concrete path behind the back lawns of the château.

Cale stooped behind the trunk of a golden maple. Six paces to his left crouched Pharaoh. They watched as Cheetah crept in silence along the rear face of the massive stone building, hidden beneath the sightlines of the CCTV cameras. These were stationed at varied angles at the château's high corners, positioned like medieval gargoyles staring down at the well-tended grounds.

In the distant area set aside for parking, a dark uniformed guard stood near a pair of black Audi touring cars, his foot on a bumper as he tied his boot.

Cale crept forward in a half-crouch, keeping tucked inside the bushes along the strolling path. Glancing across to where Jacek was positioned, he watched him issue Cheetah a hand signal. Cheetah advanced—silent as a shadow—sliding up to the guard and incapacitating him within seconds. The man slumped to the manicured grass.

A gunshot rippled through the air. A roar rose from the far-off crowd, riding on a breeze that reached them from the low south lawns.

Cheetah acted fast. Another guard went down near where the Audis were stationed. Cale found himself moving again, bent behind Pharaoh. They slipped to the place where Jacek had been moments earlier. Jacek, by this time, had disappeared inside a produce truck they had targeted. He was working on the inner wires—Cale imagined—beneath the steering column.

Now they were advancing again. No sign of Cheetah, but as he followed Pharaoh's muscular haunches, Cale caught sight of her stooped alongside a security jeep. She signaled them, and they headed in her direction.

The sounds from the racetrack below the sloping lawns grew louder, more intense. A loud rumble started as Jacek got the truck going. Cale dodged in behind a long meat truck, and nearly slammed into the back of a third security guard.

The man raised his hands, startled, exclaiming in startled French, "Sacre bleu—"

Cheetah's hand covered the guard's mouth from behind while her knife-like fingernails ripped through the man's larynx and adjoining carotid artery. He gurgled, clutched his throat, and dropped to his knees. Blood spurted, spraying Cale's lower legs as he leaped backward. A puddle was already forming around the guard's torso, leaking beneath the truck, dark like an oil spill. The guard's body dropped to the ground and jerked, air rattling from the hole in his throat. His fingers clawed at his neck.

At last he twitched and went still.

Cale followed Cheetah's silent lead. If he hadn't believed it before, he did now. Jacek and his partners played for keeps. He heard the produce truck's gears shift, the engine chug as it moved along the driveway. The sounds blended with the intensifying roar of the crowd down the hill, rising like the clash of a battlefield.

No shouts. No sirens yet. Cale wondered why they had not been spotted by the CCTVs. Perhaps the guards were busy watching the race on their monitors, as Jacek had predicted. Human beings, after all, when faced with either diligence or sloth will often choose the latter.

A security jeep swept in a circle in front of the château's main entrance. Spotting Pharaoh at the wheel, Cale ran hunched-over and slipped into the passenger seat, staying low. Glancing around, he failed to spot Cheetah. She had disappeared. Pharaoh pulled the jeep to one side of the massive spouting fountain, which highlighted the front of the chateau's main driveway—five satyrs chasing three wood nymphs—and parked there, shaded by the cover of a broad-limbed oak. Beyond the stretch of trees, the emerald lawn sloped downward, sparkling in the afternoon sun. In the distance, angled far to the left, Cale could see the large crowd gathered around the racetrack.

Pharaoh cut the engine, and they stayed low together. They watched as Jacek backed the produce truck into position thirty yards away. Three guards were down already by Cale's count. How many of their comrades—by now alerted—might be rushing their way? All he could do, however, was watch. And wait. And perhaps pray.

The voices of the colorful crowd down the hill rose up in another massive roar.

———

Inside the central surveillance room of the security building, the array of monitors blinked through their customary automated sequentials. One by one they displayed the usual bland footage. A man named Philippe was head of the electronic surveillance unit. He made it no secret he'd placed a hundred-euro wager on the favored Belgian pony team. He and his partner, Francesco, had isolated nine of the motorized CCTV cameras, aimed them at the track to capture the race.

They watched the monitors now, the variety of different angles, cheering and guffawing at the four carts being pulled by latex-garbed females, as they navigated their way around the large oval track.

Eyes locked on the action, muscles tense with the ebb and flow of the contest, the guards remained oblivious to the other cameras that were scanning the château's vast outer grounds. These unwatched cameras revealed, at the moment, far more than their usual bland inconsequence.

———

Leslie's knees were raised, the *clop-clop-clop* of her hooves pounding the smooth, even surface of the track. The thin harness straps were snug about her shoulders and midsection. They allowed her to pull the cart with her entire body and not just her shoulders and hips. Around them the clamor of the crowd was deafening. Though the blinkers impeded her peripheral vision, as the team moved around the curve of the oblong track, Leslie could see people yelling and screaming, clapping, cheering furiously. She held her head straight, chin high—as Mr. Anselm had taught them. Her steady breathing with an audible "hitch" was the cadence the others required to remain in lockstep.

The German team had lurched off the starting line, their sulky rolling past, a tiny female Prussian at the reins. Leslie hadn't let it bother her. Their plan was to run a consistent first two-hundred meters, then increase the pace. It didn't matter what position they were in—it was third place now—as they rounded the first turn.

Entering the long backstretch, the Chinese team was making some odd noise between a bark and a whinny. They had also pulled ahead of the Belgian unit. Leslie watched the flexure of their taut flanks as they breezed past, intent on keeping pace with the über-Germans.

Leslie felt her arms locked behind her in the long leather glove. Perspiration pooled between her breasts and along her lower back. No matter. Their training had been superb. She could hear the voice of Mr. Anselm drilled into her head: "Keep your pace—do not panic!"

Along the seemingly never-ending backstretch they ran with intent, heads held high, breathing in unison. Huffing in; huffing out. The crowd around them stretched like a undulating ocean, wave after wave washing against the borders of Leslie's mind. No pitch, no ebb. Just the continuous white noise drone deep inside her head.

———

Green Bay, Wisconsin

It was a bright and pleasant midmorning, and Chloe pulled her Buick to a halt in the shaded apron of Maggie's driveway, near the garages. She expected to see her younger sister outside, kneeling on the ground, tending the flowerbeds. But she also understood the strain Maggie was under. Pregnancy could do that to a gal. Though Chloe had never had the pleasure herself—their two kids were from Ed's first marriage—she heard about the condition every day from her clients at the Mood Indigo Beauty salon. Every day for fifteen years now.

With a courtesy rap, Chloe let herself in the back door. In a high voice, she called out, "Special delivery for Maggie... Live from Chippendales!"

Silence. No answer.

After moving through the kitchen, she spotted Hank down the hallway, sitting just outside the open bathroom door. The feline stared up at her but didn't react, remaining stiff as a porcelain statue. Quickening her pace down the hall, Chloe glanced inside the bathroom.

Spotting the prone figure lying on the floor, unmoving, she shouted: "Oh my God! Maggie!"

She rushed forward and knelt beside her sister. Chloe, frazzled and flustered, felt Maggie's neck. The skin was warm, pulse steady. Gathering herself, she flipped open her large handbag and dug out

176

her phone. In doing so, Chloe's fingers also pulled free the scented, rose-patterned handkerchief, and before she could punch any numbers...she felt herself swoon.

She toppled to the floor like a bowling pin, just inside the doorway, mere feet away from where Maggie lay. As she fell, Chloe could hear the thoughts of Leslie Dowd as they reached her from somewhere through the ether:

The crowd roaring, closing in. Have I been running for five minutes or five hours? The sweat on my thighs, my forehead, between my shoulder blades...a thousand insects crawling. Swish them away with my tail...Eyes stinging from the sweat—the blinkers—not seeing, time fading away, a clock running backward, tock-tick, tock-tick...not caring about what I should or should not do. Rewards, no rewards. Sickness in my stomach, the sour taste of bile again, nothing, everything at once, the universe pulsing and endless.

The bit in my mouth is the dry taste of leather jerky. I remind myself to swallow, to breathe, pumping thighs searing with burn. Horses blowing steam, a mountain pasture, coats white with salty lather, chugging along.

I dream of ice-cold mountain streams, always so far, far away, where wild horses wander off to die on their own. Alone. Forever. One last drink of cool water, then I'll lay my head in the soft and silent snow of the meadow, the ground hardened beneath winter's pale sky and stark bone moon...where all the pain washes away into a sea of white and frozen nothingness.

Alone...forever and always. Alone.

CHAPTER 35

Château du Carthairs, Belgium

Inside the main security building, Prince Mir's security techs remained glued to the closed-circuit monitors, watching the race as it unfolded down on the track. Several of the patrolling guards had paused in their surveillance rounds, hovering at the edges of the enthralled crowd. Others watched the contest play out from higher ground, caught up in the action, paying little heed to their patrol duties.

The crowd's roar was building, like a jet preparing for takeoff.

A good distance from the running track, near the western edge of the inner grounds—at least forty yards from the serpentine stretch of tree-lined driveway—a lone guard was patrolling a modest glade near the walking path. He seemed oblivious to the proceedings on the far-off racetrack, intent instead on performing his rounds. Without warning, Cheetah emerged from the high bushes and kicked the man's legs out from under him at the knees. She elbow-locked the man, forcing him into a thick clump of vegetation.

Another guard had spotted the commotion, however, and was moving toward where his mate had disappeared. He had his weapon drawn, talking into the com-unit on his wrist.

"We've got a problem," Pharaoh informed Cale, studying the incident through his monocular as they sat in the parked jeep. "Cheetah's been made." He continued searching the area where the incident was taking place, staying low in the driver's seat.

"If she's compromised," Cale said, "I'll have to get to the truck—open the rear door for Jacek."

Pharaoh continued to peer through the scope. In the distance, the second guard rushed headlong into the cluster of tall bushes, disappearing as if swallowed.

———

Moving at a steady pace, knees high and clomping hoofs, haggard breaths, *running, running, running* as they moved into the long oval track's final turn. Voices shouted and cursed and implored all four sulkies on as they rolled forward...and the race shifted into slow-motion now to Leslie, as if she were watching a soundless movie.

Does anything matter? she caught herself wondering. When you're a prisoner in your own life?

The melancholy she had felt for the past two months seemed to be catching up to her. Yet she was *not* alone, was she? Not really. She had her pony mates running alongside her, counting on her...counting on her *to focus*.

Somewhere around the final turn, Leslie snapped out of her trance. It was Marina, the Latvian, to whom she gave credit. Young flaxen-haired Marina who was running with true grit alongside her. Without turning her head, Leslie could discern the girl's latex-covered legs matching her own high stride, hooved boots slapping the track surface step for step.

She remembered passing the Germans moments earlier, when they had broken wide coming out of the turn. And here was the Chinese team—matching dark ponytails flogging their upper backs as they chugged along, running slower, legs stiff and heavy as if plodding along a wet sand beach. And here now came the magnificent blond Belgian team, spurred on by the crowd's incessant deafening roar.

Leslie spotted the finish line thirty meters ahead. They were coming on fast, fast, fast, a mirage out of the desert...wind at their back, their flashing golden sails on display...thighs firm, knees high, matching strides...the sky above bluer than any ocean.

They broke the tape.

Although Leslie could not manage a gasp air for a full minute, as the sulkie rolled to a stop, she found herself hunched over, bent at the waist, sweating like a marathoner. A single thought kept leaping through her mind: *We won the fucking race!*

Then as if on cue, her thoughts began to shift ever-so-slowly from victory to freedom. And this was followed, the next tick later, by the most intriguing thought of all:

I'm going home!

———

What happened to Leslie next was a blur, a movie fast-forwarding. The opposite of how it had been while journeying around the track.

Around them grooms and trainers were assisting them, steadying them, removing the bits from their mouths, sponging sweat from their faces and necks. In the midst of the commotion was Mr. Anselm, giving her water to sip-spit-sip-swallow. He unclipped her harness, removed the long glove that bound her arms together, separated her from her pony mates.

Leslie doubled-over from exhaustion. Her chest heaved and her vision was blurry, sparkled, blotchy from fatigue. With one arm around her waist, the trainer was guiding her away from the crush of the crowd, steering her off toward the infield grass.

Around them clusters of strange people—guests of the prince, Leslie supposed—were celebrating as if a World Cup soccer match had been won in the final seconds. Leather running this way and that, tight midriffs, bare buttocks, spandex tights, spike heels unable to walk well on the infield sod. Leslie ignored everything. She was content to let Mr. Anselm guide her. She still had her halter on, and he was leading her by a single rein. Someone clapped him on the back: Great job, great job; Congratulations; Splendid show; Jolly good; *C'était magnifique!*

With Anselm nodding yes, yes, yes, thank you very much.

All this while they were moving away at a steady pace. He was taking her somewhere to receive post-race recovery care, she guessed, perhaps the prince's private medical tent. They crossed the back of the track and began climbing the sloping lawn up in the direction of the southern wall of the main house. In her hooved shoes, Leslie's calves were screaming like a pair of opera singers who'd just been gored.

She was coming around to where she could think straight. Her faculties were beginning to clear. Her adrenaline tank was empty. She'd left it all out on the track, like the experts say you should. Every ounce of energy had been spent trying to win the race. And for what?

Her freedom.

It's what Prince Mir had promised, wasn't it? Without the blinkers impeding her vision, Leslie could glance around, notice people vectoring off in every direction. Most seemed headed back to the beer tents, back to the party. The band was kicking in where they'd left off, launching into a snarling punk version of "We Are the Champions." Leslie and Mr. Anselm were heading opposite the flow of people, moving in the direction of the parking bay. He was leading her with a rein, cooing to her all this while as if she were a real horse. She couldn't hear his actual words. Was unable to process them.

As they climbed the modest slope, Leslie noticed a delivery truck had been backed to the edge of the concrete loading area. A man in army fatigues flung wide one of the two loading doors. Leslie balked. With huge eyes she studied Mr. Anselm. She remembered now. He was leading her somewhere dangerous, some ill-conceived escape attempt, leading her—Leslie was now certain of it—to a painful death.

She nicked, fighting the reins like an old mare unwilling to accept convoy to the soap factory.

"Leslie, please!" Mr. Anselm's tone was low, imploring. His eyes scanned the area, panicky, though trying not to appear suspicious. "We don't have time. We must do this. Now!"

Thirty yards away Leslie saw a pair of the Prince's security guards freeze. One was talking into his walkie-talkie. Together they began surveying the grounds around them, eyes searching.

Her mouth was still raw and dry, parched from the leather bit. "No. I can't...the Prince..."

Leslie swung her head around, panic coloring her eyes as she searched the far-off distance. She could see the stripes of circus colors stretched out beyond the spacious lawns and playing fields. One of the massive hot-air balloons was being launched. It pulled at its final pair of tethers, as if attempting to escape. Just like she was?

"He promised me my freedom." She adjusted her eyes back to Mr. Anselm, pinning him with a tight look.

"His promises are meaningless." The old trainer shot a wild glance back down the slope. "He will give you nothing—you know as much."

Ahead of them, Leslie looked up the slope again at the man in army fatigues. He appeared to be anxious, waiting. He held one hand concealed beneath his armpit, scanning the area for threats. Tension narrow his eyes.

"No." Leslie's voice remained defiant. "We *won* the race!"

"Don't be a fool, Leslie," Mr. Anselm snapped, prodding her forward, advancing in the direction of where the truck remained parked. They were now twenty yards away.

He was correct. Leslie knew it in her heart. Prince Mir would never allow her freedom. She was his prize, his favorite piece of horseflesh. For all she knew, he'd have her stuffed and mounted on the front lawn, like the life-size statue of the famous Barbaro at Churchill Downs.

What am I thinking? Leslie's mind screamed, chastising herself for her naiveté.

In her sudden haste to stride forward, she tripped, falling to her knees on the grass. Mr. Anselm still held the rein and he moved to assist her to her clumpy feet. The army man at the truck also left his post, rushing to her aid. A nice-looking man, she saw, with dark hair and gentle gray eyes. He slipped up to her side, helping her along. Her pony shoes continued to slide on the slick grass, her legs heavy with fatigue.

Both men were assisting Leslie now, guiding her forward. They neared the back of the parked truck, one of two rear doors half-open, and she could hear its engine already rumbling low.

Footsteps. Running. Coming nearer by the second. Leslie turned, and her eyes searched the immediate area behind them. A cocoa-skinned female in camo fatigues, similar to the army man, rushed past them, headed toward the front steps of the château. She appeared to be bleeding from a wounded upper arm.

A pair of guards was hastening after her. "*Arrêtez! Arrêtez!*" they were shouting.

The petite female stopped and rounded on them, quick as could be, sweeping the legs out from one before he could draw his weapon. She subdued the other with a pair of fist strikes. But in the distance, more guards were rushing in the direction of the female attacker, who sprinted off and climbed the broad front steps, disappearing inside the château.

"Stop where you are, horse trainer!" shouted a sudden thick voice. It came from thirty yards behind them, moving up the grassy slope of hill.

Leslie felt Mr. Anselm freeze at the command, and his shudder matched her own. She did not have to turn to recognize the gruff tone of the large Liberian, the man who had threatened to carve away pieces of her buttocks like roast turkey and feed them to her cold.

To her relief, the dark-haired soldier did not hesitate. With surprising strength, he grabbed her waist and lifted, setting her knees-first onto the rear bed of the truck. Was this the American detective? The one Mr. Anslem spoke of? The man sent here to rescue her?

"Stop! Now!" shouted the bulky African, fast approaching. His handgun was outstretched, and he fired once, twice, with the shots pinged off the second, closed rear door of the truck.

Glancing behind her, frantic, out the open door in the distance, Leslie noted the colorful balloon now rising over the treetops. She could hear the cheers and clapping of the watchful throng, their singsong voices carried along on the sun-kissed breeze.

A meter from where she knelt, the dark-haired man spun around, crouching low. He returned fire, his weapon appearing as if from nowhere. Leslie could see the large Liberian ducking for cover behind a thick clump of hedge bushes. A moment later, the American was hopping up inside the truck's open door. Leslie scooted aside. She peered around him, watching as he extended his hand back down to assist Mr. Anselm up through the door.

To Leslie, he shouted, "Get farther up front! Stay behind the door."

The elderly Belgian had one foot up, was almost inside, when the front of his chest exploded. The warm wet spray of blood spattered the inside of the shadowy truck. Mr. Anselm's eyes flashed at Leslie, meeting her gaze, then he toppled back out of sight. Another bullet whizzed clean through the compartment as the army man swung the heavy door closed. The truck's engine revved, and Leslie found herself pitched down to the hard floor as the vehicle lurched forward.

With the rear doors now closed, she could see nothing. The quilt of darkness trapped them in its folds, black as the inside of a coffin.

———

They were speeding, rocking sideways, and Leslie found herself flung across the truck's flat inner bed, and into the arms of the man working to assist her. He held her tight as she heard bullets zing off the truck's side and rear panels. The engine was roaring. Another loud crash. Then they were squealing around an unseen curve, downshifting, accelerating. Leslie was jolted again, banging her head on some exposed shelving. There were no windows, so she lay huddled with the stranger in the darkness, enfolded by his arms, each of them holding on for dear life.

Gears ground, shifted, and they were headed down what Leslie imagined was a narrow country road. They were speeding away from the château.

"Your parents are Gene and Laureen Dowd. Green Bay, Wisconsin." The army man spoke this in a firm voice. His hands were working to free her from the halter. "I'm a policeman. My name is Cale. I'm here to help you."

"Mr. Anselm..." A glance toward the closed rear doors in the blackness, eyes frightened, watery.

"Gone. Sorry. We can't help him now." The words stung her, striking as sharp as slaps. "I have to ask you this, Leslie—please, it's important—is there another girl? A Mary Jane Moore? From Green Bay?"

"Mary Jane," she repeated the name distantly, as if she'd been asked to recite the constellations in the heavens.

"Yes! Mary Jane!" he pressed. "Is she somewhere? Is she alive?"

Leslie was quiet. Then in a soft voice, she said, "They killed her. They *roasted* her like an animal." Unable to hold back any longer, she began to sob in the dark. "They...they *ate* her."

The strange man held her close as the truck rocked back-and-forth. They swayed together as it accelerated. Leslie felt his strong arms and wished he could somehow teleport them both away—in wizardly fashion—over four thousand miles back to her home, back to her bedroom.

He could tuck her in beneath the thick warm quilt of her bed, like her dad used to do when she was little, and she would once again be safe and warm.

CHAPTER 36

The produce truck barreled along at a speed where missing even a modest curve in the road would prove perilous. The flickering leaves of the high trees twirled in the breeze, and sunlight poured down through the forest, yellow brush strokes splashed across the asphalt road.

In the back of the produce truck, Cale helped Leslie remove her awkward footwear. She still had on the latex bodysuit and she shivered in her white stocking feet. She was more frightened than cold, he imagined, and he discovered a tattered old blanket in a corner that he slipped around her shoulders. The truck swerved again, and they both were rocked, grasping the empty shelving once more to regain their balance.

Rising, Cale advanced unsteadily toward the front of the truck. He managed to swing open the half-size cab door. He stooped his head and shoulders into the front. Jacek was at the wheel and Cale watched the vegetation on each side of the two-lane road whiz past like some Tilt-A-Whirl ride. Blotches of green, amber and brown flashed amid sprinkles of buttery glow.

"Everything copacetic back there?" the Czech asked, his tone revealing the seriousness of their mission.

"Shaken a bit. Unharmed for the most part." Cale exhaled. "The old man, Anselm. Didn't make it." He decided that no comment on the history of Mary Jane Moore was necessary. "Any word from Cheetah?"

"Battling with the guards," Jacek reported, "on the steps of the château. Half-dozen of them. I imagine the rest are on our tail."

Cale watched as Jacek cut his eyes to the side mirror. Pharaoh was following behind them in the stolen jeep, having fled the security guards' gunfire when their truck had blasted through the gated barricade of the château's service entrance.

"We've got a ninety-second lead. Maybe," Jacek said. "They'll catch up in a mile or so."

Cale glanced out the side mirror, a worried look on his face.

"Don't fret about Cheetah, Mr. Packer." Jacek advised this in a confident tone, though his eyes narrowed, unable to hide his concern. "Even if she's wounded, she'll make it to the château's roof. How she escapes from there will be a thrilling story. One she'll tell some night over warm brandies."

"Does Agent Fronteer know we made it out of there?"

"Couldn't get through on the SAT. Not without pulling over." He pointed his elbow at Cale's pocket. "Give your mobile a try."

Cale worked his way into the cab, angling himself with effort into the empty passenger seat. Jacek goosed the accelerator and Cale felt the speed. He withdrew his phone, pressed auto-dial.

The ICE agent answered on the first ring with an abrupt, "Give me your status!"

"Coming in hot," Cale reported, holding his breath. "Hostiles right behind us. Not a friendly bunch."

"Have you got the package?"

"Affirmative. Single delivery. The second girl's not alive, and the old man didn't make it."

"Can you out run them?"

"Negative. Hostiles will be gaining fast. And this heap we're in doesn't have much oomph."

"Copy. We'll send you ground support, soon as you clear the geography of the château grounds. The Belgian soldiers have been ordered to stand down until then."

Cale gritted his teeth. "We don't have time to play politics."

"I'll do what I can—just get free of the forest in one piece."

Powering off, Cale shifted half-around and poked his head back through the cab's opening. Leslie was a shadowy bundle, covered by the blanket. She appeared paler than before. Shock was settling in, he guessed. Her eyes glistened, and Cale felt a pang of guilt slice through him. Already they were referring to her friends as statistics. In a matter of minutes, he and Jacek, along with Cheetah and Pharaoh and Leslie herself, might all be joining them.

Jacek broke into his thoughts. "Sounds like we're on our own out here, eh?"

"Got to get free of Prince Mir's land before they can do anything to help us."

Jacek blew a frustrated sigh as he navigated a tight curve inside the funnel of trees. "That big African bastard?"

"Back there with them—maybe leading the chase, for all I know. He emptied his clip at the truck as we were busting through the gate."

Leslie's frail voice reached them from the dark recesses. "Don't underestimate him! He's...he's not even *human*."

Cale watched as she balled herself even tighter, knees to her chest. "No worries," he said, measuring his confidence as he spoke. "We'll send him back to hell, where he belongs." He didn't miss Jacek's fervent nod.

Leslie peered out at Cale through the bleak darkness, her eyes moist. "Maybe if your name is...Jack Bauer...or something."

"I'm his first cousin." Cale deadpanned the comment, and it summoned a humorless smile to her lips.

———

It should have been one of the finest moments of his life, but as he breezed up the wide front steps of the château, Prince Mir Al-Sadar was fuming. Two of his suited bodyguards flanked his sides, matching his stride, itching to fire their weapons at anyone who looked at them cross-eyed.

As the trio approached the tall front doors—chaos reigning around them, guests in leather or fetish gear scampering about, confused as headless fowl—they could see the spatter of blood on the steps. The female invader had been struck by at least two bullets. They hadn't stopped her, however, and she might be lying in wait around any pillar, any corner, prepared to fire a fatal round at them. This fact made the guards both cautious and nervous, and they kept their assault pistols set on hair-trigger.

Twelve minutes earlier, amid the turmoil of Leslie Dowd's escape, Prince Mir had phoned in his orders. His private pilot—on call twenty-four-seven—was already at the controls. The engines were whining, the roto-blades beginning their slow whir, where they would build toward liftoff in a matter of minutes. The prince was taking no chances. If his ground troops failed to capture the intruders, then his helicopter would overtake them in a matter of minutes, force them to abort their futile escape attempt. Force them to surrender.

He would take his prized pony girl back. If he was met with resistance, well, they had a pair of rocket launchers aboard, locked and loaded. He would blow the escapees into clumps of charred remains, road kill on the pleasant Belgian countryside.

Climbing the final steps to the third floor, the prince led his entourage through the secure steel upper doors, where after another small set of steps, they arrived on the roof's launching pad. They covered their eyes, squinting into the too-bright sunlight. The screech of whirling blades caused their eardrums to spasm, the wind forcing the guards to crouch as His Highness, alone, moved to board the shiny black Bell.

Inside and belted, sound blockers in place, the prince shouted his orders to the pilot.

Sixty seconds later, with the bodyguards looking on from the rooftop and shadowed by the château's high spires, they were an ever-shrinking speck against the afternoon sky.

———

Cheetah found herself trapped inside a second-floor bedroom, which overlooked the front of the château grounds. Staring out the window below, she could better examine the chaos their daring rescue mission had created. Confused revelers were milling about in small groups, talking animated among themselves. Others moved in more haphazard fashion, as if uncertain whether to flee the estate, or take their chances being protected by the prince's security force.

To their credit, the Mod Starlings continued to play from the far-off band shell, as if the shooting and disruption might be distractions their dedicated fans, somehow, were used to. They were professionals, after all. Despite the crowd size being reduced to a fifth of what it had been earlier, the show must go on.

Cheetah could discern the music, muted by the thick walls, from the upstairs bedroom she was hiding in. There, after securing the door, she had taken a minute to assess her physical condition. Her left calf was bleeding—but it was a graze, nothing serious. Her left shoulder had taken a through and through shot, a few centimeters outside her protective vest. Using her knife to slice strips of bedsheet, she'd fashioned a tourniquet around the wound to staunch the blood flow. Rotating it, testing it, she was satisfied that her shoulder still worked.

With soldiers closing in, searching all floors, Cheetah was filled with adrenaline. It would have to suffice, as it had always done for her in the past.

Now all she needed was a plan.

"Search the bedrooms," she heard a distant voice bark, giving orders in French. "The entire second-floor. Even the closets."

Moving toward the room's tall windows, Cheetah peered down at the front grounds, the fountain and curling driveway, the mature trees that stood guard like sentries. Hearing a thunderous throbbing from above—drowning out the music for fifteen seconds—she noted the shadow of a helicopter as it lifted from the rooftop. Prince Mir.

Cheetah turned her eyes to the lawns, where they sloped from the trees and down across the open playing fields. In the far off distance, she watched the second hot-air balloon being fired up. It remained tethered to the ground. Despite the earlier chaos and gunfire, it was still preparing to go airborne.

She focused straight down through the window, considering her options.

Cheetah hadn't paid it much heed at the time, but stretched above the chateau's front entrance, the wide canvas banner had been fashioned in an oversized sign, which beckoned the prince's guests to his fabulous event:

WELCOME BELGIUM FETISH FESTIVAL

Through the window now, she noted that the banner had been secured to the stone facing by strong metal pitons—the kind used by mountain climbers. The twenty-foot stretch of canvas, she decided, provided her with the best—and perhaps only—means of escape. But the guards were searching, coming nearer by the minute, and she had to move fast.

Grabbing a small vanity stool, Cheetah crashed it through one of the windows. She employed the stool to clear away most of the residual glass. Moving to the window's edge—the thudding boot steps of guards clomping along the outer hallways—spotting the canvas pinned to the wall five feet below, Cheetah leaped through the window like an adroit spider monkey.

She caught hold of the banner with both hands and it held her weight for two long beats. Then the canvas split at its outer piton, tearing free from the end she was holding.

Cheetah came swinging down over the front entrance steps. Below her, a dozen startled festival-goers were staring with astonishment, as if bearing witness to a circus act. She landed feet-first, with an awkward thud on the edge of the château's steps, but never slowed her pace. With her handgun drawn, she limped across the drive towards the stone protection of the fountain. Shots came blistering after her, ricocheting off the masonry. Fired from the guards at the open window, she could see. Around her people were shrieking, hunched down, shouting, scrambling for cover behind whatever nearby bushes and tree trunks they might find.

From the opposite side of the gurgling fountain, Cheetah did not hesitate. She loped down the grassy incline, her calf protesting, until she was moving over the manicured lawn of the track's circular infield. The music from the band shell was louder here. The smell of fried food seasoned the air.

Cheetah sprinted onward. In the adjacent field, beyond the running track, the balloon was straining at its moorings. She could see the glow of the gas jets as the rainbow-striped monstrosity began to lift from *terra firma*. Its final tether, dangling free, reminded her of the tail of an African elephant.

Cheetah outran a trio of adolescents and caught hold of the rope. Clutching the line with both hands, wrapping it around her wrists, she felt herself yanked from the ground.

A minute later, she was up-up and away, sailing through the cool air above the leafy emerald treetops. A half-dozen scattered shots sprayed from below. Cheetah did not glance down at the security guards, hearing the whisper of rounds as they whizzed past her twisting, swaying form.

The racetrack below her shrank. The band shell took on the shape of a beached clam. The treetops grew smaller, along with the fading echo of the music.

The puffy white cumulous clouds above grew closer. First then did Cheetah accept that she had pulled her escape stunt off, and she reminded herself—as she'd long suspected—how she might just be a little crazy, after all.

CHAPTER 37

The vehicles speeding ahead of them were spewing dust. The afternoon air was thick with shimmering sunlight, darting shadows, and other than the sounds of the chase, quiet as an afternoon cemetery.

They had gained ground fast. From his spot in the passenger side of the prince's SUV, in spite of the road dust, Kinsella could make out both the stolen jeep's and the produce truck's license plates.

Two more security jeeps were behind him in pursuit. He still had his 9mm, three fresh ammo clips, and one of the guard's machine pistols, which he had grabbed for better effect. He couldn't wait to spray ten rounds into each of the bastards who had invaded the prince's private fortress.

Not to mention stealing his prized pony girl.

Kinsella knew the road was flat for the next quarter mile, before dipping and curving beneath the interlaced ceiling of branches. The road would be unoccupied. The forest on each side was heavy with trees and twisted bracken. Hansel and Gretel territory, the Belgian version. Twenty feet in and you'd lose sight of the road.

Once they cleared the forest, they could overtake the escapees without much effort. The farm roads were flat all the way to Casteau, and the intruders were outnumbered six-to-one. They'd blow them away and recover the girl. With any luck, they'd be dining on her lean and muscular flank by this evening. So much for Prince Mir's precious prize. Human flesh, Kinsella knew first hand, was tastier than any delicacy on the planet.

The narrow old forest road dipped through a series of twists and turns. He decided, however, that he didn't have time to wait for the clearing to ram these bastards off the road.

"Let's end this now!" Kinsella barked to the driver.

The SUV swerved right and accelerated, gaining on the target vehicles in a matter of seconds. The jeep swerved into the right lane, blocking the SUV's attempted pass, and this maneuver enraged Kinsella. He leaned out the passenger window and let loose a volley from his machine pistol. The jeep swerved, evading back into the left lane, just as the SUV's driver slammed on the brakes.

Kinsella's weapon was jerked left, then right, but he knew he'd hit pay dirt, nailed the jeep's driver in the upper shoulder. He'd watched him spasm and yank on the steering wheel.

The antilock brakes of the SUV lost traction on the road's gravel shoulder, and the vehicle bounced near a culvert, sliding, the driver fighting to maintain control. It skidded to a stop on the soft dirt and gravel. Kinsella cursed the driver, pulled himself back into his seat, grabbed the dashboard with both hands. The military jeeps speeding behind them had also slammed on their brakes, lest the SUV overcompensate and come careening back across their lane.

The trio of vehicles gathered themselves like angry bulls.

"Goddammit!" shouted Kinsella at his driver, his Liberian accent thick. "Get your ass in gear, mon! They're getting away."

The guard pressed the gas pedal and the SUV spun a rooster tail of dirt and stones, the suspension rocking as it zoomed back onto the road in pursuit. The pair of jeeps stayed close behind.

———

Glancing at the truck's side-mirrors, Jacek decided it was now or never. They had lost sight of their pursuers, however temporarily. The next part of the plan had to be put in play in seconds. It might be the one chance they had before leaving the protective cover of the forest.

He had witnessed the roaring SUV coming fast behind them, heard the *rat-tat-tat* of gunfire. Pharaoh's jeep had lurched back across the road in evasion. It had shimmied, moving erratically, and Jacek guessed his friend had been struck by at least one round. He couldn't guess how badly he was injured—but if more than one bullet had struck home, it wouldn't take long before Pharaoh bled out and crashed.

They still had twenty-four miles to go before reaching Casteau. The pursuing vehicles would catch them in less than three. As the produce truck rounded a curve, dipped into a shallow gulley, Jacek calculated the odds of his maneuver.

He shouted to Cale in the passenger seat, "Call Pharaoh! Tell him Barcelona Twist. Forty seconds."

Cale did as ordered, and Pharaoh replied, "Copy that," before hanging up.

Cale shot a look at Jacek. "Barcelona Twist?"

Jacek explained in shorthand: Cale was to get the girl ready to move out the front passenger door on his, Jacek's, command. As soon as the truck skidded and stopped.

Ten seconds later, with the produce truck sweeping around a narrow, shadowy bend, Jacek called out: "We're coming about! Get ready!"

"What about weapons? All I've got is my Glock."

"Take the AK. I took it from one of the soldiers. On the floor there."

Cale grabbed the long weapon, holding onto the door-handle and dashboard, bracing for the truck's desperate action. To Leslie in back, he called, "Hold tight. We're spinning around. Then jump up here with me, as soon as we stop."

When he glanced at her frightened eyes in the dimness, she nodded.

With Pharaoh's jeep maintaining a safe distance behind, Jacek slammed on the truck's brakes, spinning the steering wheel like a stunt driver. He skidded across the asphalt surface, sliding into the oncoming lane, rocking the large vehicle to a shuddering halt in the middle of the road. It was aimed sideways, blocking both lanes.

"Hurry. Out the door!" Jacek commanded, a captain giving orders in a firefight.

Pharaoh shot the jeep off the road behind the produce truck, bouncing into the soft ditch, brushing a tree trunk and snapping a thin silver birch like a matchstick. He pulled the jeep back onto the road on the opposite side, skidding to a stop in the middle.

Cale had already exited the passenger door, the large truck serving as a shield, and he helped Leslie step down sock-footed onto the asphalt. He slammed the truck door closed. Clutching the AK tight, Cale ran to the backseat of Pharaoh's running jeep, pulling Leslie with him.

Jacek shouted out the window behind them: "Here they come! Get going!"

The truck was still running. It hadn't stalled. Jacek revved the engine loud enough to send a flock of sparrows shrieking airborne from the trees.

———

Cale helped Leslie into the back of the open jeep and handed her the assault rifle, telling her to duck down. He quickly sized-up Pharaoh: the man was slumped forward, gripping the top of the steering wheel with one hand. His breathing sounded labored.

"Pharaoh! You're hurt, damn it—move over! I'm driving."

Pharaoh shook his head. "I'm okay," he rasped.

Cale noticed the side of the man's shirt was dark with blood. No time for heroes. Placing one knee on the passenger seat, he took hold of the large man beneath his armpits. Cale pulled with all his strength, managing to sandbag the grimacing Pharaoh halfway across the front seats.

"Get the hell out of here, Mr. Packer!" Jacek shouted from the truck's open window behind them.

Hopping into the driver's seat, Cale pushed Pharaoh's legs aside, slammed the door closed. He threw the jeep into gear with his opposite hand. Leslie held on tight in the back. With a sharp spin of the wheel, they accelerated down the narrow road.

In the jeep's rearview mirror, Cale saw Jacek moving the truck once more. He chugged it forward three yards, then backward again. He was creating a blockade, advancing the long truck just enough off the road to impede any end-around passage. Then he flipped the vehicle into reverse, doing the same, backing the truck to prevent the pursuers from circling around the other side.

The Barcelona Twist. Jacek was buying them precious time— enough to increase what little advantage they had to escape.

CHAPTER 38

Roaring up the narrow road, the SUV in the left lane, the pair of jeeps in the right, all three vehicles were forced to slow as they were confronted by the produce truck's erratic behavior. And where, Kinsella wondered, was the stolen jeep with the wounded driver? The man had likely lost consciousness, skidding off the road somewhere back in the trees. They had sped past the point where his vehicle had been swallowed by the forest.

Or had they?

Ahead of them now, the truck reversed itself, lurching backward. This sudden action blocked any chance at passing on the shoulder, either ahead or behind the truck. Kinsella's driver goosed his brakes, easing to a halt, engine running.

"He's blocking the fucking road!" Kinsella shouted, eyes narrow and pissing anger.

The Liberian leaned out the window and began firing his MR9 into the driver's cab, spraying the door with gunfire. The guards in the jeeps did the same, emptying their ammo clips into the truck's cab and rear compartments, blasting the truck as if it were a barn ripe for target practice. The tires exploded. The truck shuddered like a wounded mastodon and went quiet.

The greasy scent of firepower filled the quiet air of the forest. Blackbirds had scattered from the uppermost branches, and now a single crow, braver than most, cawed in protest. The guards approached the produce truck on foot, cautious, weapons ready. One flung open the driver's side door.

"Empty!" he called back to Kinsella.

"No one back here!" shouted another guard, as he examined the opened rear compartment.

Kinsella realized they had been played for fools. He felt a bitter taste rise in his throat. The jeep—he now guessed—had gotten away clean. Miles ahead of them by now.

"Search the woods," one guard called. "The bastard's got to be around here somewhere."

"Forget about him!" Kinsella was incensed. "It's the jeep we want."

The SUV navigated around the truck's front, where it bounced through the narrow ditch just shy of the trees. Spewing loose dirt, the vehicle careened back onto the black ribbon of asphalt. It accelerated up the road like a rocket, forest flashing past on both sides. Kinsella's robust shoulders were pressed to the seat's back, a pilot fighting g-force. His radio cackled, and he listened to Prince Mir's voice:

"We're airborne, headed in your direction. Are they still in the truck?"

Kinsella shouted: "Negative! A stolen jeep—the soldier and girl are aboard. A mercenary, we think, is driving."

"Mercenary?"

"He's wounded. They're sitting ducks. Little firepower to speak of."

Kinsella could feel the Prince's smirk, as the royal commanded: "Overtake them and kill them. But keep the girl alive for me."

——

Free of the forest, the jeep swept along the narrow asphalt roadway, past farm fields, pastures, a herd of brown cattle, black-faced sheep moving in lockstep on their left. Above them the Belgian sky was a vibrant blue canvas laced with low thin wisps of cloud. Every three seconds, Cale glanced in the rearview, making certain the trio of pursuing vehicles remained out of sight.

"Keep pressure on the wound," he ordered Leslie, who was leaning forward into the front passenger seat. She had discovered an oil rag in the backseat and was pressing it against Pharaoh's bleeding shoulder. The man mumbled, incoherent, and Cale issued him a worried look.

"Hold on to it, Pharaoh. Dig deep," Cale said, encouraging the man. "Eyes open. Keep blinking. A few more miles. We've got a med team waiting."

"Will he be all right?" Leslie asked. "Your other friend? Back in the truck?"

Good question. Cale decided that if there was one thing he'd learned about Jacek Tumaj, the man was resourceful. If anyone

198

could escape a band of sadistic armed guards blasting at him with automatic weapons, it was Jacek. Still, he had only to glance at Pharaoh, to be reminded that none of them were invincible.

The large man clamped his eyes closed. He cleared his throat, a raspy rattle, and a clot of blood escaped. Cale understood that if a bullet had struck bone, fragmented into his lung, it would be collapsing. Deprived of adequate oxygen, one by one his vital organs would begin shutting down.

"My daughter..." Pharaoh groaned, weak from blood loss.

Cale kept the jeep aimed down the road's center. "Try not to talk," he said. "We're getting close."

They'd soon be approaching the farmlands bordering the outskirts of Casteau. Maybe twelve or less miles to go. Leslie wiped away the sweat from the injured man's brow with her fingertips.

"Christie," Pharaoh mumbled, faint. "Her name...Chris-tie."

Cale realized that without Jacek or Cheetah around—if either was even *alive*—he had no way of notifying Pharaoh's next of kin. "What's your name, Pharaoh? Your *real* name?" he asked, casting an eye at Leslie. "So I can call Christie for you."

Pharaoh coughed blood again. Darker this time. "Keith," the man said, his voice dry and delicate. "Keith Farson. Irvine, California."

Cale was surprised. All this time, he'd thought Jacek's partner was Egyptian. Or Moroccan. Maybe a Turk or a Spaniard. Some exotic ethnic mix. And here he was, a California homeboy.

"Hold on." Cale's tone was stiff. "You can do...make it, Pharaoh—*Keith.* Just hold...another five minutes. Okay?"

———

"We've got a visual," said the helicopter pilot, pointing down at the rural landscape for Prince Mir, who sat belted in the front passenger seat, headset covering his ears. They were still ten miles out from the village of Casteau, sailing above cow pastures and quilted, beige-colored fields of wheat and alfalfa.

"Splendid," said the prince, adjusting his Zeiss field glasses. "Come in low. Cut them off near that fence gate a half-mile ahead. Yes. Right over there."

"Roger that."

——

"Son of a..."

In the rearview mirror, Cale watched the dust cloud of the SUV come roaring out of the tree cover, accelerating after them. The pair of jeeps followed close behind. At the same time, high above the pine forest, a dark wasp with whirling rotor blades came flying high against the background of wispy white clouds.

One guess—Cale thought morosely—Prince Mir Al-Sadar. And with the man's extraordinary wealth, he was sure his private helicopter would be equipped with the latest weaponry. A laser-guided missile could blow them to bits. Scatter their DNA across three farm fields.

Tending to the bleeding Pharaoh, Leslie lifted her head to see what nightmare Cale was cursing. "Oh my God," she whispered with disbelief.

Withdrawing his phone from his pocket, Cale speed-dialed Agent Fronteer's number. When she answered, he shouted, "Where the hell's our ground support?"

"Belgians can't comply. Orders from—"

"Assistance requested. Urgent!" Cale interrupted, his voice frantic. "We're seven miles out...hostiles closing. One's an armed helicopter."

"Hold on—" Cale could hear her harried voice shouting in the background. Back on the mobile, she said, "Can you attempt evasive action? Get back under trees? Buy yourselves some time?"

"That's a negative, Agent," he said, desperate. "Repeat. Chopper's closing fast."

"Damn." She seemed to be thinking. "Do whatever you can—I'll get back to you in a sec."

"Roger that. A sec's about all we've got."

Cale rang off and glanced at the approaching enemy. The SUV was gaining fast, an exhaust cloud billowing behind it like dust on a salt flat. The chopper had crossed over to the opposite side of the road ahead, getting a better angle for its rocket launcher, was his guess. Cale decided he could slam the jeep's brakes a moment after the missile was fired. If he guessed right, at such close range the guidance might not have time to realign. Perhaps it would explode on the highway ahead of them. The SUV, coming up fast from behind, might not be able to avoid a rear-end collision.

It was the last evasive maneuver he could think of.

———

Agent Fronteer knew it was a long shot. She also understood she hadn't a moment to spare. She dialed the US Chièvres Air Base, which was twelve miles north of Casteau, praying: Please, no typical Army bureaucracy.

When a voice answered, in a crisp voice, she said, "This is SAC Amy Fronteer, ICE, Homeland Security. I need to speak to your base commander. *STAT,* damn it!"

The switchboard operator verified her ID. She was informed the commander was a Lieutenant Colonel Orrie Hammel. "Tell him code word *Broadsword.* I'm requesting an immediate RRF." It stood for Rapid Reaction Force.

A moment later, Lieutenant Colonel Hammel answered. "How can I help you, Special Agent?"

Agent Fronteer kept the panic from her voice. She put in her request.

———

While Agent Fronteer worked the phones, Sergeant Berceau was summoning his remaining men to their remaining trio of military jeeps. Moments earlier, after hearing the desperation in the American agent's voice, Berceau had decided he could wait no longer.

He summed up his decision, expressing his frustration to the ICA agent, shouting: "Damn it to fuck. King Alfonse can go to hell."

The three jeeps roared out of the feed storage parking lot, careening onto the sleepy afternoon street. Breezing around a corner, they accelerated through the quaint village, crossed a bridge, and turned left onto a country road.

Minutes later, they were headed through the bucolic Belgian countryside.

CHAPTER 39

Cale had the jeep's accelerator pinned to the floor. The farmlands rushed past in a blurry montage of rusts and browns, golds and greens. Etched against the summer sky like a hawk on the prowl, the black helicopter swooped low enough for him to study the face of the man buckled in the passenger seat: his sharp goatee, slicked-back hair, the smarmy sneer on his lips. It was not difficult to recognize Prince Mir from the photos they had studied.

Glancing at the backseat, he noticed Leslie looking up. The sheen off her tight black outfit matched the color of the Bell.

"Don't look at him, Leslie—it's what he wants." Cale's voice resembled a growl. "Stay low. Stay focused."

"Focused on what? Getting blown to bits?"

Turning to Pharaoh, Cale noticed the man's face had gone pale. Fluid bubbled on his lips with each faint breath. "Stay with me, Pharaoh. A few more miles to go."

Cale gazed at the side mirror, where the SUV was gaining fast. Kinsella was now leaning out the open passenger window, and he let loose a barrage of gunfire from his machine pistol. Cale swerved across the road to the left-hand lane, hearing rounds ping off the rear bumper. He begged God not to let them hit a tire; or the fuel tank. Or Leslie.

Before Kinsella could draw another bead on them, Cale lurched his jeep back to the right lane and slammed on the brakes. The maneuver caused the SUV to counter his actions. Speeding by, moving too fast, it careened across the gravel shoulder and bounced through the culvert, scraping the side panel along the edge of a barbed-wire fence as it bucked along, not giving up.

The other pair of jeeps also shot past on the roadway. Brakes squealed as they skidded and spun ahead of them in expanding circles, fighting to stay under control. Cale wondered how much longer he could hold them off.

Pharaoh was rasping something. With their vehicle paused, Cale cast his eyes at his large comrade. "My pocket...knife. Take it."

Cale frowned. They were fleeing for their lives, chased by machine guns, helicopters, laser-guided rockets...and Pharaoh wanted him to have his pocketknife? Like bringing a slingshot to an Uzi battle. He could not, however, deny the wounded man's request. It might be his last.

He fished inside Pharaoh's thigh pocket with his left hand, gripping the steering wheel with his right, until his fingers withdrew the long, folded knife.

Jacek had informed Cale of the "wasp" knife's properties. It not only stabbed with deadly results, but also possessed a unique secondary feature: after the blade was thrust into the target, a tiny trigger could be depressed to inject a pellet of compressed CO_2. The gas would fast balloon to the size of a basketball, freezing a mammal's internal organs on contact. It worked on dry land, as well as underwater, and death from internal bleeding or asphyxiation could result in under a minute.

Cale slid the knife into the thigh pocket of his camo pants just as a burst of weapon fire sprayed down from the swooping helicopter. He ducked low and stomped on the accelerator again. Beside him, he felt Pharaoh's body jerk, slammed by rounds both into and outside his vest, hitting home. Leslie was screaming, flinging herself into backseat, as she cowered for cover.

Both the guards' jeeps and the SUV had swung back around. Far ahead, two hundred yards away, the SUV came to a complete stop in the center of the road. It held its position. One of the jeeps now came roaring back at Cale head on, intent on doing serious damage.

"Sweet Jesus!" Cale muttered.

His hands gripped the steering wheel as he drove forward. He didn't alter his direction, but instead accelerated down the middle of the road at the charging vehicle. The enemy jeep swerved at the last moment to avoid a head-on crash, lost control, and plunged into the nearby culvert. Stagnant water sprayed as the jeep nose-dived into the muck. The traction-less tires spun angrily, as the driver attempted to free the vehicle.

Cale slammed on his brakes again, skidding, causing Leslie to grip the back of the seats to keep herself from going airborne. They came to a stop, angled in the road's left lane, engine running.

Above them the helicopter zipped past. It swept low over the flat farm fields and banked around, preparing for a return encounter.

The second jeep now came roaring back at them. Cale fired multiple rounds from his Glock and bullets pinged off the grill, the front hood, the roll bar, causing the driver to swerve at the last second. The open vehicle rocked, teetered on two wheels, then toppled to its side as it screamed past. It slid down the road behind them, sparks spraying across the asphalt.

Prince Mir's helicopter hovered a hundred feet above now. Its nose was pointed menacingly down at the roadway, blocking the path to Casteau. The black SUV remained in the center of the road, positioned below the chopper like a snorting bull.

Cale recognized his adversaries were prepared for the *coup de grace*. The final kill.

He also realized, at long last, that he had run out of options.

———

Inside the dusty office room of the Casteau feed warehouse, Agent Fronteer had received the callback from the Air Base. Affirmative. Help was on the way.

She'd hung up her phone. Now all she could do was wait.

———

Time seemed to freeze. Faced with what appeared to be his final curtain call, Cale's thoughts drifted to Maggie. Would he ever see her again? It sure as hell didn't look like it. The odds—as they stood—were not in his favor.

Was this, he wondered, that moment people talked about? Where your life flashes before your eyes? All the things you've done? All the things you should have done differently?

Cale considered his last phone conversation with Maggie. She had sounded so frustrated, so disappointed in him. He'd heard it in her voice as well as her undertone. And when she'd asked about starting a family, his answer had been less than supportive. When times get tough, the tough do what? They bail out? That sort of thing.

If it's another man's child, was it wrong to walk away?

Cale blocked the dark voices in his head. It was not Maggie's fault that a monster had raped her. It was not her fault she'd gotten pregnant. If anything, he reasoned, couldn't it be argued it was *his* fault? For not doing a better job protecting her? Wasn't that the sad truth of the matter?

Strange as it seemed, he found his thoughts returning to his former girlfriend, Mary. It was a tragedy how her life had been cut short. And hadn't that been his fault, as well? If he hadn't gone for the gun during that ill-fated robbery attempt, wouldn't she be alive today?

He felt the stab of failure in his heart.

He could hear Mary's voice now, as if reaching him from the ether. She was telling him: "It's nobody's fault, Cale. It was an accident. The past is the past. If you have a chance at happiness, at love, take it. No looking back; no regrets."

"No regrets," he whispered to himself. Mary was right—he had to let go of the past. The pain was like a tumor lodged inside of him, brooding like some chancre, threatening to never let him move on until he gathered the courage to put it behind him.

Rubbing his eyes with his shirt-sleeve, Cale guessed the moisture there was caused by road dust, or maybe motor oil, or gas fumes. Sentiment? Regret? Blame? He pushed them all aside. Deal with them on some other day.

"What are we going to do?" Leslie's hysterical voice jarred him back to the present. "We've got to do something! Please!"

Staring up the road at the snorting SUV, at the angry helicopter as it hovered above the vehicle, in a tight voice he said to her, "Plan Z."

"What the hell does that mean?"

"You'll see." He doubted his words even as they left his lips.

And there it was. Cale's inner voice—his own voice this time—informing him like a gut-shot trench soldier: "End of the line. All you've got left is one final play, a final desperate heave: The Hail Mary pass."

That was Plan Z.

——

Perched in the pristine May sky above, Cale could hear the whir of the black Bell's rotors. He could see Prince Mir sneering down at them. He heard Kinsella's driver *revving* the engine of the SUV, preparing for a final run at the jeep. Cale glanced across the passenger seat at Pharaoh's riddled body: silent, motionless, leaking blood like a punctured oil pan. He looked into Leslie's frightened eyes, before raising his own back to the hovering helicopter.

Just as old Moses himself must have, once upon a time, he was searching the heavens for a sign.

And at this exact moment, Cale's prayers were answered. It was the nearest thing to a miracle he'd ever seen. It appeared as if a mirage, shimmering, highlighted against the golden backdrop of afternoon sun. Over the crest of a small hill, behind the Bell and the SUV, an Apache attack helicopter rose. The *thwup-thwup-thwup* of its rotary blades cut through the air, churning steamy currents of heat against the blue afternoon sky.

Above them the Bell continued to hover sideways like an angry black wasp. Unaware of anything amiss, the prince was leaning out the open passenger seat, belted, aiming his AK-47 down at the jeep. Cale couldn't help himself; he flashed Prince Mir his raised middle finger...just as the Apache let loose an air-to-air missile.

The explosion rocked the landscape. Debris and pieces of metal sprayed from the massive fireball at the epicenter. The blast sent shockwaves down like a nuclear wind. It picked up the SUV as if it were a child's toy and flipped it onto the center of the road. It flung Cale's jeep aside as well, toppling it into the opposite culvert.

The explosion's aftershock roared in their ears, and the Armageddon sky rained down chunks of flaming, glowing slices of hot-charred metal.

Cale clambered from the jeep, shin deep in muck. He pulled Leslie free of the vehicle and carried her up the slope to a barbed-wire fence. She'd been knocked unconscious, with a bloody gash across her forehead. Her left arm was bent at an odd angle. Cale positioned her on dry ground. He propped her head on a discarded seat cushion. Rising, glancing skyward as he stepped away, he issued the Apache pilots a salute of thanks.

The hovering helicopter's rotors cut through the afternoon air, as the airship lifted and banked for home. And an instant later, Cale was hit from behind as if by a blitzing linebacker.

Slammed to the soft ground of the field, he could feel the massive arms pythoning around his torso. No doubt. He was in Kinsella's grasp. Trapped on his stomach, the Liberian monster behind him, Cale felt the larger man's forearm pull tight against the front of his throat, hands locked together at the wrist—a classic choke hold. Feeling the pressure on his windpipe, he tried a reverse kick. Nothing. Cale managed to roll to his left and attempted to elbow the larger man's rib cage. It was akin to trying to dent a refrigerator door.

He raised his hands to scratch and claw at the meaty arm pressed against his airway. His oxygen flow was ebbing, his thoughts disjointed. Seeing sparkles, each breath dragged through flared nostrils, Cale guessed he was about twenty seconds away from blacking out—likely forever.

His pants pocket.

He had forgotten about Pharaoh's weapon. Freeing one hand, still pulling at the grip at his throat with the other, Cale fished inside the thigh pocket of his camos and found the folded handle. Withdrawing the knife, he pressed the button. Seven inches of killer blade *snicked* out. With the giant concentrating on compressing his neck, Cale's thumb found the injection trigger.

He jabbed the blade behind him in reverse motion, sliding it in through the thick intercostal muscles that bound Kinsella's solid rib cage.

The Liberian grunted but did not ease the arm-bar pressed across Cale's throat, until a moment later, when the compressed pellet expelled its frozen gas and the man's lungs, spleen, liver and heart all spasmed in instant deep freeze. His opponent's robust arms—in a matter of seconds—turned to rubber.

Cale pulled free and crabbed away on his hands and knees. He gulped air like a drowning man who'd found the water's surface.

Vessels began dissolving inside Kinsella's torso as he struggled to his knees. There came a lengthy, fifteen second interval...that seemed to take forever...before a torrent of blood vomited from the large man's mouth. His eyes and nose swelled and burst, blood gushing forth, as if he'd been stricken by a violent strain of Ebola.

Seconds later, flesh and blood exploded from inside the man's torso. Crimson bits of bone and tissue sprayed in all directions.

Fifteen feet away, still on his hands and knees, Cale continued to gasp for breath. When his head managed to clear, he staggered to his unsteady feet, gripped a fence post with trembling hands. There he doubled over and expelled a mouthful of bitter bile, trying his best not to lose any more of his insides.

Goodbye, Kinsella. And good riddance, he caught himself thinking. Couldn't happen to a sweeter guy.

———

Sirens blared now, growing louder by the second. Cale watched as two Belgian military jeeps came speeding up the country road, advancing toward the scene. Not far behind them rushed a pair of ambulances, and they were followed by two police cars from Casteau, lights flashing, ready to render assistance.

The vehicles angled off the road and stopped, the medical personnel exiting and rushing forward.

From two hundred feet in the air, Cale watched as the Apache helicopter banked west and clipped regally away from the scene. She had done her part. He reminded himself to thank Agent Fronteer—and everyone else involved—for her hasty action in summoning the air support.

His senses just about clear, Cale stumbled toward where Leslie lay. She was on the ground, unconscious from the force of the explosion. The paramedics beat him to her side, kneeling to assess her vital signs. Cale remained a step away, allowing them to work. His muddy face was tight with concern.

Leslie's heart rate, they informed, was steady, her breathing unobstructed. They covered her with tight blankets to ward off shock, established an IV line, then began examining her shoulder.

With reinforcements arriving en masse, in the distance, Cale watched the prince's single functioning security jeep extract itself from the muddy culvert. It spun around and accelerated in the opposite direction, with one of the military jeeps giving chase.

The carcass of Prince Mir's helicopter was a flaming metal heap, where it had crashed in the farm field opposite the road. A dozen small brush fires continued to burn.

The lead military jeep now arrived at the site, maneuvering around the smoldering pieces of metal and debris, which littered the terrain. Flashing lights flickered; walkie-talkies cackled around them. Sergeant Berceau extracted himself and began barking orders in French to local police and rescue workers: he wanted roadblocks erected a quarter mile in every direction. With no unauthorized traffic in or out.

He wanted this crime scene secured.

With Leslie in good hands, Cale directed another pair of EMTs over to his toppled jeep. Pharaoh's body lay twisted in the front seat. The air around them smelled like molten copper, flavored by the tang of motor oil and burning brush.

One of the EMTs checked Pharaoh's condition. The man raised his eyes to Cale and shook his head, then solemnly stepped away.

Sergeant Berceau strode across the field to the fence line. His eyes searched the ground as he moved, assessing a bloody body part here, a dripping clump of flesh there, before at last resting on the steaming heap of reddish human pulp.

Cale had limped back across the field to join him. They both stood peering down at the scattered viscera of what had once been a formidable human being. There was little point in the medics attending to the Liberian. Only God—or whomever the psycho cannibal had worshipped—could help him now.

Sergeant Berceau asked, "What did you do, shove a grenade up his ass?"

"Something like that," Cale said. He withdrew the blade handle from what was left of Kinsella's torso. He wiped the blade clean on his camo pants and handed the knife handle-first to the sergeant.

"Wasp knife?" Sergeant Berceau examined the lethal object in his hands. "They say these things will fell a rhino."

Cale cut his eyes to the chunks of steaming flesh and bone scattered around them. It appeared as if cans of crimson paint had been slopped over the weedy turf.

Cale said, "Is that a fact?"

A faint nearby coughing sound alerted them. Cale saw Leslie had regained consciousness. She was sitting up now, looking as if she'd just awakened from a dream. She eyed Cale where he stood fifteen yards away, calling out: "Did I miss anything important?"

"Nothing much."

With his cheeks grizzled, covered in mud and clothes stained with flecks of scarlet detritus, Cale knew how he looked—fresh out of some nightmare. He would fill in the missing details of the story later. They had a long flight together ahead of them.

A flight Leslie Dowd had only dared dream about in her most desperate hours.

CHAPTER 40

After two hours of medical attention and debriefing, they were transported from the NATO headquarters to the US Air Force base at nearby Chièvres. There Cale and Leslie were granted showers and issued fresh civilian clothes.

Sitting in a visitor's lounge, for the first time in three days, Cale felt close to human again. He nearly failed to recognize Leslie when she entered, wearing jeans and a gray ARMY sweatshirt. Her left shoulder was secured by a wrapped white bandage. A smaller strip over her forehead. Her hair was bronze, brushed back, and still damp.

"Hope that's not your craps-shooting arm," Cale said with a smile. "They added some new tables at the Green Bay casino."

Leslie shook her head. "I don't think I'll be gambling much my first week back."

"Smart girl."

The meal in the officers' mess was highlighted by their reunion with Jacek and Cheetah. The duo had been picked up on the forest road by a Belgian military jeep. They'd been issued civilian clothing, as well. Cheetah had limped into the room on a bandaged left leg. Her wounded arm was immobilized by sling, matching the one Leslie was sporting.

Beside her, the resilient Jacek appeared little worse for wear. After introducing them all, Leslie had hugged Cheetah. Then, over coffee and sandwiches, Jacek brought them up to speed. He reported that the police—aided by the Belgian military—were extending their investigation (with King Alfonse's reluctant blessing) to include the château of Prince Mir Al-Sadar.

"A team of exterminators couldn't scrub that place clean," Cheetah said with a shudder.

"Hope they burn it down." Leslie frowned, searching their eyes. "Those fetish clowns...bunch of sickos..."

Jacek added, "They're like cockroaches. Just show up months from now at the next fancy castle."

Cale remained silent. Jacek was right. He understood enough about human nature to know that attempting to legislate morality was a low percentage play.

They were silent for a minute, seeming to ponder a sick world becoming even sicker...and it allowed the bizarre events of the day to hit home.

Cale focused his gaze on the wily Czech—the man who had saved his bacon more than a few times during this trip. "Speaking of survival." His look at Jacek was tight. "The 'Barcelona Twist'? Escaping from those guards?"

Jacek gave a dismissive flick of his hand. "*Pshee*. They never think to check the truck roof."

Cale shook his head in amazement. Yet the comment allowed a dark cloud to pass over his eyes. "Sorry about Pharaoh," he said soberly. "He saved our lives."

The large mercenary, Cale imagined, would frown upon any display of pity. His had been a soldier's death: he died with his boots on.

Jacek's brown eyes were moist, appreciative for his words. He matched Cale's serious tone with his own. "I'll arrange to have his body flown to California. He has a daughter there."

"Not a chance!" Agent Fronteer called this out, striding into the hall the way a stiff breeze masters an open door. She announced:

"Your comrade—Keith Farson—sacrificed his life while in the service of the United States government. His remains will be returned home by military cargo. We'll make all the necessary arrangements, as well as contacting his next of kin."

Jacek nodded his thanks.

Agent Fronteer's phone buzzed. Turning away, she spoke a few words before turning back to them. She motioned for Leslie to take the phone. Leslie arose, and her voice was tentative as she spoke into the mobile. A moment later, tears flooded her eyes. It was the first time she'd spoken to her parents in over a year. Speaking low, she slipped off to a distant part of the mess hall.

Agent Fronteer turned to Cale. "We've booked you and Leslie on a direct flight, Detective. Brussels to Chicago. Then up to Green Bay. It leaves in two hours." She extended a warm hand to him. "Great job. And thanks again for your service."

Cale felt like saluting. He decided a handshake and nod were more appropriate. He watched her stride away and wondered if their paths would ever cross again.

Twenty minutes later, he and Leslie were summoned by a corporal for their transport to the Brussels airport.

"You stay in touch, Mr. Packer," Jacek said, rising. He clasped Cale's hand with both his own, adding a playful wink. "Your life will be very, very dull without me around, eh?"

"Thank God for that." Cale grinned.

He pecked goodbye to Cheetah on both cheeks, Euro-style. With final waves, he and Leslie departed the mess hall for the first leg of their long journey home.

———

The Brussels International Airport was a cauldron of late-afternoon chaos, sporting enough costumed travelers to fill a Hollywood backlot. Temporary passports in hand, stamped by the Belgian authorities and the US State Department, the Americans were scanned by a TSA agent before being ushered to the boarding area. They had their own security escort. Cale's loaner shoes were a half-size too large, but he wasn't complaining. Anything was better than the blood-and-gristle-soaked combat boots he'd traded them for.

They were seated now in hard plastic chairs, the fifth row of the departure section. Leslie had developed a nervous twitch in her upper cheek, like an aviophobe being forced to fly against her will. Her darting eyes scanned the terminal in all directions. Anyone studying her for longer than a few seconds might suspect she was a first-time smuggler carrying contraband.

Cale decided he had time for a couple of phone calls. Using a disposable mobile, courtesy of Agent Fronteer, he made sure Leslie was glued to the seat next to him. He punched in Slink Dooley's number. Tabulating the time—seven hours earlier in Green Bay—his partner answered on the third ring.

Cale informed Slink he was on a burner phone. He didn't have time to replay the highlights of his ordeal, only that he had located Leslie Dowd, and they were flying home. He'd fill in the colorful details in due time. He requested a favor from Slink: he needed him to visit the Overnight Air storage site at the Green Bay airport. Although it was Saturday, he wanted Slink to retrieve the pair of items he'd had shipped there.

When his partner questioned about the lack of a pickup invoice, Cale suggested he could claim the objects as evidence in an unsolved murder case—part of the Chemist/Tobias Crenshaw investigation.

"You almost sound serious," Slink said, dubious.

"I might've found the missing head." Cale's voice was a mixture of fatigue and intensity. "The Vanderkellen girl."

"I'm waiting for the punch line, kemosabe."

"There is none. Not a joke."

Cale explained what the rep from the air-transport company had told him: how the artifacts he'd sent from Anzio over twenty-four hours earlier would have arrived in Chicago late last night. Then they'd be flown to Green Bay earlier today, Saturday. Placed in storage. Ready for pick up.

"One obvious question: this can't wait 'til Monday? Two days from now?"

Cale glanced at the strangers moving around them. Half of them appeared to be character actors, fresh out of some European spy thriller. Maybe called *In Bruges*.

"My gut's saying to grab them sooner than later. Something about that Liberian colonel I told you about—something I don't trust."

"They won't let me just stroll in. They'll demand a warrant."

"Shouldn't be too difficult. Guy with your skills," Cale said.

"I'm sure there's a compliment in there somewhere."

Cale shifted topics. "By the way—almost forgot—I solved your case for you."

Slink snorted. "Right. There was no courthouse assassination. It was all a dream, like *Wizard of Oz*. Crenshaw didn't get shot in the head four days ago."

"I'm not saying any of that."

"Didn't think so."

Cale kept his tone flat. "What I'm saying is even better: Your suspect—Kinsella—met his unfortunate demise a few hours ago."

Slink whistled. "No forked tongue, kemosabe?"

214

"I just saved you a thousand hours of paperwork."

Spinning his tale of daring rescue and escape, the Cliffs Notes version, Cale realized it sounded straight out of a Jason Bourne thriller.

Like a boy scout sitting cross-legged around a campfire, Slink listened in attentive silence. Coming back to the part about shipping Mabutu's stolen artifacts, Slink now conceded: "I'll get on it." Cale could discern his partner's smirk, as Slink added: "I can't wait to see what your little trinkets look like."

Finishing his call, he turned to Leslie, who had remained silent in her seat the entire time. She appeared small and helpless, her bandaged shoulder adding to her vulnerability. Cale guessed the shock of everything she'd been through was at last penetrating her defenses. She had been issued a prescription for painkillers, along with a beginning heroin detox dose. Assured by the military physician that the meds were compatible, she was told they'd also function as a sedative during her lengthy flight back to the States.

Good news for them both, Cale had decided. Leslie wouldn't be itching, perspiring, or climbing the walls with delirium. And she wouldn't imagine the plane was filled with spiders and slithering snakes.

Maybe they could both get some decent shut eye.

He watched as she browsed through a local newspaper she'd discovered on an empty seat. He guessed that by this time, she could read decent French. *Damn, she's a trooper*, Cale caught himself marveling. His heart swelled with remorse for what the young woman had been through: ripped from her normal life, drugged, assaulted, transported thousands of miles away, beaten and abused even more, locked up in a fortress.

Then forced—against her will—to perform like some circus animal.

When she glanced up at him, Cale held up one finger. "One more phone call, then we'll board. Okay?"

She gave him a brittle smile. "No worries, Detective. I'm not leaving your side."

He punched in Maggie's number and waited as it rang four times. He was hoping she'd answer her cell, despite the unfamiliar international number. Her voice sounded tentative when she did.

"Hey. It's me." Cale forced enthusiasm into his voice, though he was exhausted. "I'm at the Brussels airport. Coming home."

"Honey. My God. I hadn't heard any…I was tearing my hair out."

"Two legs and upright. All I ever promised."

Maggie's laugh came back genuine, and he could hear the moist tears in her smile. It was the tender smile he'd memorized the first time they met over two years ago. "I wanted to say…" she said, halting, as if uncertain which words to use: "I'm sorry about our last talk. What I said…Jesus! it wasn't fair to dump on you like that."

"I'm a big boy."

Cale wondered if he sounded like his regular self again. He was so, so tired. But he decided it didn't matter: he was speaking to Maggie. His "normal" Maggie. Not the irrational lady who'd grilled him about the "future" and "wedding plans" and about "starting a family." And the rest of it—most of which he'd chalked up to her hormones doing the talking.

"I've got Leslie Dowd with me," he added, allowing himself a sigh of relief. "We're connecting through Chicago. So, it'll be pretty late when I get back. I'll catch a cab home."

Maggie protested. She'd be happy to pick him up at the airport. She'd be waiting up regardless, wouldn't she? Cale insisted he wanted her to remain at the house. He had a few things he needed to take care of before returning home. Not to mention the possibility of flight delays. He didn't reveal the oily sense of unease that seemed to be growing inside him like some dark premonition.

He wondered if he was avoiding the pregnancy talk by design. Or the discussion of "them" in general. He supposed so. Now was not the greatest time for it. Nevertheless, Cale marveled at how being splattered with half of Kinsella's innards didn't made him as anxious as talking about their future together.

"What sort of things? It'll be well after midnight," Maggie said.

"Evidence. In my case. I just need to do this, all right?" Cale chose not to elaborate.

"Are they coming home with you? Both girls?"

"Just Leslie."

Silence swallowed the distance between them, allowing the news to speak for itself. "Want me to call her parents?" Maggie asked. "I'm sure they'll want to be at the gate when she gets here."

"Thanks," he said. "But hold-off notifying Mary Jane Moore's family. I'd like to tell them what happened myself."

"Oh no." Maggie shuddered. "Not good, I'm guessing?"

"Not good."

Perhaps it was the soberness of the moment. Or maybe the need to shift topics. Cale asked, "You feeling all right? Still under the weather?" Loaded questions, he knew, but he guessed he was on solid ground. They were minutes away from being called to board their flight.

"I'm okay. Chloe's den-mothering me. When she isn't driving me nuts with her so-called visions." Maggie's sigh was audible. "If she tells me '*He is coming*' one more time, I think I'm going to scream."

A beat of silence. "Maybe it's *me* she means? That I'm coming home?"

Even as he threw it out there, Cale didn't believe it. *"He is coming."* No. The words carried a more ominous ring. He felt his guts knot as the image of Mabutu rose in his mind.

But with all that had happened in the past forty-eight hours, Cale decided his concern was likely some form of delayed shock. Still, the more he played Chloe's dire warning over in his mind, the more his thoughts kept looping back to the sadistic Liberian colonel. A witch doctor.

Maggie said, "I'll give you the whole play by play when I see you."

"Can't wait."

With the promise he'd be home as fast as the international flight would allow, Cale flipped his phone closed. With her microphone in hand, the ticket agent was summoning them for boarding.

CHAPTER 41

Green Bay, Wisconsin

Maggie set her phone on the dining room table. She'd been pacing the room while speaking. After hanging up, she plopped down on one of the chairs. She placed her elbows on the table, face in both hands, and closed her eyes. She said a quiet prayer of thanks. Cale was all right. He was coming home. It would take hours for him to arrive, but who cared about time? He was alive and safe and headed back. What more could she ask for?

When she opened her eyes and looked out at the sunlight slanting through the living room windows across the way, her first thought was she should contact Slink. Perhaps they could cobble together a welcome-home party. Maybe even make it a surprise. But the more she considered the idea, the less sense it made on a practical level. It would be too late, wouldn't it? Cale might not even arrive at the house until three, maybe four in the morning.

Maggie weighed the plusses and minuses. She needed to talk to Slink, regardless, about getting her handgun back from the police. The Kahr PM9 remained in the forensics lab. She had to admit that since she'd fired the weapon at the shooting range—becoming somewhat proficient at hitting where she aimed—she felt vulnerable without it.

Chloe's strange warnings weren't helping any on that count. Maggie decided she had to stop giving credence to her sister's visions of impending doom. Maybe stop listening for good. They always seemed so...so *negative!* The next time it happened, she'd simply shout: "Chloe! Just shut the hell up! I don't want to hear it, all right?"

Still, if she had her gun in the house, she'd feel much less exposed. Was it her hormones talking again? Maggie shook the thoughts of vulnerability from her head, chastising herself for being paranoid. She couldn't allow her mind to go there. If she did, the next thing she'd be remembering was how Tobias Crenshaw had invaded their home; how he kidnapped her, raped her; how near he'd come to ending her life.

She warned herself to stop it! Now! To stop the looping, self-destructive thoughts before she drove herself crazy.

Cale would be home tonight. So what if it was late. Regardless of when he arrived, they'd wake up together tomorrow morning. He would protect her and Hank (and the baby, she reminded herself) and everything could return to normal.

As normal as things were ever going to be going forward, her inner voice nagged.

In a few days, when their lives became routine again, perhaps they could have their State-of-the-Relationship discussion. Now that she was sure, Maggie would tell Cale about her "situation." That's how her mom (she knew) would have termed it.

They could talk it over the way couples did. They had shared so many heartfelt discussions in the past—most of them months ago, when she'd questioned whether he was taking their relationship seriously enough—so this would be yet another one, wouldn't it? Couples had these kinds of talks every day: about finances, chores, the kids...their future together.

Sometimes you had to clear the air in order to move forward.

Before Maggie could stop it, however, the snarky voice in her head jumped in: "Oh Cale, by the way, there's an eighty-twenty chance you might not be the father of our baby. What's that? The real father? Ha. Funny you should ask. Remember the man who raped me? Yes? He's now brain-dead, if it's any consolation...Yes. When I was drugged, if I had to take a guess, tied to a bed, barely conscious.

"You remember how it happened—of course you do. No, I'm not certain. Just a *feeling* that women get, you know? An intuition?

And more: "Sure. I suppose you'd say it's 'hormonal.' But how clichéd does *that* sound? No, you wouldn't know. How could you? What? Of course, I'm keeping him. He's my baby. How couldn't I? And by the way, do you still want to get married, or what?"

Maggie rose from the dining room chair and made her way into the kitchen. Hank was moving down the hallway, and he paused, giving his back an arching stretch. Maggie reached down and plucked him from the floor. She nestled her face against his head.

Hank began to purr, oblivious to the salty tears she was shedding on his neck.

———

Brussels, Belgium

The trans-Atlantic flight leaving Brussels for Chicago lifted from the runway as if shot from a sling, headed backwards in time. Fifteen minutes in the air, and Cale found himself already fighting to stay awake. The day seemed too surreal to be believed. It had begun, predawn, in Italy. Then he'd spent the remainder in Belgium—tramping through the woods, laying siege to a glorious old chateau, getting shot at, chased, shot at again, almost blown up, then choked to death's brink. He'd barely escaped with his life. Now here he was, headed home. Safe and, he supposed, somewhat sound.

Cale accepted the pair of small pillows he'd purchased from the flight attendant and burrowed himself against the window.

There would be no secret posing as an air marshal this time around. Not like he'd done on his flight to Europe. No Wyatt Earp attempts to detain any drunken passengers. No excitement whatsoever. He'd had enough this past week to last a couple of lifetimes.

The sun was sinking in the west, so Cale pulled the shade down and decided to keep it that way. The drone of the engines was beginning to lull him into a fugue. He struggled for comfort in his makeshift nest, but as much as he tried, he couldn't prevent the day's events from performing a running montage in his head.

After five minutes, however, Cale recognized the futility of the replay. What happened had happened. And he accepted that there was nothing he could do about any of it. He offered up a prayer of thanks for being alive—with Leslie in the seat beside him, earphones plugged in, her eyes closed. Maybe asleep; maybe not.

As if sensing his gaze on her, she blinked them open. "What's Green Bay like these days? Since I've been gone?" She asked this in a husky voice. Maybe the sedatives were kicking in.

Cale shrugged. "Same as always. Thank God."

"I figured as much."

"End of May. By the time you get settled, in a couple of months it'll be the start of football season."

"I'm a huge Packers fan. You guessed that, didn't you?"

He attempted to slide his narrow seat further back. No luck. "I know your file by heart, Leslie. Read it a few thousand times."

"My file." Her voice stayed soft, a near whisper. "I was already a statistic, wasn't I?"

"We're all statistics."

She thought about it and said nothing.

Cale handed her the extra pillow and allowed his eyes to close. Leslie remained silent for a full minute, as if contemplating asking something further. Something, he sensed, that was still bothering her. Perhaps it was about the monsters who had kidnapped her, or maybe about the other victims—girls like her—who'd been abducted in the case.

Instead, she said, "You're not really Jack Bauer's cousin, are you? You know? The guy who rescues everybody?"

He feathered a smile. "No. We're not related."

Then Leslie closed her eyes, tucking the small pillow beneath her ear, and fell into the rhythm of the airplane's gentle sway.

Cale did the same, deciding he could run through the bizarre events of this day some other time. Perhaps when he wasn't quite so exhausted. *"Pleasant dreams, Mr. Packer."* He could hear Jacek's voice in his head, as if the man were sitting right beside him. Or maybe out on the wing like some gremlin. Wing-surfing, no hands, tempting fate—that would be Jacek.

With the plane's turbines groaning peaceably, Cale slipped into the welcome embrace of sleep. For the next six hours, he moved not a muscle—save for a few twitching moments, when his dreams replayed the life-or-death struggle that he'd had with the thuggish giant called Kinsella. His was a face, Cale understood, which would haunt his nightmares for many months to come.

———

High above the Eastern Seaboard, the hum of the plane's engines remain steady. The knife-like pain deep in his brain returns, the rattles and shakers, the frenzied jungle drums.

221

Tazeki Mabutu's voice echoes inside Cale's head one final time: "Our story comes to its *finis*, Detective. So much for my teasing you with what might have been."

Cale is frozen in his seat, eyes closed, and the voice continues with a snake-like hiss: "But rest assured, I am coming for you—and for your friends, your family, and everyone you care for. I will carve open your chest and consume the meat of your steaming heart."

The echo of laughter penetrates Cale to the marrow...before fading, fading, fading...along with the pulsating drumbeats...until the shakers have surrendered their final, ghost-like rattle.

Cale blinks his eyes open and stares at his hands, which grip both armrests, his knuckles white as polished bone. He's like a man suffering from a fever, and his forehead is slick with swampy perspiration.

PART THREE:

A LONG DAY'S JOURNEY INTO NIGHT

"Now they lay thee down to rest, no rhythm beating in your chest; Your coffin opens 'fore the light, and out you walk on moonless nights."

—- *Nzambi* hex of witch doctor Tazeki Mabutu

CHAPTER 42

Green Bay, Wisconsin

With a glance in her rearview mirror, Chloe swung into the left turn lane on Main Street, on the city's East Side. At the stoplight, she eased to a halt. She frowned while glancing in the Buick's driver-side mirror, and with her right hand she lowered the radio volume.

From the passenger seat, Maggie gave her a questioning look. "Something the matter?"

"Just because you're not some double-naught spy," Chloe said cryptically, "it doesn't mean you're not being followed."

"What are you talking about?"

It was Saturday evening, and the sun was still strong in the western sky. Traffic was modest this time of day, families eating dinner or firing up backyard grills. It made for a comfortable and uncongested drive through the city. They were headed to St. Phillip's for the six o'clock mass, with confession before, if they could make it in time.

Maggie ignored her sister, choosing to shift her gaze back out the window. Her eyes were locked in a thousand-yard stare.

Chloe wondered if Maggie might be trying to catch a glimpse of the future—her own. She lifted her eyes back to the rearview mirror and said, "A car's been following us for the last half mile. A little white Smart Car." She glanced at Maggie, then back to the mirror. "Any ideas would be appreciated."

Maggie started to turn her head, causing Chloe to bark: "No! Don't! Keep looking straight."

Maggie froze in the passenger seat, her eyes bugging as she stared forward. "You're either crazy or paranoid," she mumbled. "Likely both."

The left turn arrow glowed, and Chloe navigated through the intersection. The snub nose vehicle stayed on their tail, sliding back to an easy three car lengths behind.

"The answer is no," Maggie said, moments later. "I don't know anyone who drives a Smart Car." She cast her eyes out her side window to study the wing mirror. "If this is some kind of test for the new detective agency, it isn't funny."

Chloe rolled her eyes. "Hello? A car is following us! So no. It's not some test." She exhaled like an actress on cue. "Speaking of which, are we still even considering the detective business thing? We haven't talked about it for over a week."

Maggie placed a hand on her abdomen. "Small wonder...with everything happening." She sighed. "I'm not sure it's a great time to be starting a new business." She chewed her lower lip and returned her gaze out the window.

Chloe reached over and patted her sister's knee. "We'll talk later. After Cale's back, and things return to normal." She regretted her comment at once. Normal? Would things ever return to normal? Especially if Cale's not the baby's father.

A minute later, the tall steeple of St. Philip's edged into view between the rooftops of the surrounding homes, and the sisters saw the reddish brick of the church and adjacent sacristy, the tall stained-glass windows. Pigeons stalked the base of the wide concrete steps and low bushes on the bordering strips of lawn, while starlings played tag near the belfry. The parking lot was half-filled. It meant they had enough time to slip inside and have their sins washed away. Assuming the line wasn't too filled with other repentant sinners.

Chloe spied an open spot on the side street, across the corner from the church. It was where she liked to park—away from the crowd. She spun the Buick left and eased into a parking spot beneath the shade of a gnarled elm, whose upper limbs had been trimmed away from the power lines.

Maggie sat unmoving in her seat, and Chloe swung her gaze back to the side-view mirror. She watched the Smart Car sneak into a parking spot in front of the line of cars across the street. A slender, thirtyish blonde emerged from the vehicle. The woman had on dressy blue jeans and a sleeveless white summer blouse. She was texting on her phone as she walked with her head down, moving toward the front steps of the church. The woman didn't look in their direction or acknowledge their presence in any way.

Perhaps Maggie was right, Chloe conceded. Perhaps she was being paranoid. The woman just happened to be driving behind them, headed toward the same church, the same Saturday evening mass.

A simple coincidence.

The sisters exited the Buick and moved across the street. Ahead of them, a handful of parishioners advanced toward the front entrance. They walked in silence, as if contemplating the blessings soon headed their way.

"Fair crowd," Maggie said with a sigh. Her eyes scanned the grade school football field across the street, before turning back. "Confession line might be long."

"We're early enough." Chloe was a half-step ahead of her sister. "Besides, Ed's already inside, saving us seats."

As they neared the wide base of the steps, Chloe noticed the blonde-haired woman with the smart phone had stopped. She raised her eyes to face them now with a generous smile.

"Hello, Maggie," the woman said, as they approached. "I'm Charity Tantram. The criminology professor? We spoke briefly on the phone yesterday. I think there was some sort of misunder—"

"You're the one who's been calling her?" Chloe interrupted, her displeasure undisguised. "Bothering her?"

Charity kept her eyes focused on Maggie. "I just want to ask you a few questions. Maybe a video snippet for my web—"

Before she could complete the word, Chloe reached out and slapped the phone from her hand. The iPhone hit the sidewalk, breaking into three pieces, its battery skidding to the curb like a scuffed stone.

Charity gave a stunned look at Chloe. "Are you crazy? Why did you—"

"This isn't a freak show, lady." Chloe's voice was stern. "Next time make an appointment."

Steering Maggie by the elbow, she marched her past the open-mouthed professor. They climbed the steps to the tall, wooden church doors, where they were swallowed by the forgiving dark shadows inside.

CHAPTER 43

Having located the Van Waring home, Tazeki parked his rented Hyundai compact two blocks up the street, beneath an awning of shade trees. It was nearing seven p.m. on Saturday night, the peach-colored western horizon a prelude to a postcard sunset.

Exiting the vehicle, he walked up the block. He had donned a dark green-fleece jogging suit, running shoes, and he moved at an unhurried pace. He carried a small duffel bag in one hand, and he kept his eyes alert, scanning the area. Birds chirped from the trees, and he could detect a hint of charcoal wafting through the otherwise calm evening air.

After crossing a quiet intersection, spotting no one around, he slipped casually between a pair of high junipers. He entered the wide lawn to one side of the property, approaching from the north. In his disguise as an innocent jogger, he imagined he'd fit right in, should anyone happen to observe him. In this city, Tazeki reasoned, wearing green didn't hurt a bit.

If a neighbor questioned his presence, he would claim to be experiencing a bout of leg cramps. How in walking off the muscle discomfort, he had wandered without thinking onto the property. No harm, no foul.

He had no explanation for the duffel he carried. He doubted he'd need one.

No one approached. No one seemed to notice him, nor care about his presence. Not a soul, that is, save for the plump gray tabby, which he'd observed sitting in the screened, first-floor window that lead to the backyard patio deck. *"Hello again, Hank. Remember me?"*

When the cat's green eyes grew larger, he added: *"Boo!"*

He watched the feline leap back and flee, scampering deep inside the house to hide somewhere safe, he imagined.

Tazeki had already made certain the house was otherwise empty. Thus he went about his business unencumbered. It took him fifteen minutes to scope out the outside property from all angles, survey the lot lines, the trees, bushes and shrubs, every nook and mound and ditch. After a while, he located the prime position for his purposes. It was an open space tucked inside the high bushes, hidden amid three tall elm trees, which bordered the lot on the southern side. From this invisible position now, glancing up, he spied a robin's nest. Across the way he noticed a pair of crows searching the ground beneath a conifer pine.

He opened his duffel bag and removed a dozen charms he'd brought with him on his journey. Tazeki proceeded to cast a repellent spell, designed to dissuade both animals and humans from approaching his hidden enclosure. One of the crows seemed to sense the presence of magical activity. It cawed and rose into the air, escaping just ahead of the reaches of the spell.

The second crow, however, was not as fortunate.

From inside the shadowed thicket, he looked out across the clipped lawns and flower beds. The avian activity within the borders of the property had ceased, the way one turns off a spigot. Yes, he decided, this secluded space would serve his plan well. All he needed now was fresh blood.

Preferably human.

Tazeki's eyes scanned out past the house, beyond the property. As if in answer to his needs, on the bordering street he noticed a small white automobile, where it sat parked at the curb beneath a chestnut tree. The loa were smiling down on him. They were one with the botono on this evening, and as if on cue, the low thrum of night drums began to sound in his head.

———

Professor Charity Tantram cruised up the street past the Van Waring residence, her grip tight on the steering wheel of her compact vehicle. She was angry at herself. No, *frustrated*—a better word. She had imagined that if she could catch Maggie Jeffers in an unguarded moment (what could be more unguarded than outside a church on a Saturday evening?) the woman would recognize that she, Charity, was not some lunatic stalker. Nor was she a publicity hound, or any sort of nut-case, thank you very much.

She hadn't planned on Maggie's sister being with her, however. Now that was one rude-crude woman. Charity had approached them as a professional, just wanting to ask two, maybe three quick questions, and to record Maggie's answers on her phone—with her consent, of course. How much more innocent could things be?

Charity was a researcher, after all. She was not some tabloid hussy who fancied herself a journalist.

Instead, Ms. Rude-Crude had intervened, slapping her iPhone from her hand as if she were some lurking paparazzo. My God, how embarrassing. And at the steps of a church, no less. And now her phone was ruined. Charity had a good mind to send Ms. Rude-Crude the replacement bill.

She stared at the broken iPhone, which sat in pieces on her passenger seat. She still had her digital recorder in the glove box. It would suffice. Charity had promised herself on the drive over that she would not give up, would not be content to drive back home like some scolded puppy. She had failed twice already—on the phone and in person—so the third time, well, it was a matter of persistence, wasn't it?

So here she sat now, parked up the block from the Van Waring residence. Charity had eased her vehicle into the shade, buzzed open the both the passenger and driver's-side windows, allowing in the soft evening breeze. She had decided she would wait until Maggie Jeffers returned from church. The woman would be calm and relaxed and on her home turf. She'd be willing to answer questions concerning the shooting of Tobias Crenshaw. And why not? The monster had kidnapped her. Held her captive. Done unspeakable things to her.

What victim wouldn't want her voice heard? Charity reasoned. She would ask if Maggie, indeed, was troubled by the shooting? Or was she satisfied? Did she feel empowered? Did she, perhaps, sense on some karmic level that justice had been served?

The Tobias Crenshaw kidnapping case—everyone knew—had swept across the nation as a lurid, sordid, headline-dripping affair. Social media, bloggers, true crime blabbers...they'd all had a field day. Securing a jailhouse interview with kidnapper—Tobias Crenshaw, himself—two weeks ago, had proved to be a significant cap-feather for Charity Tantram, PhD. She couldn't wait to put it up on her podcast site.

Her larger plan, however, was to reveal both sides of the story.

Using the internationally famous novel *The Silence of the Lambs* as her guidepost, Charity recognized that the public's appetite was hungry for details not only about the psychopathic killer, but of his innocent victims, as well. And who better to reveal how it felt to be a fly trapped in the web of a serial killer, than attorney Maggie Jeffers? Crenshaw's final victim?

The person instrumental in leading the police to his capture?

Charity studied the neighborhood where she was now parked. The homes were older here, spaced comfortably apart, near double or triple the city's standard lot size. Many were blessed with mature trees and dense clumps of bushes, which served to protect and isolate many of the houses. Charity decided the layout worked to her advantage. She could approach the front door of Maggie's home without her feeling threatened—not blind-sided, as she'd no doubt felt outside the church, an hour ago.

Gazing out her window, Charity noticed a lone figure, as he emerged through the trees of the adjacent lot. He was a slender black man wearing matching, forest green workout attire. The stranger grinned at her, offered a polite wave. When he veered in her direction, however, Charity tensed. She felt as if she'd been caught doing something illicit.

Coming closer, the man appeared to be admiring her vehicle. He called out: "What a chipper little car. Great mileage, I'll bet."

Charity smiled at the compliment. Her desire was to appear nonthreatening, show she was a regular in the neighborhood. She leaned across the passenger seat, saying, "Yes. Thanks. We just love it." Give him the impression she was not on her own.

"Very Euro," the jogger said, his grin still in place. As he moved from the sidewalk to the patch of grass near the curb, he slipped a hand inside his pocket. He leaned in close to the Smart Car's open window.

Charity sat frozen, not wanting to arouse his suspicion, not wanting to reveal what she, in truth, actually was: a cheesy, publicity-hound stalker, lying in wait.

The man withdrew his hand from his pocket. He raised his fingertips to his lips. Charity watched as the stranger blew on his fingers; and as he did, he popped them open, wide and stiff, in the *voila* fashion of a stage magician.

She remained staring at the man as if hypnotized—the way a rabbit is paralyzed by a snake's eyes—watching his odd, hypnotic movements without flinching.

Alarm bells were clanging deep in Charity's head. Get *away, away, away*... At last she pulled herself in, leaning as far from the window as she could manage. She turtled herself down in the compact seat. Her fingers sought the control panel—missing the button once, twice, again—as she attempted to close the windows.

They buzzed up, at last. There was a glass barrier now between the stranger and herself. Yet her gut was telling her that it was too late. Gray and greasy shadows were gathering in the confined area of her vehicle, and they clutched at Charity's throat like the bony fingers of a ghoul. She attempted calling out...but only a rasping sound escaped. The air seemed unable to rise up through her windpipe.

Though twilight had not yet engulfed the evening, Charity's vision had become dull and blotchy. Seconds later, she felt her head thump against the driver-side window.

It was the final sound Charity Tantram heard.

CHAPTER 44

Organ music blared. Triumphant voices lifted. Father Ambrose Larchezi blessed those in attendance at the Saturday evening service. Maggie rose from the pew and followed Chloe and Ed—along with Cato and Katya, their two kids—toward the exit doors. She was pleased that they'd arrived early enough to offer their confessions.

They had each received the priest's absolution and taken Holy Communion. Like a newly baptized infant, Maggie felt clean again.

They paraded now with the other patrons toward the open doors of St. Phillip's, where they emerged into the warm and pleasant May evening.

Ed drove off with the kids, after informing Chloe they'd chosen a local pizza parlor for dinner. They would meet her back home later—if she decided to leave Maggie's house at a reasonable hour. They'd already planned an animated Disney movie, which awaited in the que. The sisters waved goodbye. They headed toward the side street, where Chloe's Buick sat nestled in the blanket of shade beneath the trees.

Fifteen minutes later, they pulled into the driveway of the Van Waring house. Chloe was humming to a song on the radio, while her sister sat in the passenger seat in contemplative silence. Maggie exited the vehicle after Chloe parked off to one side on the driveway apron. She walked toward the house, thinking of Cale, calculating the time his flight was scheduled to arrive back in town—very late, well after midnight.

As she neared the backdoor, surveying the shrubbery, Maggie let loose a shriek. "What on earth is *that!*" she shouted, one hand flying up to cover her mouth.

"What the hell—" Chloe echoed. She was frozen a few steps behind Maggie.

Streaks of crimson zigzagged across the backdoor as if painted there by some crazed derelict. Shiny black feathers were embedded in the slashes, stained and sordid, looking as if they'd been dipped in motor oil. A sacrificed bird had been nailed to the door upside down. The result, perhaps, could be imagined as an attempt at conceptual art. But only if the artist was Charles Manson.

A slaughtered crow. The thought lodged in Maggie's head as if implanted there. She took a step closer.

"Don't touch it!" Chloe warned. "I know what it—it's a voodoo hex."

Maggie shifted her gaze to Chloe, then back to the door again. "This is...crazy! Why would anyone do something like..." Her voice trailed off, as if unable to finish the thought.

"Not why. Who."

Maggie stayed silent.

"Remember? 'Someone's *coming*?'" Chloe shifted her eyes from the door to the cluster of high bushes around the side of the house, peering as if drawn to the spot. Moments later, she focused her attention to the tall trees at the edge of the property.

Maggie followed her sister's gaze. Through the leafy foliage, she could discern the fresh-clipped lawn of the neighboring lot. The scent of charcoal wafted on the breeze, and it made her shudder. It all brought with it the illusion of nonchalance, of normalcy. Maggie wasn't fooled. A bloody and butchered bird tacked to her backdoor might mean any number of things, but "normal" wasn't one of them.

"What are you thinking?" Maggie asked. Her lungs felt tight, and her heart was still running laps in her chest.

"He's no longer coming," Chloe said theatrically, turning back to face her sister. With a dark glint to her eyes, she whispered: "He's already here!"

———

The evening light was blotted with purple shadows, and Tazeki Mabutu had a game plan. He knelt enmeshed within the jungle clump of tall bushes, assembling his pieces the way a general plans a battle's every outcome, long before the first shot is fired.

He had spent time during the lengthy flight with his eyes closed in deep meditation, scrying the whereabouts of Pazuzu. It hadn't taken him long to figure out the puzzle: the brisk wind, the stars in the night sky, the confined and compact space—it could mean but one thing: Pazuzu had been traveling. His small statue, Tazeki had realized, was packed in a box or a shipping crate, and was being flown somewhere.

Shipped by the detective. Van Waring. Shipped to his home city in the States, most likely. Where else would he ship the items he had stolen? He allowed himself a contented smile. It made the most sense.

He didn't just want his possession back. He *needed* it back. He needed his old friend Pazuzu returned to his side. He had to recover his gris-gris: his sacred personal objects were encased within the hidden pouch, tucked deep inside the base for these many, many years.

To the witch doctor, little else mattered in the physical world. Still, the botono was no fool. He understood that one must have in place a contingency plan. A clever strategy—like playing chess at a master level—always required a backdoor, an escape hatch, where you could maneuver free if your best-laid plans went awry.

Tazeki further decided that he had the perfect place to hide: His old friend Tobias. *Ha.* That warm squishy spot in his brain, if need be. But only while Tobias Crenshaw remained alive. (Which he still currently was.) Yet with the significant injuries the man had suffered—being shot in the head was considered "significant," after all—that plan could not be relied upon for too long.

Besides, it would never come to that, Tazeki assured himself. Not in a hundred years. How could it? He had both foresight and strategy, had both superiority and surprise...these all working in his favor. Like a grandmaster, he was invulnerable in this contest.

Or so he imagined.

He stood hidden now, tucked deep inside the high clump of bushes along the border of the Van Waring property. Tazeki was masked by the growing darkness, one with the cover of night. He had ditched the fleece tracksuit in favor of a pair of dark, three-quarter length canvas pants and no shirt.

Above him the tree branches swayed in the wispy May breeze. Insects flitted about, mosquitoes, fat flying bugs, crickets calling: nothing he didn't experience in Africa each day times ten thousand. High above, the clouds swept past, casting a gray veil of shadow across the corn-colored moon.

From inside his duffel bag, Tazeki withdrew a few magical items. He set them at his feet on the ground he'd cleared. With no need for a flashlight, he stripped the bark from a slender sapling with his razor-sharp knife. He created a *poteau-mitan*, a center post, and planted it in the pliant, musty soil like one would a gravesite marker. Around its base he sprinkled white corn flour and scattered a handful of potent charms.

He created a makeshift altar by laying down a rectangular piece of scarlet cloth, weighting it with a handful of fist-sized stones, which he'd discovered embedded in the moist dirt.

These tasks complete, he reached for his mobile phone and punched the number for Kinsella. Tazeki allowed the phone to ring twice before clicking it off. Their method of communication had never failed in their many years together. His henchman would call back in less than ten minutes.

Kinsella would have flown from Brussels after Prince Mir's sordid little fetish party, he imagined, and be somewhere in Italy by now. He'd be seeing to the disposal of the American detective's body. Good riddance. The man was but a boil on the ass of a leprous zebra. And he was hardly worth the brain cells that he, Tazeki, had already wasted on his amateurish meddling.

Not far from where he now knelt, placed inside a separate set of bushes, he had secured the blond-haired female's head atop a four-foot pike. Her clouded green eyes stared vacuously into the night, seeing nothing—yet seeing all. Her vision was now guided by the loa. She would be his "watcher," eyes and ears scanning the darkness for any threat.

Tazeki had dumped the headless body somewhere off in the thicker bushes, half buried, angled so her blood could seep back into the earth. The insects were already flocking to it, as if a dinner bell had rung. Later, after he'd removed the hex and departed, the night birds would come to investigate, drawn by the coppery scent. They'd be followed, in turn, by the smaller mammals. The remains of her drained and blackened body would be discovered days from now, by then little more than a putrid and picked-over carcass.

Ten minutes came and went. Then fifteen. No return call from Kinsella.

Glancing at his phone, Tazeki willed his partner to respond to his summons. The phone, however, failed to vibrate, remaining quiet in the tall bushes. While this proved annoying, it did not alter the botono's plan. Not in the least. If there was one person on the planet he trusted, it was his old childhood friend Nmanu.

Darkness had now descended in earnest. He gazed off into the backyard of the property. Tazeki could discern one entire side of the house, along with the back driveway and wide apron, which ran in front of the home's connected, double-stall garage. In the opposite direction, maybe a quarter of the front lawn was visible, where it stretched towards more tall bushes and, at last, the front street corner.

The outside security lights flicked on. They cast a frozen spotlight on the backyard and upper driveway, stopping at the edge of the tree-line, with its more skittish night shadows.

From his pocket, Tazeki withdrew a small vial of crème-yellow powder. Holding it to his nose, he inhaled, before pocketing the vial again. He would bide his time. Patience was a quality that the botono—like every other houngan and witch doctor worth their salt—was familiar with. He believed in the age-old aphorism:

"Vengeance done best, is vengeance worth the wait."

———

Inside the house, the living room furniture had been pushed aside, the rugs raised. Chloe had drawn a chalk circle on the maple wood floor of the living room. Within the circle she drew a pentacle. She scribbled a series of elaborate lines and Latin words alongside the five-pointed star.

"Chloe?" Maggie fought to control her voice. "Do you mind telling me what—"

"It's a protective circle," Chloe said, looking up. She still had on the blue slacks and purple blouse she'd worn to church. Yet from her oversized handbag, which she always kept inside her car, she had accessorized her look with rings on eight of her fingers, four silver bracelets per arm, and an ivory scrimshaw necklace. For protection.

Chloe had put on these adornments after they'd discovered the bloody horror nailed to Maggie's backdoor. They warded against evil.

Hank leaped up onto the pushed-aside couch, an excellent observation point. "If we can lure his ass into the circle," Chloe continued, knowingly, "close off the portals of escape, we should be all right."

"'Portals of escape'?" Maggie frowned. "You can't be serious."

"Doors. If that works better for you."

Maggie measured her words. "And who are we trying to trap in the circle, again? This...this Mr. Voodoo Man?"

Chloe's look at her sister was narrow. "He's here—remember? The same witch doctor who fancied-up the backdoor?" She placed six white votive candles around the circle, lighted them, mumbled an incantation beneath her breath. More protection.

"And you know how to draw this, uh, 'protective circle' and stuff...how, exactly?"

"It's in Aunt Fay's old journals. I read them on nights when I can't fall asleep." Chloe swiped her brow with the back of her hand. Her bracelets jangled. "It doesn't take a law degree, you know."

Maggie stayed silent for a few beats.

"But Father Larchezi was here yesterday. Blessing the house? Wasn't that the point?"

"And you saw what happened to the backdoor, didn't you?"

"Are you—are you saying it didn't work?" Maggie's words expressed her concern, and her frown remained. "It kept Mr. Voodoo Man outside, didn't it?"

Chloe puffed her cheeks and exhaled. "That's just it—we can't be sure. What if we're dealing with super strong juju? Or even worse, demonic entities?" Her tone left little margin for debate. "We've got to try everything we can. Right now—for real. For every protective measure we put up, this bastard might have a counter-hex."

She glanced at Maggie and narrowed her eyes. "Especially if he is who I think he is."

"Who you *think* he is?"

"Very powerful. A voodoo priest." Chloe took a breath. "An Obeah man, a conjurer. *Enorme juju.*" She had reported this without hesitation. As if to emphasize her point, she added: "A houngan. Or a botono, if you will."

Maggie was nibbling one knuckle, her thoughts chasing around in her head like coyote pups after their tails. She needed Chloe to stay rational—at least until Slink got here.

She had phoned Detective Dooley within minutes after finding the bloody bird tacked to the backdoor. She'd left a message. When Slink returned her call, she'd asked him to come over—at once—to check on them. Make certain that they were all right. When Slink accused her of sounding "spooked," Maggie had laughed away his concern.

After hanging up, however, she'd decided Slink was right: her laugh had sounded closer to the cackle of a crazy woman.

"That colored chalk won't stain the floor, will it?" Maggie now asked.

"Everything will be back to normal. Once he's vamoosed."

"Vamoosed?"

"The hell outta here!"

Slipping away to the kitchen, Maggie poured herself a glass of merlot. She'd be damned if she was going to wait for Cale another five hours without fortification. Chloe was driving her insane. If the "witch's circle" could offer protection from her sister, she'd be happy to hop inside herself.

With one hip against the countertop, Maggie took a sip of wine. She was pleased that she'd changed into jeans and a light summer sweater after returning from church. This was going to be one long, long night.

And it didn't take a psychic to figure that much out.

CHAPTER 45

Slink Dooley parked the pewter Taurus behind Chloe's Buick on the apron of the Van Waring driveway. It was approaching ten p.m. and the outside security lights were as stark as the kliegs on a film set. It had taken longer to run Cale's errands than he had imagined, but it was Saturday night, and Slink's wife understood he was out working a case. Consequently, the time mattered little. He decided that a beer or two before heading home would be a splendid idea.

Dressed in casual jeans and an untucked polo shirt, Slink carried a large cardboard box, balancing a plastic evidence bag on top. As he approached the house, he studied the backdoor, the walkway, the shrubbery, all for signs of recent vandalism. Nothing appeared amiss. The ladies had tidied it up, scrubbed the area clean. It didn't require much detecting skill to notice the lingering odor of Clorox.

At least he wouldn't have to write up a report.

Crickets sounded their chorus from the lawns and adjacent bushes. Rapping twice, Slink let himself into the house, calling, "Anybody home?"

He was trying not to startle the inhabitants. He wondered why they hadn't bothered locking the door, with as rattled as Maggie had sounded earlier. She'd practically told him Jason Voorhees was stalking the neighborhood in his hockey mask.

"We're in here! The living room," Maggie called.

Closing the door with his foot, Slink set the large box on the kitchen countertop. He placed the evidence bag alongside it. He headed through the dining room and stopping beneath the arch that separated it from the living room. He blinked as he took in the moved furniture and the ornate drawing on the floor, where Chloe knelt, a blue piece of chalk in one hand a few shades lighter than her blouse.

Not knowing what to say, Slink blurted: "Good thing I'm not the Chemist." He put a cop's edge in his voice.

"Meaning?" Maggie asked. She was sitting on the edge of a sofa and held a glass of merlot in one hand. It appeared nearly full, Slink noted.

"Meaning your door's unlocked. Any monster trolling the neighborhood could've walked in here unannounced."

Stopping her art work, Chloe sat back on her haunches, frowning. She pointed her piece of chalk and narrowed her eyes at her sister.

"I locked it. I swear." As she protested, Maggie's eyes roped them both, one to the next. "When I flicked on the security lights. After what happened—earlier."

Maggie rose from the sofa and stomped into the dining room in her stocking feet. Slink watched her as she moved across the kitchen and checked the backdoor lock again. Flicked it open and closed. She bolted it, the metal slapping into place.

By this time Chloe had risen and, carrying her own mug of tea, trailed after her sister. She moved past Slink, mocking Maggie with a head shake as she stepped through the dining room, then into the kitchen.

Slink followed dutifully behind Chloe. He stopped just inside the kitchen. Hank sauntered after them both, arching his furry back, brushing against Slink's ankles where he stood, as if now accepting that the detective was no threat to the household.

Maggie leaned against the kitchen counter edge, facing them, holding her wine glass in front of her chest like a weapon.

"You Chlorox'd the evidence off the door." Slink stated this, knowing what had been there. Maggie had texted him a picture from her phone. Nasty art work, all right. Vandals. No evident gang tags—unlikely, as they were, in this suburban neighborhood.

"Kids, no doubt. Go figure." Chloe waved a dismissive hand, and the flash of her bracelets caught the light.

Slink studied them both, his detective skills being tested. Law enforcement and psychics, he understood, did not have a great history of working together. And vandalism was seldom considered a serious crime. Slink imagined that Chloe might not want to get involved, not want to provide any sort of official statement.

He could already hear the jokes down at the station: "A famous psychic like Chloe Jeffers? Shouldn't she have seen it coming?" Along those lines. Cops' humor.

Best to let it go, Slink decided. Sleeping dogs and all that.

As if of the same mind, both ladies shifted their attention to the presents Slink had deposited on the kitchen counter. The large box and the smaller plastic evidence bag.

The bag contained Maggie's handgun, the Kahr PM9, along with a half-full box of ammo and the spare clip. He had retrieved the weapon from the department's forensics lab late that afternoon, before heading out to the airport to pick up the items Cale had requested.

"At any rate, Merry Christmas from Italy." Slink pointed at the large box and stepped over to the refrigerator. He fished out a bottle of beer. Twisted the cap, took a healthy swig. "I put your gun on the counter, there." Pointing with the bottle, speaking to Maggie, he said, "Clip's loaded, safety on. Got it back from Evidence. You're officially cleared in the Crenshaw shooting."

"Hooray." Maggie shrugged, unenthused. The entire mess had been a mistake in the first place, as far as she was concerned,

"The bastard dead yet?" Chloe asked, an edge to her voice.

"Holding on. Far as we know."

"Somebody pull the plug. Put him out of his misery." Chloe harbored no sentiment for the man who'd kidnapped and raped her sister. She lifted her chin at the box. "Cale shipped this here? Did he say why?"

Maggie stepped over and slid the bag with the handgun against the wall beneath the upper cupboard. With a steak knife, she slit open the large box's flaps. She peered inside like a ten-year-old with a birthday gift.

Slink lifted an indifferent shoulder. "He said it was *importanto*. Overnighted it. Had me pick it up at the airport."

"See, Mags?" Chloe chortled. "Your fiancé hasn't forgotten you."

"Hopeless romantic, ain't he?" Slink winked at Chloe. Reaching down, he scratched the fur on Hank's back. "I dropped one item off at our forensics lab. A female shrunken head, in case you're curious."

Maggie crinkled her face. "Tell me you're kidding."

241

"I never kid about shrunken heads."

"I find them fascinating. Personally." Chloe reported this with a lilt to her voice. "They have a pretty cool *je ne sais quoi* factor."

"Maybe to you." Maggie reached into the box and lifted out a fifteen-inch statuette. Held it in the air. "This is so *not* Gucci!"

"Whoa." Slink took a pull from his bottle. "Hope Cale doesn't draw my name for Christmas."

It was a bronze-colored, ceramic, Buddha-like creature. The eyes seemed to possess a life-like, charcoal glint; and it bore the sinister smirk of a bobcat who'd just swallowed a juicy pigeon.

Hank arched his back, and his hackles rose. Emitting a throaty growl, he sped from the kitchen, disappearing down the hallway. Chloe, for her part, reacted not much differently. Before Maggie could utter a word, her sister grabbed the idol from her hands and dashed off in the opposite direction. She headed toward the living room, bracelets jangling as she moved.

"Chloe! What the...?" Maggie shadowed after her sister, moving from kitchen to dining room to living room—the way a mother trails a nap-resistant four-year-old.

Slink moved behind them both, sipping his beer, watching the ladies with a bemused look.

———

In the middle of the living room, Chloe placed the foot-high object in the center of the pentacle. Trapping it, she knew, inside the witch's circle. Maggie watched as her sister recited a series of foreign words she'd never heard before. Latin? Maybe something older? A hex of her own? A protective spell? Or an incantation? She'd learned long ago that with Chloe, she could seldom be sure.

Finishing her odd chant, Chloe then beelined from the room, heading back through the dining room and into the kitchen. Maggie could hear her rummaging through the cupboards near the stove and glanced over at Slink. She gave him a helpless shrug. Chloe rushed back into the living room, where she began pouring salt from a carton of Morton's. She encircled the witch's circle and pentacle, further trapping—she explained—the statuette inside.

"Salt. Double protection." This was her explanation.

242

At last she stepped back from her handiwork. Chloe observed the mess on the floor with the same tight-lipped satisfaction a French chef reserves for a perfect soufflé.

"Bravo!" Slink clapped like he'd just viewed a live performance. "I knew coming here would be better than anything on TV."

Maggie shook her head. "Don't encourage her. Please."

Slink confirmed the time: ten-forty now. He strode back to the kitchen, where he set his empty bottle on the countertop near the sink. Having followed behind him, Maggie grabbed the empty and rinsed it out. She placed it in the recycling bin inside the closet and closed the door.

Slink stepped halfway down the hallway and disappeared into the bathroom. He mumbled something about renting beer instead of buying it, while closing the door. But Maggie wasn't listening.

———

In the kitchen, she gathered all the discarded wrapping tape and crumpled newspapers and packing filler. She pressed the bundle back inside the cardboard box and closed the flaps.

Maggie pictured Cale packing the items. Like many men she knew, he had little talent when it came to gift wrapping. It didn't escape her how snugly he'd managed to secure the inner contents, despite his usual irreverent style. Maggie decided to leave the box on the countertop, figuring it was out of the way where it was. While all this was happening, Chloe remained in the living room, preoccupied with the diminutive statue, as if she was catching up with a long-lost acquaintance.

Three minutes later, Slink emerged from the bathroom. He informed them he was bidding them farewell for the evening. Cale would be home in another few hours. He could resume command of the Van Waring Asylum for the Mentally Challenged.

"Keep the security lights on," he advised Maggie in a fatherly tone. "And be sure and keep little Bubba there locked inside the magic circle." He'd made finger quotes saying this, and pondering the moment, Slink added, "I don't think I've ever spoken those words out loud before."

Maggie issued him a wan smile.

With the assurance that Chloe would watch over them like a mother hawk, she opened the door and ushered Detective Dooley out into the cool, fresh air of the night.

A thumping bass sound was coming from somewhere not too far off. It sounded low and distant, as if from blocks away. Maybe teens having a graduation party. It sounded like that. Maggie decided it wouldn't bother her. She'd be staying up late waiting for Cale, regardless.

"Tell Janet I'll call her," Maggie said with a nod.

"I'll do that." Slink was thoughtful for a moment. "You need anything, call me on my phone at once. Got it?"

"Got it, Dad."

"Cute."

Slink turned from the house with a wave. He called back over his shoulder: "Don't wait up too late. Any sort of flight delay, he might not make it home before daybreak."

She nodded again and bid him goodnight.

Mindful of moths and flies and other airborne insects, Maggie closed the door. This cut the noise of the distant bass sounds. Pulling the small curtain aside, she watched Slink's lean figure cut across the driveway apron and disappear around the edge of the garage, where he vanished from sight.

CHAPTER 46

Across the neighboring streets and lawns, the houses and adjacent parks, it was just another Saturday night. The shadowy trees stood tall, like guardians at a castle wall. The bushes around them were swollen and prickly. On the quiet streets, traffic had become sparse with the setting sun, and the homes showed faint flickers of light from within. Yet beneath the umbrella of his spell, all sounds of nature were controlled by the maestro, the dark botono.

No noise, in fact, was being emitted from inside the Van Waring house. While outside the home, the low thumping of the log drums played—a summoning sound that opened the gateway to the Old Gods.

Deep inside the high bushes, Tazeki was now in full houngan mode. He had applied white ringlets around his eyes and matching streaks along each side of his face. He was shirtless. Paint smears ran down his smooth, dark torso. He knelt before his makeshift altar on the ground with his head lowered. His hex had been cast out to the furthest edges of the property, an invisible bubble designed to encapsulate all that he desired to control.

Raising his head, the witch doctor now called on Papa Legba to open the gates of the Underworld—to summon forth the loa that he sought. He expressed his desire through the intercession of Matre Kalfu, for a sinister *baka* to assist him: a poisonous loa, a serpent.

Despite the low persistent drumming, Tazeki was alert to any foreign noise, to any movement in the dark that he did not wish to be there. From twenty feet away, through the unblinking eyes of the blonde's head, elevated on its pike, he watched the man in the polo shirt emerge from the backdoor of the house. The man walked toward the pair of vehicles, which were parked at the far edge of the driveway's wide apron.

Tazeki watched, and he waited.

———

Slink crossed the driveway, heading toward his Taurus. He could hear those damn party drums thumping again.

As he moved, he felt a cool tremor of premonition slide up his spine—his internal detective's instinct. For a moment, he considered turning back, reentering the house and staying on guard. At least until Cale arrived home from the airport. But Slink's common sense got the better of him, and he decided the idea was silly. Especially the way Maggie's sister was behaving, as if she'd been smoking hashish.

A pentacle? Morton's salt? A witch's circle? Then sticking the little Buddha statue inside the ring, trapping it as if it might be Hannibal Lecter. Perhaps she was loopy on pain meds, as well?

She must be floating on some kind of high, Slink reasoned. Maybe sniffing too many perm fumes down at the beauty salon.

Near his car now, Slink heard a different noise. It sounded like the pounding music he'd heard earlier, but now it was issuing from the far side of the property. Or was it from down the block? With the low cloud cover, he couldn't be sure. Probably kids camping out, having harmless fun. A graduation party? A birthday bash? Slink imagined that if he listened close enough, he might hear splashing in a backyard pool. Voices laughing in the night.

His detective senses on alert now, he noticed how sweet and summery the air smelled, like lavender or lilac. At any rate, it seemed to be issuing from the high bushes across the way, near the property line along the side of the house.

Once again, he considered Chloe's odd behavior. Slink shook away the thought—it was not his problem. But something strange was in the air tonight. Perhaps he shouldn't just accept that it was vandals who had defaced Maggie's backdoor. Maybe there was more going on here. Something he was missing.

Slink stopped in the middle of the driveway. His vehicle was fifteen feet away. He considered his weapon for a moment, knowing it sat holstered in the car's glove box. He shrugged away the paranoia. Why would he need his gun? This was his best friend's house on a Saturday night. Besides, he wasn't even clocked in, and this was hardly a crime scene. It was just some kids having a party down the block. What else could it be?

For no reason he could put his finger on, Slink decided to cut across the lawn. Something about the high bushes seemed to draw him.

As he approached the tree line, the sweet odor of jasmine—yes, that's what it was—became stronger. The drumming sounded more intense over here. He noticed a dozen tiny lights flickering inside the dense vegetation. Fireflies? Lightening bugs?

Without warning, Slink felt his body jerk. It was as if something heavy had fallen from the clouds and landed on his upper back. Whatever it was, it was clinging to his shoulders like an invisible weight. His muscles spasmed. He felt his face grimace and contort. Slink's arms and legs went rigid, as if he'd been injected with a neurotoxin. His body lurched, and he felt himself propelled forward, heading straight into the thick bushes like a man walking blindly into a forest.

And then, Slink Dooley felt nothing.

———

Tazeki slipped from the cover of the bushy thicket, the lofty elm branches swaying above him in the night breeze. He ramped the drumbeats up a level and sized-up the *nzambi* he had created.

With the invisible loa riding his back, the man's face bore a likeness to the baka serpent. It made Tazeki smile. He moved away from the bushes, striding across the grass, keeping inside the shadows and out of the glow of the security lights. Behind him, moving with a dead-legged gait, the zombie followed like an obedient pet.

Tazeki looked over his shoulder, back at the thicket. He could see the blonde-haired female, her head on its pike. Her dull green eyes followed their progress, watching owl-like, as if with some vague and undefined interest.

At the zombie's car, he searched the man's pants pockets, locating his set of keys. He clicked open the door locks with the remote fob. Leaning inside, he fished the .38 special revolver from the glove box. He closed the door without making a sound.

Handing the weapon to the zombie, Tazeki led the way across the lawn, moving in silence around the shadowy side of the house. They strode to the backbeat of the *tanbu* drums, which pounded their rhythm beneath the canopy of stars, of curling clouds, of the peeking, butter-eyed moon.

———

Candles flickered around the magic circle. Standing a few feet away, watching with a keen eye, Chloe stood with her arms crossed. She studied the fifteen-inch demonic figure. It seemed to now be glowing a soft orange, as if somehow lit from within. She decided she must be imagining it.

Hearing the thumping sounds from somewhere outside, Chloe strode back into the dining room. She eased aside the curtain and peeked out into the darkness alongside the house. Nothing there. Was it bass speakers she was hearing? It was a dull percussion that sounded like a gangsta SUV, as it performed a slow cruise through the neighborhood.

"What's with that noise?" Maggie asked, emerging from the bathroom. "Did you turn on the TV?"

"It's from outside somewhere," Chloe reported. She allowed the curtain to slide back in place as she watched her sister open the refrigerator door. "Think you've had enough wine?" she asked. Then, as only a sister can snark: "You're pregnant. Remember?"

"I told you—that Swedish study?" Maggie rolled her eyes at her sister. "Moderation, remember? Nutritional flavonoids. A couple nips are healthy."

"Flavonoids. Right. You believe everything you read?"

"Hello? Swedish!" Maggie frowned. "I believe it because it makes sense."

Chloe couldn't stop herself from feeling skeptical, but who was she to talk? She was someone who believed in magic and hexes, in psychic visions and voodoo spells, and yes, in witch's circles. She also believed in evil demons warning her that *He is coming!*

She decided it best to keep her comments to herself. Maggie seemed edgy enough, as it was. So maybe not a good idea to push

248

her buttons tonight. Cale would be arriving home very late. He and Maggie had more than a few issues they needed to discuss. Her sister, Chloe understood, wasn't in the mood for any additional stress on her plate at the moment.

"Smart move, Chlo," her inner voice chided. "Keep your big trap shut."

"Besides—two glasses can't hurt." Maggie held the half-filled bottle of merlot aloft. "I thought we were celebrating. Cale should be here in another few hours."

Chloe shook her head. "I'm not your mother."

"You act like it sometimes."

"What's that supposed to mean?"

Standing at the edge of the living room/dining room, beneath the ceiling arch, Chloe shifted her eyes past where Maggie stood. She peered down the long hallway that led up the small steps to the family room. And beyond that, the sliding doors to the adjacent outside deck.

She could see the Weber grill in its usual spot. Hank, she noticed, was sitting steadfast in his lookout at the top of the steps. His ears were perked. Chloe knew he could hear the thumping sounds, but the fur on his neck was not hackling. No evident danger. Not at the moment, anyway.

Jesus! Chloe wondered. Why did she feel so stressed? What was going on here tonight?

Maggie remained in the kitchen, bending over, still peering inside the refrigerator door. She must be feeling better, Chloe decided, if she was searching for something to eat. She didn't like the way Maggie had allowed herself to get so thin. Yet she understood the pressure her sister was under, not to mention the morning sickness. Eating something couldn't hurt—even if it was due more to nerves than actual hunger.

Maggie called over her shoulder: "Can we put some music on, at least? Macy Gray? Or something soft?"

"I like it quiet. Helps me think."

Chloe remained standing where she was. She shifted her attention back into the living room, staring over at the evil bronze statue. There was no denying it: the diminutive Buddha was ever so slightly beginning to change. Was it possible? An optical illusion? Some trick of the flickering candlelight?

No. Chloe decided that she was not mistaken. The object was beginning to take on a faint reddish glow.

She watched as the demon's fixed smirk seemed to turn into a more sinister scowl. She heard her inner voice caution: "Keep it together, Chlo. Now's not the time for your imagination to start performing cartwheels."

CHAPTER 47

"You have no power over me, witch!"

The greasy, tremulous voice spoke deep and clear. It came—Chloe understood—from within the diminutive statue. Yet, the worst of it was, it did not speak out loud. It sounded only inside her head.

She was shocked and surprised, and when Chloe stumbled backward, the edge of an end table scraped her knee. She gripped the tall leaning mirror standing against the wall, holding it with one hand, using it to steady herself.

She stared at the smirk-faced, short and sinister little idol. Was she imagining it had just spoken to her?

Glowing brighter, as if unable to remain silent any longer, the scratchy voice from deep within the statue rang inside her head once more, alive in a venom-reeking gust of breath: "I am Pazuzu! King of the Wind Demons! Master of fornicators and liars and thieves!"

Whoa! Chloe thought darkly. She hadn't been drinking—so maybe Maggie was right? Perhaps this was a good time to start.

A sudden, whirling breeze swept through the room, causing the candles to dance and curtains to flap. A misty gray haze steamed out from the idol's petulant lips. But trapped by the protective circle, the noxious fog drifted up to the room's ceiling, where it lingered, brooding like a miniature Chernobyl cloud.

Chloe was thankful she was a safe distance away. She remained at the junction between living and dining rooms. A crossroads, she reminded herself grimly.

"Did you open a window?" Maggie called from the kitchen. She was standing, facing the sink. She grabbed her glass of merlot and turned, eyeing her sister twenty-feet away.

Chloe's inner voice warned: "Don't tell Maggie the crazy statue spoke to you—she'll freak!"

She called to Maggie, her voice trembling: "No! Just checking the locks."

A screeching howl sliced through her comment, freezing them where they stood. Chloe gazed back down the long hallway. Up on the stairs landing, Hank's back arched like a Halloween cat. His eyes were as round as two green traffic lights. He was looking up at a distorted face pressed against the glass of the outside deck doors.

The face was expressionless, with its black button eyes peering dully into the house.

Hank bolted down the steps, the hallway, then disappeared into the kitchen. But Chloe wasn't watching the cat anymore. Her eyes were locked on the contorted face looking in through the glass— Slink Dooley's face.

"What in the—" Maggie cried out, standing frozen as the cat shot past her feet. She tripped and the wine glass dropped from her hand. It shattered, spraying crimson liquid and shards of glass across the floor, the lower cabinet doors, and the hallway baseboards.

Hank, a frightened blur, scampered into the dining room, where Chloe stood beneath the ceiling arch. His padded paws slid across the wood floors. He careened past her, darting wildly into the living room.

Chloe felt a sense of dread sweep over her. She witnessed the feline in a skid, sliding like a base-stealer...heading straight toward the protective ring where the diminutive statue stood. She screamed, "*Noooo!*" as she watched the cat blast through the salt ring, smearing the markings. He hurtled past the idol and out the opposite edge of the circle.

Two of the candles had toppled, spraying hot wax. They were left in his trail as Hank vanished from view, diving into the dark bathroom at the far end of the living room.

Laughter pierced Chloe's brain, a stabbing ice pick of sinister glee. She dropped to her knees in pain, grabbing her head as she peered up at the ceiling. The greasy gray cloud drifted beyond where the circle's boundary had been. It reminded her of a genie set free from its urn.

Chloe understood now that the cloud, itself—and not the bronze statue—was the demonic entity named Pazuzu.

———

Maggie was confused. Something had frightened Hank senseless. She stared down at the crimson puddle spreading across the floor, and the bits of glass around her stocking feet. In the living room, Chloe was shouting, panicked. And she could hear heavier glass breaking—the outside deck doors?

A dark thought invaded Maggie's mind: Someone (maybe more than one) was breaking into the house.

Her eyes studied the kitchen, where grabbed a long knife from the wooden block near the stove. Should she dash toward the family room? The outside deck? Investigate? No, not smart. The intruders would spot her. Where she now stood, she was hidden in the kitchen's low light, and they might not have noticed her yet.

Could she use this to her advantage? Maggie wondered. Should she stay hidden, then rush forward at the right moment and attack with the knife? Or was it better to run headlong straight at them, ready to slice and dice?

Her dilemma, her choice...and she had five seconds to decide.

It took an instant for Maggie to realize that chancing either of the above would rank high on the stupidity scale. Both choices added-up to the fastest way of getting herself killed.

Her and the baby.

She knew she had to remain silent. Cale, she remembered, had always advised her to get away from any unknown threat. To find a weapon and assess the situation from a safe distance. But what about Chloe? She couldn't just abandon her sister, leave her alone in the house, could she?

She could—but only as the last available option.

The backdoor was just five steps away. Maggie pictured herself escaping outside, running to the neighbors for help. Then again, no. The invaders—multiple?—would have anticipated such a move. They'd have the back exit covered. She would run straight into their arms the way panicky teenagers did in horror movies.

Trying to remain calm, Maggie's eyes searched the room, spying the basement door. Downstairs. It was the best chance she had of escaping unseen, of calling for help. She wondered where she'd left her phone. No matter. There was a landline in the basement. She could call 911. Or better yet, call Slink. He had left just ten minutes ago. He could return faster than any first responders could manage. No questions asked.

Queasy with terror, overwhelmed by guilt for abandoning Chloe, Maggie tiptoed across the kitchen. Unseen in the low light, she stepped on a sharp piece of broken glass, slicing the arch of her foot. She winced, gasping, ignoring the pain. Limping on her heel, she continued forward and eased open the door that led to the basement.

Maggie peered down into the throat of narrow darkness. It was the smartest move she had—away from the threat—and she slipped on through.

Gentling the door closed behind her, she flicked on the light switch. She hobbled down the steps as quiet as she could manage, knife in one hand, using the railing like a crutch. She glanced back at the red imprints trailing behind her. She was unable to discern if the spots were blood or spilled merlot. The cordless phone was on the table, next to the old couch. She lifted the receiver. From memory, she pushed the buttons for Slink's mobile number and thought she could hear a faint ringing sound upstairs.

When his voicemail message ended, she whispered as loud as she dared: "Slink! Someone's breaking into the house. Get back over here! Now!"

She next dialed 911. No answer—nothing but dead air. Maggie could hear heavy footsteps moving through the house above. She limped back to the base of the stairs and killed the lights. She dialed 911 once more. Silence—no dial tone. Standing in the dark, panic closing in, her mind screamed: What the hell is happening?

Calm breaths. Deep and silent breaths. Her heart thudding in her chest, Maggie set the phone on the carpeted basement floor. Rescue wasn't answering, but it didn't matter, did it?

Slink would get her message and be back here in a matter of minutes. She was sure of it. Slink was the cavalry. He would return, and he would save them.

Standing frozen in the dark, holding the knife to her chest, her foot seeping blood, Maggie wanted to slap herself.

Why hadn't she grabbed her gun from the countertop?

CHAPTER 48

Shattered glass. Glinting shards flying in all directions. The *nzambi* kneed open the outer deck door, splintering the wooden frame as he entered. He held the handgun loose at his thigh while he lurched his way forward. The jungle drums were pounding the background rhythm, shakers rattling, and Tazeki followed his henchman into the house.

With the *nzambi* moving stiff-legged, his eyes glazed, together they descended the steps from the family room, down to the first-floor of the spacious split-level home. Staying four paces behind, Tazeki surveyed the rooms as they progressed. He was familiar with the house's layout, having seen it during his astral journeys and scrying, of course—his crimson pinprick eyes.

They moved down the hallway, past the bathroom, then into the open kitchen—where an explosion of burgundy and glass shards had splashed across the floor and lower cupboards. And at last into the larger dining room area.

Now standing beneath the high ceiling arch, Tazeki eyed the disarray in the living room—and he studied the witch-woman standing alone amid the clutter.

His zombie stood to one side, awaiting orders, as if on pause. Tazeki eyeballed the redhaired harlot, as if sizing up her potential as an adversary.

The female stood in the center of the room, positioned inside a damaged protective chalk circle. She'd placed her feet on each side of the diminutive (crudely smirking) statue of Pazuzu. She had grabbed a plain wooden crucifix from somewhere, and now clutched it to her chest. The same cross the priest had used, Tazeki imagined, during his comical house blessing.

The percussion continued its pounding, the house filled with throbbing rhythm. The witch doctor gave her a rueful smile. It caused the witch to cringe, taking a half-step back, staying inside the circle—which had been breached, and no longer offered the slightest protection.

The witch now extended the crucifix out like a weapon. She appeared to have attempted a hasty repair of the broken salt ring, and seemed uncertain whether to flee, or to stay and confront the intruders.

"Slink?" Chloe called out. Her voice trembled. "What's going on? What are you doing back here?"

The zombie looked at her, mute, cocking its head to one side.

Tazeki watched as the witch swung her gaze back to him, fixing him with the crucifix as if it were a Colt .45.

"I called 9-1-1, asshole!" She barked this over the relentless throbbing sounds. "The police—they're on the way!"

Tazeki offered her a sadistic grin. "My hex on the house...the entire property. No signal will reach outside the bubble."

Pazuzu's wheezy breathing seeped down from one corner of the ceiling, sounding like an infected bellows. It was thick, wet and raspy, dripping with evil. He was a moldy-gray haze now, hovering above them like a noxious cloud.

The witch doctor studied his demon friend, said nothing, then swung his eyes back to the witch.

"Stay back!" Chloe waved the cross protectively.

The painted psycho stood twelve feet away, standing at the border of the dining room. She shot her eyes up at the ceiling demon, then over to Slink, standing like an upright corpse.

"Slink! What are you... Snap out of it—we need your help!"

The zombie continued staring at her with his black-button eyes.

"Your safety ring?" Tazeki shook his head, making a *tsk-tsk* sound. "And that stupid piece of wood... Amateurs."

"You think you're hot shit," Chloe spat. "But you're something else, aren't you? Something more than evil."

Tazeki smirked. "Care to enlighten us?" He looked about the room at his two partners.

"You're also *insane!*"

Chloe fired the crucifix at him, then spun around and broke from the circle. She was heading for the back of the living room. Dodging furniture, she ran toward the rear hallway—an escape route.

The witch doctor placed his fingers to his lips and blew them open again *voila!* As if he'd fired a blowgun, his action sent Chloe airborne. She tumbled into an end table, crashing the lamp, landing hard on her back and moaning in pain.

To the zombie, Tazeki commanded: "The basement. Bring me the other one. Alive!" The zombie stomped away toward the kitchen, the handgun held low in his fist.

When he glanced back at the witch, he saw she was attempting to pull herself to her knees. Time to put her out of her misery, he decided. Watching her head and shoulders lift groggily above the back of a sofa, he withdrew a pinch of red powder from the front pocket of his pants.

Tazeki blew the powder in the witch's direction and watched her drop to the floor with a discernible thud.

Then all he heard was the guttural throb of the *tanbu*.

———

He had no concept of time. An hour was a minute, a minute a day. For Tazeki Mabutu—for any botono casting a voodoo spell—time was as irrelevant as graveyards and fairy dust and wood ash blowing in an autumn wind.

His zombie had carried Van Waring's dark-haired bitch up from the basement: breathing, unconscious, unharmed for the most part. He'd placed her on a couch up in the family room. The sister-witch—as of anyone cared—lay frozen in the living room, where Tazeki had left her.

Pazuzu was an odious gray cloud drifting room to room, free of the statue's prison for the first time in centuries. Tazeki didn't mind if his friend was loose. He wasn't going anywhere. Even if he did manage to slip outside, and attempt to fly off, the invisible enchanted barrier would keep him trapped. He allowed the demon—an evil, psychopathic entity—to drift through the air like a ghost ship cruising through midnight waters.

Seeping in between the open window blinds, high in the night sky, *Lshne* cast silver slices of moonlight down into the room. Her glow was aided by the security lights ablaze across the outside deck. The drumbeat was softer now, subdued, as if in preparation for the serious ceremony about to take place.

The time had arrived for Tazeki to perform his examination.

In the same room he'd spied upon before, he now approached the unconscious female. He remembered her name was Maggie. Tazeki nudged aside the wooden coffee table with his foot, creating space for himself. He knelt beside the couch, where the *nzambi* had placed her.

Her capture, he knew, had been quite easy. She'd been unable to slice the man with her knife—incapable of inflicting harm on her fiancé's closest friend, his partner, the man scheduled to stand as best man at their upcoming nuptials.

Not much chance of that happening now, Tazeki knew. It was difficult to marry a man currently floating face down in the Mediterranean, courtesy of the assassin Tebbi Qa.

After taking the knife from the woman, the zombie had choked her into unconsciousness. He been careful not to snuff away her final gasp of breath. She was dreaming now, he imagined, perhaps of her most frightening childhood nightmares. Or maybe of monsters lurking in closets. Or of boogiemen poised in the dusty darkness beneath her bed.

If she only knew how real, they were.

Withdrawing the serrated, curved blade from his waistband, Tazeki leaned in closer to the female. He listened for her breath, inhaled it through his flared nostrils, as around them the shakers rattled, and the drums continued to pound out their rhythm.

Her socks were soiled where she had stepped through the glass and wine on the kitchen floor. Her hair had been pulled back, clipped in place, but it was mussed now, and a few stray strands had fallen loose across her forehead. With his left hand he raised the thin fabric of her sweater above her rib cage. The pale skin of her stomach thus exposed, Tazeki unsnapped the top three buttons of her jeans, flaying them open the way a rib cage is spread during an autopsy.

He placed his ear on the warm, bare flesh of her stomach. He flicked his tongue, tasting her salty skin as a viper would.

Pulling his head back, he studied his patient. Focused on her eyelids, watching them flicker as she struggled with some deep inner torment. Raising the knife in the air, he swept the sharp blade inches above her abdomen in a figure-eight pattern. He was surprised to see her hands rise up—not to fight, not in defense—but as if to welcome the blade.

Her slender fingers wrapped over his own as he poised the knife mere inches above her firm, smooth flesh.

Tazeki saw tears seep from the corners of her eyes, cascading down her pale cheeks. Her lips mouthed the words "Do it! Please. Do it!" And when he lifted the blade away, her hands fell back to her sides, the spell broken.

Ahh, he told himself. I know now who the father is.

"A fat baby boy." He whispered to the darkness, more than he said this to himself. "Seasoned with the proper spices, I'm certain he will taste delicious."

CHAPTER 49

The green-checkered taxi pulled into the driveway, tires rolling over the weathered gray concrete. The vehicle eased to a stop halfway up the drive. Cale spotted Slink's Taurus up ahead, bathed in the dull wash of the cab's headlights. Further up was Chloe's Buick, equally pale in the shadows.

His and Maggie's vehicles, he guessed, were parked inside the garages.

Cale gazed out the side window of the cab. With the security lights dimmed, the house was cast in late-night shadows. Faint flickers of light escaped from the closed curtains of the dining room.

Somewhere far off, he could discern the thumping of a bass beat. It sounded blocks away. As if a basement stereo had been left on somewhere. This reminded Cale, darkly, of night drums, and in a panicky moment his thoughts flashed back to Liberia—where he had been inches away from losing his life. He shook away the memory, but the thumping sound persisted.

Something didn't feel right. Could it be kids? A quarter-mile away? Throwing an all-night party?

He glanced at his watch: 1:34 a.m. Why hadn't the neighbors complained? He damn sure would have. In fact, he was surprised there weren't uniforms knocking on some address right now, advising the occupants to turn off the racket.

Still, summer was almost here. A Saturday night. So maybe no one minded. Cale decided he was too worn out to care.

He carried no luggage. He had on the loaner clothes he'd been issued in Brussels, and a light windbreaker courtesy of Agent Fronteer. He had prepaid the cabby with cash he'd been issued, and now watched the vehicle drive off.

As he moved along the narrow walkway, which led to his backdoor, the thumping sound seemed to grow louder. Coming from inside his house? All of a sudden, the entire strange scenario made sense to him. A surprise party. Slink had no doubt bribed the cops to ignore the music, until Cale had arrived home.

He cursed to himself. Of all the stupid pranks. And being dead tired on top of it—this was not what he needed right now.

Cale located the spare key from beneath one of the flower bed rocks. He keyed the lock and steeled himself. His jaw tightened. Nevertheless, he was prepared to grin like an idiot, when they all leaped out of the shadows shouting *Surprise!*

———

In the family room of the split-level home, Tazeki tossed the blade aside. He rose and stepped away from the sofa, then eyed the ceiling, where the sentient fog that was Pazuzu had watched, while he'd examined the pregnant female.

He issued the demon an abrupt command. "Do it!"

Pazuzu did not hesitate. The clammy ooze swept down from the top of the room, an odious cloud bearing a hint of sulfur. The gray stream seeped into the female's nose and between her parted lips, as it invaded her body. Her skin took on the sudden chalky pallor of a corpse, and for a moment, she seemed content in her peaceful repose.

Looking on, Tazeki decided he'd seen enough. From one vessel to another, now his demon friend could do his blood work.

As he began to turn away, however, the woman's chest lifted and shuddered with a convulsion. Her face contorted, and her mouth grew wider than one would imagine possible. The greasy smoke that was Pazuzu came oozing back out of Maggie Jeffers. It sought the ceiling, where it hovered, watchful and resigned.

"What the hell's going on?" demanded Tazeki.

"*Ahhhhhhh. Botono...*" Pazuzu's mental voice was wet and raspy. "Your bitch is *tainted*. Her blood runs thick with *His* own."

Tazeki leaned forward and placed two fingers on the woman's arm, near her elbow. The flesh was warm. A clear image flashed into his mind: He pictured Van Waring's bitch standing in the communion line at the Catholic church, accepting the host from the priest on her tongue, swallowing it. Making the sign of *The Christ*.

Still in its blessed state, her soul-body was resistant to the demonic spirit's invasion. Resistant to evil.

261

The entity Pazuzu began to gather force. It swam in a giant gray swirl about the room, round and round, as if now a shark too big for its tank. Without pausing, it gusted through the shattered deck doors, breezing out into the fresh air of the chilled night.

The demon's voice sounded from afar. "Do with her what you will, Botono. I am escaped from my prison. I no longer do your bidding."

Tazeki was about to curse, to say something vengeful, or perhaps try what he could to prevent the demon's escape. Instead he stayed silent, and he felt the breeze and listened to the sound of the backdoor, as it swung quietly open.

CHAPTER 50

Pocketing his key, Cale stepped into the shadowy kitchen and closed the door at his back. The strange sound of low-thumping backbeat continued. Could it be coming from the basement? He wondered if Maggie had moved the party downstairs. He'd likely find his friends asleep on the worn couches there, beer cans scattered about, the flat-screen spinning some late-night cooking infomercial.

Faint light bled in through the edges if the adjacent dining room windows, Cale recognized the outline of the large cardboard box on the countertop. Near the wall behind it, he spotted a plastic evidence bag. He guessed it containing Maggie's handgun: the Kahr PM9. Slink had come through as promised. He'd procured the items Cale had requested from the airport storage facility. Hopefully, he had already handed off the shrunken head to the department's forensics lab.

So much for that prick Mabutu's precious African artifacts.

He stepped into the kitchen, and another dark thought struck: perhaps his friends were all cloistered in one of the nearby closets? Prepared to jump out like college kids in a frat house? Scare the hell out of him—great fun.

Cale flicked on the recessed kitchen lights and his breath caught in his throat. The grisly sight assaulted him, appearing like many of the crime scenes he'd studied over the years. A pool of slick blood, with glass and debris spread across the floor, with footprints smeared this way and that. Add in the red-brown spatter, which stained the walls and the adjacent baseboards.

Like a thousand different crime scenes.

And yet, upon further review, a more discerning look told a different story. Cale felt himself relax, and he exhaled.

This was not a scene of slaughter. No. He knew enough to understand that he was not looking at a pool of blood. The broken bits of glass and thick bouquet of merlot told him otherwise. Someone had had an accident here. But it had been a wine spill. Nothing more. And they'd failed to clean up the mess.

Cale felt his heart unclench. Still, something was not quite kosher with this picture.

Heavy footprints, he saw now, had clomped their way through the auburn puddle. Smeary tracks leading one way—to the basement door—then back the other, before trailing off down the hallway. They appeared headed toward the family room. But did the pattern make sense?

Cale's instincts were on high alert. For the first time since he'd boarded the plane in Brussels, he wished he had his gun.

Cautious now in the low light, he stepped with care around the wine spill. Instead of following the footprints toward the steps, he chose the opposite direction—playing a hunch. He made his way into the dining room, casting wary eyes as he moved, and when he peered into the living room from beneath the ceiling arch, he could not believe his eyes.

A pair of candles still flickered, throwing faint shadows against the far wall. Other candles had been knocked over, extinguished, lying like slain soldiers on a battlefield. The room was a nightmare. Furniture was toppled, lamps, tables and chairs flung about.

And standing alone in the midst of it all—inside some half-smeared ring of powder on the floor—was the diminutive idol: Colonel Mabutu's prized little Buddha statue.

What the hell had happened here?

With the hollow drums thumping, a rhythm matched by his own pounding heart, Cale was about to call out, when a rush of shadow pummeled him from behind. He found himself tackled, knocked off-balance, falling against the hard chairs of the dining room table.

His aggressor followed suit. Cale felt a pair of strong hands fighting to grip his throat. Despite the dimness, he recognized his attacker.

"Slink! What are you doing?" he shouted. "It's me—it's Cale! Get the fuck off me!"

In the initial attack, a large potted plant had toppled, along with two dining chairs. Crusty mulch sprayed over both men, and Cale spit the dark loam from his lips, as he fought his opponent. But Slink stayed on top of him, relentless. As they wrestled chest-to-chest, Cale could feel a hard object poking against his rib cage. It felt solid, like the butt of a handgun.

He swung an elbow, trying to connect with Slink's cheekbone or chin. Anything to knock some sense into his partner.

"Slink! Christ! It's *me*, damn it!"

Slink continued his attack, however, ignoring Cale's words, swinging, punching, grappling like a relentless martial arts fighter. Cale vacillated somewhere between halfway letting-up, versus taking the assault for what it was. Slink couldn't be serious, could he? His partner? His best friend? The whole thing must be some joke.

How could Slink fail to recognize him?

"Stand down, you moron!" Cale barked the command in anger. "What are you...doing? *Stand down!*"

The *tanbu* pounding increased in tempo, trapping both men inside a throbbing pulse of aggression. Slink had his knee lodged in Cale's groin, both hands struggling to grip his opponent's neck. Cale countered—keeping one arm locked inside Slink's elbows—grabbing at his wrists and forearms, forcing the pressure away.

But for how long? How long before this crazy wrestling match turned into a fight for survival?

———

Up in the family room, Tazeki was finished with the unconscious female. At least for now. He focused down at her bare midriff from a few feet away. He imagined that he could see the evil growing cell-by-cell inside her abdomen.

Just desserts, he told himself.

Downstairs, he could hear the commotion. It reminded him of two grunting male lions trapped in a struggle for pride supremacy. His new *nzambi*—unlike that fool Kinsella—would dispose of Van Waring.

Tazeki smiled. Murdered by your partner. Having your life choked out of you, while staring into your best friend's eyes. He'd call it "justice served."

The detective's bitch, lying unconscious here on the couch, had a grim future ahead of her, as well. Bearing Tobias Crenshaw's love child, the man who'd kidnapped her, drugged her, tortured and raped her. Each time she gazed into her newborn's eyes—or at her own reflection in the mirror, for that matter—she'd be face to face with her private version of hell.

Game, set, match to Colonel Mabutu. Revenge complete. He decided not to gloat. He'd have ample time for celebrating later.

On the minus side of the ledger: Pazuzu had fled. Perhaps forever. That is, if the demon managed to break through the invisible enclosure of Tazeki's spell. And what of Kinsella? He would find out in due time, of course, what had become of his dear old friend. But did the botono care?

Not so much. All that mattered to him now—*truly* mattered—was getting his gris-gris back. It was where his true powers were hidden.

A gunshot exploded, slicing through the charged atmosphere.

He turned and fled the room. Tazeki sped down the steps and hallway, past the wine-splattered kitchen, and stopped short of the dining room. The two men remained locked in their desperate struggle. He calculated what had happened: the .38-caliber service revolver, which the zombie had tucked inside the waist of his jeans, had been pulled loose. Van Waring had managed to fire a single shot before the weapon was knocked from his grasp.

Moving into the living room, he was horrified to see the results. The ceramic statue of Pazuzu had been blown to bits. He rushed forward and began searching through the rubble like a bomb-blast survivor.

"My gris-gris!" Tazeki mewled with despair. "Where the hell is my gris-gris?"

——

Cale had wrested the revolver from Slink, managed to aim and fire a lone shot across the room. His suspicion was that the diminutive statuette was in some way controlling his partner, forcing him to fight like a cyborg on meth. It had to be the evil little idol behind Slink's attempt to strangle him.

What other explanation could there be?

The blast from the handgun nearly fractured Cale's eardrum. But his aim had been true. The bronze statue had exploded into a thousand bits of shattered porcelain.

An instant after he'd fired, however, Slink had slammed a fist into his chin that left Cale dazed and seeing stars. The statue's destruction, it seemed, had zero effect on his partner's unrelenting attack. The heavy weapon had dropped from his grasp.

Now Slink's punches were raining down on him in earnest. Cale felt like a fighter trapped against the cage mesh. Struggling to maintain consciousness, he felt a tsunami of darkness threaten to take him under. It would be so peaceful, like a stone dropped into the cool waters of a lake, drifting down, down, down...where the pain would shut off and he could let himself go, sinking to rest at the clear, cold bottom.

Another fist landed hard against his jaw. Then another. Cale's sight was dimming, but he blinked it clear, and in doing so, laid eyes across the living room on the one person in the universe he least expected to see:

Tazeki Mabutu? Could it really be him? The Colonel?

Streaks of paint were smeared across the man's face and body. He was in full witch doctor mode. Cale told himself that he had to be hallucinating. Why would the Liberian be here? At his house? In his living room?

Cale wondered if, perhaps, he had already died? Been choked to death? Was this his first vision from beyond?

Mabutu rose from the rubble of his shattered statue. He looked like a man who had located a treasure among the ruins. "My gris-gris!" The Liberian's voice cried, like the desperate tenor of a lunatic. "I found it! I found it!"

Cale watched awestruck as the spook-faced witch doctor pried open what appeared to be a weathered leather pouch. His fingers probed inside, until they emerged, holding up a web-like piece of flesh-colored parchment.

"My caul!" the wiry colonel cried with glee. "I've got it back!"

Cale snapped back to the present. He could feel Slink's hands compressing his neck now. Only this time, he could offer little resistance. He recalled his partner's words a day ago, when he'd professed his desire to "choke the last living breath" out of Tobias Crenshaw. Was this what Slink was thinking now? Doing the same to him?

On the verge of letting go, he kept his eyes focused on the witch doctor across the room. And the strangeness of the man's very presence here, gave Cale a thought more poignant than anything he could recall:

He was staring at the embodiment of insanity.

CHAPTER 51

Tazeki was beside himself with pleasure, like a nine-year-old on Christmas morning. Gazing at the object of his sacred birth, holding it with loving fingertips—as one might cradle an injured baby bird—he realized his caul had dried out over the years. Shrunken over time. But it mattered little. What did matter was that this precious, web-like piece of uterine tissue, which had clung to his newborn skull at birth, was back in his possession.

Of course, it would have shrunken. It had been trapped inside the airless base of the little statuette for decades. How could it not show signs of weathering? Still, it was his caul. His birthright. His secret source of strength as a powerful dark botono.

He fingered the frail tissue with a lover's touch. Making a magic gesture over the dried relic, Tazeki watched as it expanded and reformed itself back into its original shape and texture. "My caul," he whispered to the room, the words swallowed by the shakers the heady thumping of the *tanbu* drums.

He placed the delicate object over the upper half his face. He chortled with glee. Reunited again—after all these years. Peering out a single gaping eyehole, like he might be the Elephant Man, he stared across the room at where the detective was taking his beating. Punch after punch slammed into the man. And now the *nzambi* was choking Van Waring.

He could feel—actually *taste*—his enemy's life force ebbing away. He motioned with his forefinger, and the *nzambi* let up on his fatal grip.

"Colonel...Mabutu." Cale's voice rasped, colored with disbelief.

"What? No clever quips, Detective?" Tazeki called out. "No pithy comments?"

"Just that I'll be...waiting for you...in hell."

"Splendid," cackled the witch doctor. "I'll see you when I get there."

"In the meantime," the detective gasped, "go *fuck* yourself!"

269

Tazeki flicked his finger and the *nzambi* resumed his death-grip. Van Waring grabbed futilely at the man's wrists, continuing to stare across the room at the witch doctor, as if mesmerized.

Despite the frenzy of drumbeats and shakers, he imagined he could hear the death rattle of the man's final breath.

——

Cale felt nothing. Not fear or blazing anger, or even frustration. It was an odd sensation, this one of surrender. It was something he'd never experienced before in his life.

His vision was blotchy and unfocused, and he guessed his oxygen-deprived corneas were beginning to cloud. Tiny petechial hemorrhages were forming. Cale blinked, knowing he did not have many blinks left.

Nevertheless, he reasoned, how could he complain? After surviving the colonel's deadly eel pit, and living through a pair of assassination attempts, followed by Prince Mir's helicopter gun barrage...these all before Kinsella's brutal blindside attack...well, Cale had accepted that he'd been living on borrowed time.

At his funeral, they might recite a laundry list of things he had accomplished at the end. How he'd tracked down Leslie Dowd and helped rescue her. Made good on his promise to her parents. And how he'd brought closure, perhaps, for the family of Mary Jane Moore.

Beyond these, hadn't he also helped rid the world of some very unsavory characters? Tobias Crenshaw; Prince Mir Al-Sadar; Kinsella; Colonel Mabutu. To name but a few.

His fight against evil—though cut short at the end—had been a worthy one.

Cale's mind now summoned forth one final image: that of the gloomy African cave. He recalled clinging to the sharp, dripping rocks, his fingers numb and bleeding, the pool filled with toothy eels swimming below his legs in circular fashion, like a team of sharks closing in on a life raft.

Cale recalled how, in his most desperate hours, his thoughts had shifted to Maggie—how much he cared for her, and how he'd enjoyed every minute of the wonderful times they'd spent together. Laughing and loving. And sometimes just smiling and holding one another, skipping the need for unnecessary words. And wasn't that the saddest part of all? How he wouldn't be standing beside her? At the altar? Wouldn't be around for the birth of their child?

His father's old aphorism came to him now, as if rising up from the grave: "No one ever claimed life is fair, have they?"

Cale could offer no rebuttal.

———

The roar of the gunshot rocked the room.

With his stare still fixed on the colonel, Cale watched a dark smear form inside the open eyehole of the odd piece of whatever-it-was the witch doctor had placed over the upper half of his face.

Tazeki Mabutu was lifted from the ground, flung backwards like a heavy meat-sack. He landed with a crash on the coffee table, on his beetle back, legs twitching...

...and then he did not move.

At this exact moment, Cale felt the pressure on his neck subside. Slink's hands released him, dropping away, and he felt his partner slump down onto the hardwood floor. Maybe also dead.

Shifting his gaze past Slink's unconscious body, Cale spied Maggie in the kitchen. She was down on one knee, elbows locked, the Kahr PM9 extended in her outstretched hands. Just as she'd been taught. She had fired a single shot clean through the colonel's webby eyehole. Bullseye.

One helluva shot was Cale's final thought. He watched his vision fade to black, while at the same time understanding that his eyes remained open wide.

With the drums now silenced, the house turned as quiet as a three-a.m. cemetery. The pungent aroma of nitro seeped through the air, trailing the ringing echo of the gunshot...and that sound, as it faded, morphed into the flatline hum of an EKG monitor.

CHAPTER 52

Alone in the middle of a landless ocean, Cale rides the rolling crests, wave after wave of jagged dream, using all of his strength to remain afloat. A giant breaker crashes over him, submerging him beneath a heavy weight of gun-gray water. He finds himself pushed downwards, backlit by the sun's faint and distant glow.

An ominous specter rises from below. Sensing its presence, Cale peers down to witness an enormous creature lifting from the black depths. Rising up and up and up, its form enlarges as it climbs. What pushes Cale beyond fear is the monster's face: it is Colonel Tazeki Mabutu, his razor teeth bared and jagged and spread in a malicious grin.

Cale thrashes his arms and legs, whipping them in a panicked swim for the surface. And as he emerges from the nightmare, he awakens with a desperate gasp for air.

———

The beeping sound raced along with his galloping heart rate. Cale could distinguish the sound of the nearby EKG monitor. He forced himself to relax, to slow the cadence down *beep-beep-beep…beep… …beep…*

He heard a familiar voice issue from across the room. "Lazarus returns. Hide the women and children."

Cale opened his eyes. He spotted Slink Dooley sitting atop the window ledge, hands splayed—the right one bandaged to the wrist. He had both feet flat on the floor.

"If this is heaven," Cale said, rasping, "I think I'm going back."

"You'll regret that decision when the Demerol wears off."

With one hand, Cale fingered the gauzy bandages covering the left side of his face. Nothing hurt. He guessed the painkillers were performing their magic. He asked, "Bad? Or really bad?"

"Contused around the cheeks, jaw, neck. 'Orbital hematoma,' it says on your chart." Slink massaged his jaw. "Like a driver gone through his windshield, I suppose."

Cale attempted a frown he couldn't feel.

"I've seen you in worse shape, kemosabe. For the record, they kept you here three nights. X-rays, patch up, and observation. Releasing you later today."

Cale scanned the room with his unbandaged right eye. "Maggie?"

"Six stitches in her foot. Otherwise, no worse for wear." Slink shrugged. "Said she'd be back in an hour."

"She clear with the DA?" Cale asked.

"Home invasion. Self-defense." Slink pulled aside one curtain and peeked down through the window. "Chloe corroborated everything."

"She's clear then?"

"As a shot of Polish vodka."

Cale remembered Slink had visited him the day before. Or two days ago. His memory was unclear. The Demerol. He'd asked Slink to procure an item from a local bookstore. Or maybe he'd dreamt it.

"Did I ask you to pick something up for me? Like a gift?"

"Like a gift—yeah." Slink aimed his chin at an ash-colored bureau across the room. "Top drawer over there."

Cale propped his head up, folded one of the pillows beneath his neck. "What day is it, by the way?"

"Monday afternoon. You've been in here sixty hours."

Slink eased the half-open drape aside and peered down at the street below like a spy keeping an eye on a tail. "A pair of Feds are waiting to grill you in a day or two. State Department. Small matter of a dead Liberian colonel discovered on your living room floor. Dressed in a Halloween outfit. Seems it's a bit beyond our local jurisdiction."

"You already talk to them?"

"Not yet. I talked to the state boys." Slink crossed his arms over his chest. "Believe it or not, I don't remember that much."

"You were a little...out of control. If I recall right." Cale let the understatement hang in the air. "Some wild-ass PCP. Just me venturing a guess."

Slink was staring at his shoes, and when he lifted his eyes back to his partner, they were heavy with remorse. "I'm sorry, Cale. I didn't mean to—you know—any of it."

"Wasn't your fault, man. You weren't...let's just say yourself." Cale fingered his jaw with one hand and worked it around like a boxer who'd just come around. "Your right cross could use some work, though."

Slink's smile was sheepish, though relief was apparent in his eyes.

Cale shifted topics. "About the shrunken head? Any word?"

"I spoke to Forensics this morning." Slink withdrew his phone, checked the screen, pocketed it. "Dusty Harold's guessing it'll match the Vanderkellen girl. Like you thought."

"Jesus." Cale exhaled. "How sick is that?" Neither man spoke for a beat. "At least it's another nail in Tobias Crenshaw's coffin." Cale said this without humor. "Speaking of which, has the bastard bought the farm, yet?"

Slink pulled a face. "Life support. Still a veggie. DA's wondering if they should skip the expense of a trial, save the taxpayers some moola...It makes sense to me—but I don't know the politics of trying a brain-dead serial offender."

Cale's thoughts drifted. He wondered if the Chemist might be lodged somewhere in this very hospital. Maybe a floor below. What would it take to sneak down there in the dead of night? Pull the plug on his respirator? Finish what he'd started two months ago?

He banished the thought from his head.

"Here's one for you," Slink continued. "I spent this morning checking the UW-Madison archives. Want to take a wild guess who Tobias Crenshaw's college roommate was? Twenty years ago?"

"Ron Dayne?"

"Close. How about a Liberian exchange student? Guy by the name of Tazeki Mabutu."

Cale's attempt at a whistle was blocked by the stitches inside his cheek, and the patchwork of bandages covering the outside. The fact he couldn't whistle anyway didn't help.

A petite nurse entered the room. She searched around for the television remote, found it, flicked it on. "We received a call at the desk, Lieutenant," she explained. She looked at them, one to the next. "A Milwaukee FBI agent named Eddie Redtail."

Cale sighed. He understood that if Agent Redtail was calling the hospital, it was for a good reason. He watched the nurse buzz through the channels, aiming the remote like a six-shooter. She settled on BBC News. "He insisted you watch this," she explained. Upping the volume, she set the remote at the foot of the bed.

On the television screen, a female news anchor was informing them of a report coming in live from the Home Office. The screen split, and the image of a second reporter appeared. He stood aboard a ship, microphone in hand, speaking in a British accent:

"Earlier today, the Liberian cargo freighter *Kwensana* was halted in international waters. In a daybreak raid involving the British Royal Navy warship HMS *Thornbridge*, in concert with the Western Sahara Coast Guard. The joint operation took place just south of the Canary Islands. According to ship logs, it is believed the freighter was destined for the UK.

"Under the cover of darkness, HMS *Thornbridge* tailed the freighter until first daylight, when she stopped the vessel and proceeded to conduct a close-quarters intercept. A group of suspected human smugglers were arrested, and the *Kwensana* seized."

Images of patrol ships seizing the older, coal-colored freighter flashed on-screen, and the reporter continued: "Concerning the outcome of the operation, *Thornbridge*'s presiding officer, Commander Mervin F. Browne, Royal Navy, gave us this statement, quote:

'Utilizing the stealth features of our Type 23 frigate, we could recognize suspicious activity underway aboard the freighter. Eleven suspected traffickers were apprehended. From below decks, we were able to free twenty-four Liberian females, all age thirteen or younger.

'Anyone involved in this type of illegal activity has received a quite clear message: *We mean business*.'

Cutting back to the reporter:

"The Royal Navy, along with the US and Italian navies, are working with the Western Sahara government, and other African countries in the region, to promote the lawful use of the maritime environment along Africa's Western Coast. This operation follows the guidelines of the EU and United Nations mandate, to increase efforts at reducing the activities of pirates and human traffickers."

Slink rose from the window ledge. Grabbing the remote, he clicked off the television, and set the device on a table. The room fell silent save for the soft beeping of the EKG monitor. The nurse moved over to the bedside and began unhooking the machine. She slid the IV from Cale's arm and applied a small gauze bandage, saying, "Marching orders. Looks like they're sending you home."

There went his after-hours sneak into Crenshaw's room, Cale decided. Certain he needed no further adventures—at least for some time—he allowed that it was probably for the best.

"Looks like your insurance ran out," Slink said, cracking wise. He stepped around the edge of the bed, making as if to leave. "Don't suppose you had anything to do with—" He flicked his head at the TV. "That freighter? The rest of it?"

"Above my pay grade." Cale shrugged. "Homeland's been on it for a while. The trafficking ring. Colonel Mabutu. I guess we can score one for the good guys."

"Finger in the dike," Slink resignedly said. "Those traffickers are like cockroaches."

He strode across the room, then paused at the door, turning back. "By the way, Captain McBride said to tell you your vacation's over. Back to work next Monday."

Cale didn't smile. He didn't cheer or fist-pump. Instead, he gave his partner a simple nod. Slink departed, leaving Cale to his private thoughts. His mind drifted to Agent Amy Fronteer, in Rome, and he wondered if their efforts had played some small role in halting the Liberian freighter, freeing the young victims from a life of living hell.

Had they made a real difference? Perhaps. Every little bit and all that. Still, like Slink had said, "Finger in the dike."

Cale harbored no illusions. He reminded himself that saving the world from evil—as Maggie had suggested, before he'd set off on his overseas journey—was not a healthy job choice.

As usual, she was right.

EPILOGUE

There came a soft rapping on the hospital door. Maggie entered with a ghost-like smile. She was wearing jeans, a summer blouse and comfortable flats, and walked gingerly on the heel of her injured left foot. She was followed, moments later, by a different nurse wearing a puppies-and-kittens smock, who pushed an empty wheelchair. Familiar with the routine, already dressed, Cale moved from the edge of the bed and took a seat in the chariot. The nurse's eyes scanned the room for personal items.

Maggie did likewise. "Sure you've got everything?" she asked.

"Oh." He remembered. "There's a bag. In the top drawer of the bureau, there."

Maggie stepped over and withdrew the package. She handed it to Cale without giving it a glance. He set the item in his lap, staring at the plastic bag. *The Reader's Loft*—a local bookstore—was stenciled in cursive on the outside. Behind him the nurse grabbed the wheelchair's handles and proclaimed: "And away we go."

Cale felt himself propelled out the door and into the extra-wide, too-bright hallway.

———

The hazy May sun caressed a gentle wind, which carried with it a hint of raspberry bushes and fresh-clipped lawns. A string of pigeon-colored clouds sat perched in the western sky. Sitting outside the hospital pickup doors, Cale closed his eyes, taking in the breeze like a cat sitting in a screened porch window.

When Maggie pulled her Mazda up curbside, Cale lifted himself from the wheelchair. He opened the passenger door and eased inside, still holding the bookstore package in his hand. He closed the door behind him, encasing them in silence.

Before shifting the vehicle into gear, Maggie issued him a questioning look, arching her eyebrows behind her sunglasses.

As if he'd been expecting it, Cale handed her the package. "Gift for you," he said, expressionless. "I never, you know, got the proper chance...with everything happening and all."

She slid her glasses up on her head and stared at the writing on the bag. "Definitely not Gucci," she quipped. Withdrawing the thin, colorful tome from the bag, she studied the title: *The World's Most Amazing Baby Names.*

Maggie's laughter was genuine. It sounded like the first honest humor she'd known in months. She leaned across the seat and hugged him, mindful of his injuries, and kissed Cale's cheek where it wasn't bandaged. Tears glistened in her eyes. When she pulled back, she brushed them away with her fingertips.

He studied her and could picture her mind sifting through a hundred different thoughts at once. "Does this mean you—? Us? You know?" The questions dangled in the air between them.

Cale raised one shoulder, and the pain in his ribs caused him to wince. "It means whatever you'd like it to mean."

"Baby names," Maggie whispered, making it sound as if the idea were a new invention. "Better than stupid Gucci, any day."

His eyes searched her face, so smooth and wonderous, that he sometimes felt frozen just looking at her. "I'm happy to give—you know—input. But it should be your call."

Her forehead creased. "My grandfather's name was Rory. A possible, right? For a boy, that is?" When he frowned, she added, "I thought you liked four-letter names for guys?"

"I should. I've been called most of them." Cale's grin became playful and he reached for her, pulling her close in the vehicle's snug inner space. "God, I missed you."

Maggie did her part, and their kiss held the lingering promise of passion.

A car horn sounded behind them, a simple goat-like bleat. They were holding up the departure line. Maggie straightened in the driver's seat with a giggle and slid her sunglasses back in place. After checking the side mirrors, and the rearview, she shifted the Mazda into gear and eased away from the curb.

They moved off down the sunlit street, happy to sit together in companionable silence. And even happier to be headed for home.

ACKNOWLEGEMENTS

A novel is not created in a vacuum. Any good story is always a collaborative effort. In light of this, I'd like to thank Kevin "The Coach" Harbick, whose passion would not allow Tobias Crenshaw (a.k.a. the Chemist) to perish; and Detective Lieutenant Paul Splawski (retired) of the Green Bay Police Department, who provided particular insight into how criminal transport, police suspensions, and Review Boards function.

To Scott Fowler Browne and Tera Thorp-Harbick, who allowed me to tap into their minds regarding the inner workings of African voodoo and witchcraft. Bart Drage lent insight into the Italian coastline and his beloved city of Anzio, Italy. Marco Lenzen, OD— a true spiritual warrior—offered me religious advice on dark witchcraft spells and hexes.

Kudos to D.P. Lyle, MD, whose text *Murder and Mayhem* helped me with zombie creation. And Steven M. Falk, MD, anesthesiologist, who aided with his expertise. Chase DeCleene, college wrestling champion, assisted with tips on hand-to-hand combat and knife fighting. Elizabeth De Baere rendered excellent advice on horror and fantasy.

I'd be remiss if I failed to thank Grant Cousineau, and the other members of the Green Bay Readers Group. And further to Ashley Emma, best-selling author of her Amish Detective Series, who encouraged me to re-cover The Chemist Series reprints

And last but not least, my thanks to Randy Rose, Tom Ebli, John Thornton, David Cowles and Dale Berg, along with the loyal members of the Green Bay Chapter of "The Corporation—a Think Tank for Creative Solutions," who continue to keep me grounded by their support. *Muchas gracias* to you all.

ABOUT THE AUTHOR

Janson Mancheski is an award-winning author of five novels. The Chemist Series (*The Chemist (2010), Trail of Evil (2011) Mask of Bone (2011)*) featuring Detective Cale Van Waring, are all set in Green Bay, Wisconsin. *The Chemist* captured first place for fiction in the Sharp Writ Book Awards in 2010. Voyage Media Productions has accepted Janson's screenplay version of his book, and casting and production offers are currently being reviewed.

Janson has authored a number of short stories and received awards for multiple screenplays. The movie script version of Janson's fourth novel *Shoot For the Stars (2016)* (an historic Green Bay Packers "What If" novel), was a finalist for the 2012 Writers Digest creative fiction awards. His latest novel *The Scrub* (a memoir featuring the ghost of Curly Lambeau) was published in December 2017.

A University of Wisconsin–Green Bay graduate and practicing optometrist (Illinois College of Optometry–Chicago, IL) from 1985

– 2005, Janson worked as the team eye doctor for the UW–Green Bay men and women's basketball teams. He also functioned as team eye doctor for the Green Bay Packers from 1990–2002.

Janson is an ardent Green Bay Packers, UW-Green Bay Fighting Phoenix, and Wisconsin Badgers fan. His newest novel *Bully Me This!* will be released in summer, 2019.

For further information on Janson's books and activity:

SEE **www.Jansonmancheski.com** (Featuring *The Chemist* movie trailer, starring Steve Golla.)

Facebook @ **Janson Mancheski author**

WANT MORE OF THE CHEMIST SERIES?

CHECK OUT THIS SNEAK PEEK OF
GREATEST HITS – THE CHEMIST SERIES

CHAPTER 1

"What the heck is a 'Greatest Hits' book? Never heard of such a thing before."

This was spoken to me at a recent writing fair held in Green Bay, Wisconsin. My hometown. The downtown event is called "Untitled Town." I was speaking on another three-person panel, this time on screenwriting. Many of the questions revolved around my first novel *The Chemist* (2009), which (as mentioned) is moving through the pre-production channels as a motion picture, being produced by Voyage Media Productions, based in Los Angeles, CA.

Most people are aware that making movies these days is very expensive. It's something we all assume, but until you are part of the process, you don't realize exactly *how* expensive. Anywhere from $4 to $50 million dollars expensive. And up! As part of the movie marketing plan, where savvy professionals are involved every step of the way, I was given movie poster art-work concepts to evaluate, and either approve or reject. Professional cover mock-ups designed to promote the film. Today's creative movie artists are experts at what they do. And viewing their work—along with members of the marketing and production teams—I was forced to admit that most of the professional renditions seemed to be more glamorous, exciting, and aesthetically pleasing than my current, staid eight-year-old book cover.

Thus, I was open to changing my cover. Upgrading, as it were. And my further decision (in line with savvy marketing, hey-hey) came when the lightning bolt of an idea struck me: Why not use the movie poster art to re-cover my original novel *The Chemist*? That way they'll match.

I know what you're thinking: *Duh!* Many sixth-grade kids could have thought of that. Maybe so. But to me it was a worthwhile idea. And what this revelation lead to was the common-sense follow-up: If you're going to change/modernize one cover, and the book is already a three-part thriller-suspense series, then wouldn't it make sense to change the second and third book covers as well? Again, the answer seemed obvious.

Considering the above, another savvy marketer (of which you may have already guessed, I am not) suggested that perhaps I should write a short informational blog-article to accompany the re-release of the books. Something to give away, perhaps, as a complimentary eBook. Something to generate a bit of (movie industry lingo here) *Buzz!* I pondered the suggestion. I imagined that I could pluck out a few scenes from my three novels and turn these into a compelling short story. Or . . . I could compile several old blog posts, shovel them into an eBook format, and call it something or another. Something catchy, no doubt.

Or Door Number Three: I could do something different.

And that, my friends, is how the genesis of this book you hold in your hands was created. So, I hope you enjoy it in the vein of which it was written. Storytelling, make-believe, fiction—soiled and dirty, warts and all. And it's my fervent ambition, above all else, to hope you are entertained enough by the "teaser" narratives to go out and purchase the actual books. Read them in their gritty entirety.

In their shiny new covers, of course.

If you enjoyed this sample, please view Greatest Hits on Amazon: https://www.amazon.com/Chemist-Greatest-Killers-Traffickers-Perverts-ebook/dp/B07NKM362F

Printed in Great Britain
by Amazon